Manu-Smṛti
A Critical Study and Its Relevance in the Modern Times

Manu-Smṛti

A Critical Study and Its Relevance in the Modern Times

Asha Rani Tripathi

PRINTWORLD
Publishers of Indian Traditions

Cataloging in Publication Data — DK

[Courtesy: D.K. Agencies (P) Ltd. <docinfo@dkagencies.com>]

Tripāṭhī, Āśā Rānī, 1944- author

Manu-smṛti : a critical study and its relevance in the modern times / Asha Rani Tripathi.

pages cm

Includes index.

ISBN 9788124608333

1. Manu (Lawgiver). Mānavadharmaśāstra. 2. Hindu law. I. Title.

DDC 294.594 23

ISBN 978-81-246-0833-3

First published in India in 2015

Printed and published by:
D.K. Printworld (P) Ltd.
Regd. Office : *Vedaśrī*, F-395, Sudarshan Park
(Metro Station: Ramesh Nagar)
New Delhi – 110 015.
Phones : (011) 2545 3975, 2546 6019; *Fax* : 2546 5926
e-mail : indology@dkprintworld.com
Web : www.dkprintworld.com

Acknowledgement

I EXPRESS my deep gratitude to the Almighty for bestowing upon me the strength and confidence for accomplishing the task of writing a book on *Manu-Smr̥ti*. I am much grateful to my two revered *guru*s, late Prof. Siddheshvar Bhattacharya and Prof. Dinesh Chandra Guha at Banaras Hindu University, Varanasi under whose able guidance I learnt the basics of research. Most of the contents of this book are based on research papers that I had presented at different conferences in India and abroad. Those papers generated lively discussions and the scholars present in the audience encouraged me to bring my research works on *Manu-Smr̥ti* in a book form. I owe a great deal to all those scholars who kept on inspiring me for writing this book.

I am deeply indebted to my father late Pandit Alakh Niranjan Pande, a great Sanskrit scholar who himself authored few important books related to Sanskrit language and literature. He always inspired me to pursue an academic career. I am extremely grateful to my husband Prof. R.S. Tripathi, a reputed scientist, who provided a scientific outlook to my work by going through the manuscript, playing the role of a critic, correcting the final proofs and by helping in giving final shape to the book. He enjoyed doing these jobs due to his great admiration for Sanskrit language and Vedic literature. My two loving daughters Anupama and Mudita were indeed very enthusiastic about the book and provided me the much needed moral support; I thank them profusely. I also thank all my relatives and friends for their good wishes.

Also, my thanks are due to Shri Susheel K. Mittal and D.K. Printworld (P) Ltd. for publishing this book.

Jyeṣṭha Śukla 15, 2072 (VS) **Asha Rani Tripathi**

Contents

Scheme of Transliteration

Vowels	a ā i ī u ū ṛ ṝ ḷ e ai o au				
Anusvara	ṁ				
Visarga	ḥ				
Consonents					
Gutturals	ka	kha	ga	gha	ṅa
Palatals	ca	cha	ja	jha	ña
Cerebrals	ṭa	ṭha	ḍa	ḍha	ṇa
Dentals	ta	tha	da	dha	na
Labials	pa	pha	ba	bha	ma
Semi-Vowels	ya	ra	la	va	
Sibilants	sa	as in sun			
	śa	palatal sibilant pronounced like the soft s			
	ṣa	cerebral sibilant as in shun			
Aspirate	ha				

Abbreviations

AitaBrā	*Aitareya Brāhmaṇa*
ĀpaDhSū	*Āpastamba Dharma-Sūtras*
AV	*Atharvaveda*
BauDhSū	*Baudhāyana Dharma-Sūtras*
BhG	*Bhagavad-Gītā*
BṛUp	*Bṛhadāraṇyaka Upaniṣad*
ChāUp	*Chāndogya Upaniṣad*
GauDhSū	*Gautama Dharma-Sūtras*
KaṭhUp	*Kaṭhopaniṣad*
Mbh	*Mahābhārata*
MS	*Manu-Smṛti*
Rām	*Rāmāyaṇa*
ṚV	*Ṛgveda*
ŚataBrā	*Śatapatha Brāhmaṇa*
SBE	Sacred Books of the East
TaitSaṁ	*Taittirīya Saṁhitā*
TaitUp	*Taittirīyopaniṣad*

Introduction

A Brief History of Vedic Literature

INDIAN thoughts and ideals are the real treasure house of the variegated products of the perennial flow of Indian culture. This tradition has acknowledged human life as a rare bliss and an opportunity to perform noble deeds. The human life was thus accorded a systematic form by framing it into different *puruṣārtha*s (*dharma, artha, kāma* and *mokṣa*). The practice of *dharma* became the main goal of life, as through *dharma* only, one might enjoy *artha* and *kāma* in a desired manner and might finally attain *mokṣa* (freedom from the worldly life) through self-realization. The four Vedas laid the foundation of this unique philosophy. The tradition of attaching due importance to *dharma* in human life was further carried through all later writings. Kalpasūtras (one of the Vedāṅgas) brought out all the rules of *dharma* in a systematic form which were otherwise scattered all over the four Vedas. The three sections of Kalpasūtras (Śrauta, Gṛhya, Dharma) dictated the rules and regulations pertaining to *dharma,* related to the different aspects of life in a true and practical manner. Śrautasūtras deal with the performance of the Vedic rites, while Gṛhyasūtras describe the numerous ceremonies connected to the domestic life of a person from his birth to death. Dharmasūtras, which are directly connected to Gṛhyasūtras, deal with *dharma* in detail. These Sūtras have expanded the definition of *dharma* in its wider sense. The meaning of *dharma* was stretched to all social concerns such as rights, duties, law, religion and even culture. Most of these Dharmasūtras had originated from different Vedic schools. Apart from that, there are many independent Dharmasūtras.

The basic content of Dharmasūtras was to assert the authority of Vedas as the source of *dharma*. They also have discussed the duties of four *varṇas* (brāhmaṇa, kṣatriya, vaiśya and śūdra), four *āśramas* (*brahmacarya, gṛhastha, vānaprastha* and *saṁnyāsa*), *saṁskāras*, governance, rules for taxation, ownerships, witness, moneylending, payment of debt and deposits, punishments for various crimes, inheritance, *śrāddhas*, sins, expiations and penance. The prominent Dharmasūtras are: *Gautama-Dharmasūtra, Baudhāyana-Dharmasūtra, Āpastamba-Dharmasūtra, Vāsiṣṭha-Dharmasūtra, Yājñavalkya-Dharmasūtra, Hārīta-Dharmasūtra, Viṣṇu-Dharmasūtra, Hiraṇyakeśi-Dharmasūtra* and *Vaikhānasa-Dharmasūtra*. Many other Dharmasūtras are the supplementary parts of Śrautasūtras and Gṛhyasūtras and are mainly written in prose.

Manu-Smṛti and Other Smṛtis

Smṛtis are the highly specialized literature focusing fully on various aspects of *dharma*. They follow the content of Dharmasūtra and are the metrical codes. The term *smṛti* means "remembrance", as they reveal the *dharma* already prescribed in Vedas. The word *smṛti* means the memory or recollection of what was previously cognized. They are the works rendered by those great sages who studied the Vedas and pondered over their injunctions and prohibitions. These sages were conversant with the codes and demonstrated the utility of those codes by practising them in their own life. Thus Smṛtis became the tool of improving man's day-to-day life for securing a fruitful future. Many Smṛtis were composed side by side to Dharmasūtras. Many times even Dharmasūtras refer to Smṛtis. *Manu-Smṛti, Yājñavalkya-Smṛti, Pārāśara-Smṛti, Nārada-Smṛti, Bṛhaspati-Smṛti* and *Kātyāyana-Smṛti* are the well-known Smṛtis.

Among all these Smṛtis, *Manu-Smṛti* is the most ancient, authoritative and systematic one. It has been said that if Pāṇini has determined the nature of the Sanskrit language for all time, Manu has determined the Hindu conduct for all time.

History of the Text of Manu-Smṛti and Its Relation to Other Texts

Manu-Smṛti is one of the most popular books that India has ever produced. It has received a high estimation for centuries. The publication of the translation of *Manu-Smṛti* by Sir William Jones cleared all the doubts which Westerners had in their minds about Indian thought. In fact, it has paved the way for many European scholars to understand the Indian notions of judiciary based on the ground of practical and systematic judicial administration. All these subjects have been thoroughly discussed in *Manu-Smṛti.* These topics became the centre of attraction and prompted numerous discoveries later on.

Sir William Jones's translation (1794) was reprinted in 1796; Johann Huttner did the German translation in 1797; it was largely used by the scholars writing on early criminal law. A number of editions of this work have so far been published in India since 1796. In this work the Nirnaya Sagara edition with the commentary of Kullūka has been used. The widely acclaimed and well-known translations of *Manu-Smṛti* have been done by V.N. Mandlik and Georg Bühler.

The content of *Manu-Smṛti* has proved that India had a rich tradition of thinking on how to bring about real harmony between the different groups of the society and how to introduce an ideal life. In spite of all its substantiality, the work is shrouded in several types of controversies. In order to assess the text in its true spirit, the following questions have to be answered first:

1. Was there a person named Manu as an author of the work and when was it written?
2. Did he write the whole content of the book at a time or was it written in succession?
3. Is the extant *Manu-Smṛti* the same work as was originally written by Manu?

It is not going to be an easy task to produce the facts related to all these questions, but even then a humble effort can be made to ascertain the facts with the help of certain available evidences.

In many *mantras* of *Ṛgveda,* Manu has been mentioned as "father" (*ṚV* I.80.16, 114.2; VIII.63.1). At another place Manu is addressed as "our father" (*yāni manur-avṛṇīta pitā naḥ*). One may also come across many compounded words like *manu-jāta, manu-prītasaḥ* and *manur-hita*. These words are occurring hundreds of times throughout *Ṛgveda.* At another place the sages pray to gods to show them the ancestral path of Manu (*ṚV* VIII.30). Manu is also considered as the light of the people (*ṚV* I.36.19). Manu offers sacrifices to the gods (*ṚV* V.35.15; VIII.30.2; X.36.10). Manu is also prayed to along with Indra (VIII.68.6). In *Ṛgveda* most of the *mantras* mention Manu as an individual sage. According to another *mantra,* Manu is a sage who offers prayers to thirty-three gods (VIII.27.4, 30.2). In *Ṛgveda* there are many stories related to Manu (X.61-63). Manu is also referred in *Atharvaveda* (XI.33) and in *Sāmaveda* (I.2.33; III.165, 145, 232; IV.123-24; VI.262). Manu has been delineated in Sanskrit literature from the early Vedic period onwards. He is regarded as father, as one of the ancient sages, a semi-divine person and a king who received law and regulation from the gods itself. *Manu-Smṛti* also mentions that Manu became a king by his own righteous conduct (VII.4).

In *Taittirīya Saṁhitā* it has been said that whatever Manu says is wholesome like medicine (*TatSam.* II.2.10.2). Further it says that "we are Manu's children" (*manavyo hi prajāḥ* II.1.5.6). In *Taittirīya Saṁhitā* III.1.9.4-5 and in *Aitareya Brāhmaṇa* V.14 there are stories of Manu dividing his wealth among his sons and the exclusion of his son Nābhānediṣṭha. *Śatapatha Brāhmaṇa* (SBE vol. 12, p. 216) relates the popular story of Manu and the great flood. *Nirukta* of Yāska (chap. III) presents a discussion pertaining to the rights of sons and daughters. Here it refers to the opinion of Manu Svayambhuva that the children of both sexes may inherit their father's property. Yāska clearly mentions Manu as law-giver. The laws propounded by Manu were well established during the Sūtra period. *Baudhāyana-Dharmasūtra* (I.21) also mentions Manu. It has been said that:

> Just as Bhr̥gu, a disciple of Manu, has complied the well-known views of Manu, a later *Baudhāyana* might have complied the views of Bodhāyana.

Āpastamba-Dharmasūtra connects Manu with promulgation of *śrāddhas* (II.7.16.1). *Vāsiṣṭha-Dharmasūtra* quotes at least sixty *ślokas* which are very much existing in extant *Manu-Smr̥ti, Vāsiṣṭha-Dharmasūtra* uses the words *mānava* and *mānavam ślokam udāharanti* many times. Many laws mentioned in this book are the prose version of *Manu-Smr̥ti*. In *Mahābhārata,* Manu is named at numerous places. It mentions Manu as Manu Svayambhuva (Śānti-Parva 21.12), Pracetasa Manu (Śānti-Parva 57.43) and many times simply as Manu. Śānti-Parva of *Mahābhārata* (verses 336.38-46) narrates:

> Supreme composed a hundred thousand *ślokas* on *dharma,* which were promulgated by Manu and later on Uṣanas and Br̥haspati composed Śāstras based on the work of Manu Svayambhuva.

The same version has been repeated in the prose introduction of *Nārada-Smr̥ti* that Manu composed a Dharmaśāstra of 100,000 *ślokas*, 1,080 chapters and 24 *prakaraṇas* and imparted it to Nārada, who abridged it into 12,000 verses and taught it to

Mārkaṇḍeya, who in turn brought it down to 8,000 *śloka*s and passed it to Sumiti Bhārgava, who again reduced it to 4,000 *śloka*s. Vātsyāyana in *Kāmasūtra* II.6 records a similar tradition of *dharma* and dealt with it in a special treatise. The similar story has been brought out in extant *Manu-Smṛti* I.32-33 where Brahmā taught the Śāstras to Manu and he imparted it to ten sages. It also says that Manu gave this knowledge to Bhṛgu who imparted it to others (I.59-60). This tradition has been maintained throughout *Manu-Smṛti*. These statements cannot be brushed aside. Later on, Medhātithi remarks in similar manner that the original work was abridged by Manu and others. *Mahābhārata* has made a distinction between Svayambhuva Manu and Pracetasa Manu. The former is introduced as the writer of Dharmaśāstra and the latter has been taken as the composer of *Arthaśāstra*. Śānti-Parva 21.12 too refers Svayambhuva Manu. Śānti-Parva 58.2 considers Pracetasa as the author of *rāja-dharma*. At few places Manu without any adjective has been associated with *rāja-dharma*.

One may find the reference of *Manu-Smṛti*, even in *Rāmāyaṇa*. Many ideas related to *dharma* and *rāja-dharma* found in *Rāmāyaṇa* are very close to *Manu-Smṛti*. It even mentions the name of Manu as a law-giver. The verses which are cited in *Rāmāyaṇa* can be seen in extant *Manu-Smṛti* (Kiṣkindhā-Kāṇḍa 18.30-32 and *Manu-Smṛti* VIII.316-18). Purāṇas owe much to *Manu-Smṛti*. *Bhāgavata Purāṇa* (XI.27.12) also refers to *Manu-Smṛti*. According to *Bhaviṣya Purāṇa*, the original text of Svạyambhuva Manu was redacted in four parts by Bhṛgu, Nārada and Aṅgiras. A verse from *Ṛgveda* has also been quoted to support the statement. The statement of Manu referred at this point opposes *Ṛgveda*. It seems that Yāska may have supported the view expressed by Manu. Kauṭilya in his *Arthaśāstra* mentions the names of few law treatises and quotes *mānavaḥ* five times. *Tantrākhyāyikā*, the earliest version of *Pañcatantra*, pays homage to Manu along with Cāṇakya,

Bṛhaspati, Śukra and Parāśara. *Hārīta-Smṛti* and *Viṣṇu-Dharmaśāstra* are fully familiar with the content of *Manu-Smṛti*. *Viṣṇu-Dharmaśāstra* is just the prose version of *Manu-Smṛti*. *Pārāśara-Smṛti*, *Kātyāyana-Smṛti* and *Bṛhaspati-Smṛti* follow *Manu-Smṛti*. *Bṛhaspati-Smṛti* is just a supplement to *Manu-Smṛti*. Bṛhaspati says that *Manu-Smṛti* occupies an important place as it represents the essence of Veda and that a Smṛti which opposes Manu is not esteemed.

Mṛcchakaṭika of Śūdraka (9.39) refers to the law of Manu that a brāhmaṇa sinner should not be given death sentence but instead of that he may be exiled from the country. An inscription of the Valabhi era (i.e. CE 571) mentions a king who obeyed the rules formed by Manu (*IA*, vol. 8, p. 303, *Gupta Inscriptions*, p. 165). Śabarasvāmin (CE 500) the commentator on *Jaimini-Sūtra* has said that Manu and others have given instructions (*Pūrva-Mīmāṁsa* I.1.2, vol. 1, p. 4). He also quotes a verse as a Smṛti passage and it is found in extant *Manu-Smṛti* (*MS* VIII.416 and *Mbh*, Udyoga-Parva 33.64). *Pratimā-Nāṭakam* of Bhāsa refers *Mānavavidyā-Dharmaśāstra* and *Pracetasa-Śrāddhakalpa*. In the first canto of *Kīrātārjunīyam* composed by Bhāravi while describing the state of Duryodhana to Yudhiṣṭhira the spy says that Duryodhana is following the path of governance showed by Manu (*Kīrātārjunīyam* 1.9). Śaṅkarācārya had before him the extant *Manu-Smṛti* as he quotes many verses from *Manu-Smṛti* in his *Bhāṣya* on *Vedāntasūtra*. *Tantravārttika* of Kumārila Bhaṭṭa offers a special reverence to *Manu-Smṛti*. He has given more importance to *Manu-Smṛti* in comparison to *Gautama-Dharmasūtra*. Kumārila treats Manu as the representative of all other Smṛtis (*Tantravārttika*, p. 165). He states that the authors of Smṛtis are generally prepared to accept as authoritative the usages of countries, castes and families that are not opposed to Vedas and he first quotes *Manu-Smṛti* (II.6) and then *Gautama-Dharmasūtra* (XI.20).

Before entering into the riddle-like debate on topics such as the authorship and the date of *Manu-Smṛti* it is necessary to know the extent of literature known to Manu or referred in *Manu-Smṛti*. Manu speaks of three Vedas (*ṚV* I.23, II.77, III.145, IV.123-24, 261, 264; *Yajurveda* I.23, III.145, IV.123-24, VI.21, 38, IX.18, XI.262, 264, *Sāmaveda* I.28, II.7, III.145, 185, 232, IV.123-24, XI.212). *Atharvaveda* has been mentioned as *Atharvan-Aṅgiras Śruti* (XI.33). Brāhmaṇa *granthas* have been considered as the essence of Vedas (XI.264). *Manu-Smṛti* mentions *Āraṇyaka* without naming it (IV.123) and even Vedāṅgas without mentioning the number (II.141). At another place (III.185) Manu uses the word *khadavidyā* but it is not very clear whether it really refers to six Vedāṅgas. Manu knew many Dharmaśāstras (III.232). The study of Dharmaśāstras has been considered a must for everyone (*MS* II.10; III.232; VIII.3). *Manu-Smṛti* mentions Ākhyānas, Itihāsa, Purāṇas and Khilas (Sūktas) (III.232). Khilas are known as additional hymns appended to regular collection. But he does not mention the name of any Purāṇa or Itihāsa. He has mentioned several authors of Dharmaśāstras, for example, Atri the son of Utathya (Gautama according to some commentators), Bhṛgu and Śaunaka (III.16), Vasiṣṭha (on the rate of interest, VIII.140) and Vaikhānasa (VI.1). Manu's description of Brāhmaṇa is very close to that of Vedānta (IV.83, 94). The reference of Upaniṣads can also be seen (VI.29; XI.262). The study of Upaniṣads is needed for self-realization. Upaniṣads are capable of revealing the mystery of all Vedas. It seems that by that time there were few groups of people who were opposed to the teachings of Vedas. It may be the school of Lokāyatas or Cārvākas. The reference of *vedabhayaḥ smṛtayaḥ* (XII.95) clears that Manu has criticized those people who distrust Vedas. He describes the heretics and their guilds (IV.30.163). He warns householders not to welcome these people. The *nāstika*s are those who often condemn Vedas and one should try to avoid their company

(IV.163). *Manu-Smṛti* brings out the different concepts very close to different schools of Indian philosophy. It mentions *tarka* without mentioning Naiyāyikas and Dharmapāṭhakas without referring to Mīmāṁsakas (XII.111).

Manu-Smṛti describes the mode of *prāṇāyāma* and suggests that *prāṇāyāma*s accompanied with *oṁkāra*s and *vyāhṛti*s constitute the highest *tapas* (VI.70). *Prāṇāyāma* destroys all aberrations of senses and mind (VI.72). *Manu-Smṛti* details the results of the withdrawal of sense-organs and holding the mind to the tip of the nose. One may experience the subtleness of *Brahman* through *yoga* (VI.64-65). The technical words of *yoga* used in *Manu-Smṛti* may also be seen in some Upaniṣads. *Manu-Smṛti* also relates many theories of *yoga* techniques in order to get the knowledge of *Param Brahman*. It brings out the traces of Sāṁkhya philosophy without mentioning the Sāṁkhya system. In fact, the origin of the universe as depicted in the first chapter of *Manu-Smṛti* is in accordance with the Sāṁkhya concepts. Manu mentions *Nirukta*, but does not mention the name of Yāska. At many places in *Manu-Smṛti*, Manu quotes or refers the views of others by using the words like *kecit* (III.53.261, IX.32), *kī* (X.10, XI.45) and *anye* (III.261). It indicates he was familiar with few other works on Dharmaśāstras. *Manu-Smṛti* refers to four types of vows prevalent at that time. The *vrata*s like Cāndrāyana (XI.117), Atikṛccha (XI.208) and Aśvamedha (XI.260) have been given much importance. *Pañcamahāyajña* is prescribed for every person. *Manu-Smṛti* also refers to Vedic *hiṁsā*. The killing of certain types of animals was allowed for sacrificial purposes (V.23-24, 31). Eating of flesh after offering that to God was permitted up to some extent (V.31-32). The names of many Vedic gods like Indra, Yama, Varuṇa, Soma along with Bhadrakālī, Lakṣmī and Brahmā are also well mentioned in *Manu-Smṛti* III.87-89. *Manu-Smṛti* also mentions the *devapratimā*, *devāgāra* and *devamandira* (IV.39; VIII.248; IX.280). No reference is found about the image of any particular god.

The word *dhyāna-yoga* can be seen in *Śvetāśvatara Upaniṣad*, I.3. *Maitrāyaṇīya Upaniṣad* brings out the details of *khaḍaṅgas* of *yoga* (VI.18). *Kaṭhopaniṣad* considers *yoga* a way to *Parama Brahman* (VI.II). *Kauṣītaki Upaniṣad* I.4 expresses the same view. Manu (VI.79) repeats the very words of Upaniṣad.

A Debate on the Existing Controversy on Mānavadharmaśāstra

Western writers like Georg Bühler, Edward Washburn Hopkins and Arthur Coke Burnell have raised numerous questions on the authorship of *Manu-Smṛti*. They did not consider it an original treatise, but a "versified recension of an older treatise in prose". There is no doubt that all the genuine Dharmaśāstras, which we possess now, are without any exception, nothing but more modern text of earlier Sūtra works on *kula-dharmas* belonging originally to certain Vedic *cāraṇas* (Max Müller, *History of Ancient Sanskrit Literature*, pp. 134-35). They argued that there were many recensions of Vedas used by the people in ancient India. The followers of the different recensions split up framing different schools. These schools had their own Brāhmaṇa *granthas*, Sūtras and law of sacrifices, which did not differ substantially from one another. They also contained a section of traditional law and customs. These authors traced a work named *Mānava-Dharmaśāstra*, a work belonging to *mānavas*, one of the six sub-divisions of Maitrāyaṇīya school of *Black Yajurveda*. They considered that this Dharmaśāstra had not yet been recovered, and was probably lost for ever. There is little doubt that it was turned into verses and added to *Manu-Smṛti* and that this is the actual *Mānava-Dharmaśāstra* (compare Albrecht Weber's *Ind. Literaturgeschichte*, p. 296, n.). According to Bühler, Vasiṣṭha's Dharmaśāstra contains four *sūtras* of *Mānava-Dharmaśāstra*, the first of which is "the *mānava* says that one may kill an animal only for honouring the manes, gods, and guests". It follows three verses and a passage in prose with *iti* at the end. Bühler agreed that all these four *sūtras* are quotations and as the extant *Manu-Smr̥ti* is in verse, these must be regarded as taken from *Mānava-Dharmaśāstra*. There are other quotations in *Vāsiṣṭha-Dharmasūtra* attributed to Manu which either contradict present *Manu-Smr̥ti* or have no counterpart in the latter. Bühler drew special attention to the fact that *Vāsiṣṭha* (19.37) quoted a *mānava* verse which was not in Anuṣṭubha and which had nothing corresponding to it in extant *Manu-Smr̥ti*. Bühler also threw light on a fragment Uṣanas quotation on Manu about impurity which is in prose. It occurs in extant *Manu-Smr̥ti* 5-78. *Kāmandaka Nītisāra* (11-13) says that according to *mānavas*, the *vidyās* to be studied by a king are three, while *Manu-Smr̥ti* (7-43) regards them as four distinct *vidyās*. *Manu-Smr̥ti* (7-54) says that the number of ministers should be seven or eight. According to Bühler, Kāmandaka had in his mind *Mānava-Dharmaśāstra* and not the present *Manu-Smr̥ti*. Weber, A.F. Stenzler, Müller and Bühler addressed this matter in depth. William Whitney concludes:

> Out of last two (Gr̥hya and Dharmasūtras), especially the last, come by the natural development the law books (Dharmaśāstra) which make a conspicuous figure in the later literature: the oldest and the most noted of them being called by the name of Manu (an outgrowth, it is believed, of *Mānava* Vedic school); to which are added that of Yājñavalkya and many others.
>
> — *Sanskrit Grammar*, p. xviii; compare also with Whitney's *Oriental and Linguistic Studies*, I, p. 72

On the strength of the presentation of the complete sets of the Sūtra works of *Āpastamba*, *Śrauta*, *Gr̥hya* and *Dharma* and similarly with *Baudhāyana*, it is regarded that *Mānava Cāraṇa* also had a *sūtra* on *dharma*. Bühler came to the conclusion that the 12th and 13th *parvas* of *Mahābhārata* knew a *Mānava-*

Dharmaśāstra which was closely similar to the present *Manu-Smṛti*. E.W. Hopkins believed that there was a floating mass of verses containing philosophical notes attributed to mythical Manu on which the earlier books of *Mahābhārata* and *Manu-Smṛti* both drew and that the matter that is common to both works was not borrowed from any systematic treatise (Hopkins, *Great Epic of India*, pp. 21-22). Hopkins held that Anuśāsana-Parva of *Mahābhārata* knew of a *Manu-Smṛti*, same as we have now. But both Hopkins and Bühler agreed that the earlier books when they referred Manu were either *Mānava-Dharmaśāstra* or the floating mass of popular verses, but not the present *Manu-Smṛti*.

According to A.C. Burnell the I[st] and XIIth chaps. of *Manu-Smṛti* form an explanatory philosophical framework to the whole text. Eighth chapter, which is an abstract of polity and conduct of life and affairs of the king, is found in the *rāja-dharma* section of *Mahābhārata* and in *Nītīśāstra* and perhaps belongs to later times; such matter is entirely foreign to the original Sūtras. The author also thinks that the text was intended for *rājā*s and similar persons, and was not intended for the use of brāhmaṇas. Burnell admits that Manu was a north Indian and probably a Punjabi brāhmaṇa, who came down to south to help and to civilize the people there. His arguments are based on 123-24 verses of the IInd chapter. The author thinks that Manu lived in a country where little was known of Sanskrit; and this also points to a place in the south of India. He further adds that the text belongs to the second class of Sanskrit law books: that is to say to the books which were intended to popularize the earlier Dharmaśāstras and for practical tribunals.

> It thus appears that the text belongs to an outgrowth of old Brāhmanical literature, which was intended for the benefit of the kings, where the Brāhmanical civilization had begun

> to extend itself over the south of India.
>
> — Introduction to *Manu-Smṛti*, p. xxvii

The author tries to convince that a modified brāhmaṇa civilization arose in south of India with many essential differences as compared to their source, and which gave rise to an enormous secondary literature; *Manu-Smṛti* belongs to that category.

Jolly Julius in his introduction to *Viṣṇu-Dharmasūtra* (p. XXVII) admits:

> Manu has little in common with *Mānava, Gṛhya*, both in *mantra*s and otherwise. Manu is recognized as an ancient writer on Dharmaśāstras in Dharmasūtras.

He quotes the verse 21.7 of *Gautama-Dharmasūtra* where it is said by Manu that "three out of five mortal sins (*mahāpātaka*s) could not be wiped out except by death". The extant *Manu-Smṛti* contains this verse (XI.89-90, 103-04).

According to K.P. Jayaswal, the reference of *Mānava* view in Kauṭilya's *Arthaśāstra* is not traceable in the present text of *Manu-Smṛti* which shows the existence of an early *Mānava Rājanītī Śāstra*. From this floating mass of Manu's verses, the present *Manu-Smṛti,* the redaction of Bhṛgu might have been taken (Manu and Yājñavalkya — Tagore law lecture). His conclusion is based on the word *senāpatya* (*Manu-Smṛti* XII.100). He thinks that Manu has given many powers to brāhmaṇas. But even in *Ṛgveda* the greatness of brāhmaṇas has been described (*ṚV* X.92.12). Even in *Mahābhārata* Droṇa, a brāhmaṇa teacher, was made commander-in-chief of the Kaurava army. The Dharmasūtras like *Gautama* (VII.25), *Baudhāyana* (II.2.80) and *Vāsiṣṭha* (III.24) have allowed brāhmaṇas to use arms for protecting themselves and cows. Pāṇini (V.2.71) describes brāhmaṇas as professional soldiers. In *Arthaśāstra* of Kauṭilya, there is a reference of the army consisting of brāhmaṇas, kṣatriyas, vaiśyas and śūdras.

P.V. Kane in his *History of Dharmaśāstra* has discussed all these theories in detail. The analysis done by the learned author is an eye-opener for the ongoing debate on the authorship of *Manu-Smṛti*. He says:

> Western scholars on account of preconceived baseless notions write about the Indian books and Indian people. How it can be possible that the wild theories about thousands of floating Sanskrit verses among people thousands of years ago, their being welded into one Śāstra and new customs started on the basis of theses verses by a sect of *mānavas*.

Further he says:

> Manu was famed as the great lawgiver of ancient times. Some practices and rules had changed in the course of the centuries. Later writers wanted changes according to their lights to be recognized, but, if that had stated that in their own names, little weight would have been attached to them, therefore they probably hit upon the plan of saying in some cases that the view propounded by them had the authority of Manu. — *History of Dharmaśāstra*, p. 324

While answering the doubts created by few scholars regarding the existence of *Mānava-Dharmaśāstra*, Kane opines that Kāmandaka in his *Nītisāra* is paraphrasing the words of Kauṭilya and not of Manu. Commenting on the use of the word *mānava*, the author says:

> Manu or *Mānava* denotes the same thing. Early writers like Kumārila and Viśvarūpa employ the word *mānavam* with reference to *Manu-Smṛti* just as they use the word *vasiṣṭhayam* to denote *Vāsiṣṭha-Dharmasūtra*. — *Tantravārttika*, pp. 167, 194; Viśvarūpa on *Yājñavalkya-Smṛti* III.245, 257

Śaṅkarācārya in his *Bhāṣya* on *Bṛhadāraṇyaka Upaniṣad* (1.4.7) applies the word *mānava* to *Manu-Smṛti*. Referring to the number of the ministers, *Manu-Smṛti* VII.60 allows more ministers than seven or eight. In the final remodelling of the *Manu-Smṛti* from its original in verse it is not unlikely that few changes have been introduced.

According to Kane:

> . . . most of the quotations attributed to Manu are found in *Manu-Smṛti*. Hence, even if few quotations attributed to Manu are not found in *Manu-Smṛti* we cannot at once jump to the conclusion that Vasiṣṭha had before him not the *Manu-Smṛti* but *Mānava-Dharmasūtra*. It is not right to say that *Vāsiṣṭha-Dharmaśāstra* 11-23, 12-16, 23-43 either contradict or find no counterpart in *Manu-Smṛti. Vāsiṣṭha-Dharmaśāstra* 11-23 correspond with Manu III.245-46. *Vāsiṣṭha-Dharmaśāstra* (23-43) has nothing corresponding to it word for word, but its echo on *Manu-Smṛti* XI.211 is very clear. Bühler's argument about *Mānava* verse in Triṣṭubha is not quite sound. The available text of *Vāsiṣṭha-Dharmasūtra* is far from satisfactory. The non-occurrence of a particular verse found in *Vāsiṣṭha-Dharmaśāstra* in *Manu-Smṛti* cannot be taken very seriously. *Vāsiṣṭha* quotes a *sūtra* of *Gautama* (4.37) which is not found in extant *Gautama-Dharmaśāstra*. In the same manner the verses ascribed to *Vāsiṣṭha* in *Nibandha*s are not found in the printed text of *Vāsiṣṭha*.
>
> The brāhmaṇas in south India were in the very early days of their colonization surrounded by an alien culture and by their alien customs. It was necessary therefore to formulate distinctly the rules of general conduct for the Aryan community in south India, that studied the *Black Yajurveda*. The same necessity did not exist in north India where the members of *sūtra cāraṇa*s knew their ordinary everyday duties very well and were more or less homogeneous community with the same ideals and culture. In the beginning when the manuals on *Śrauta* and *Gṛhya* were first composed, it was not necessary to compose set treatises on *dharma* for each *cāraṇa*. — Kane, *History of Dharmaśāstra*, p. 145

The discovery of writings on *Mānavas* cannot solve the problem of the authorship of *Manu-Smṛti*. First, the existence of *Mānava-Dharmaśāstra* itself is in doubt. Kumārila, the great scholar of all the branches of Sanskrit studies, has not mentioned that the followers of *Black Yajurveda* studied *Mānava-Dharmaśāstra*, though he mentions that they studied *Baudhāyana* and *Āpastamba*. He expresses high regard for *Manu-Smṛti*. Viśvarūpa, the renowned pupil of Śaṅkara, does not agree with the existence of *Mānava-Dharmaśāstra* (p. 18 of Viśvarūpa Commentary on Ācāra section). Second, the doctrines as propounded in *Mānava-Ghṛyasūtra* (ed. Knauer) do not tally with *Manu-Smṛti*. For example, the first verse of the IIIrd chapter of *Manu-Smṛti* prescribes that a student should study Veda till the age of thirty-six. It has opposed *Mānava-Ghṛyasūtra* II.12.1-2. In the same manner, *Mānava-Ghṛyasūtra* I.4.7 opposed *Manu-Smṛti* IV.95; *Mānava-Ghṛyasūtra* I.20.1 opposed *Manu-Smṛti* II.34, *Mānava-Ghṛyasūtra* I.211 to *Manu-Smṛti* II.35, *Mānava-Ghṛyasūtra* I.22, 1 to *Manu-Smṛti* II.36, *Mānava-Ghṛyasūtra* II.12.1-2 to *Manu-Smṛti* III.84-86. The ideas related to domestic rites presented in *Mānava-Ghṛyasūtra* are totally different from the present *Manu-Smṛti*. The details of the funeral rites widely differ in both works. Hence, it cannot be determined that the extant *Manu-Smṛti* is the recast or versified version of *Mānava-Dharmaśāstra*.

The problem of the occurrence of the words like *manuaha* or *manurasbravīta* in *Manu-Smṛti* cannot prove that these are the quotations from some other works. There may be many reasons for this type of usages. Manu was a very ancient law-giver. He designed many social codes befitting to the contemporary society. Many practices may have been changed in the course of time. Since the later writers might have desired to proclaim those old codes in a new light and in order to make them more emphatic, these phrases might have been added. In order to avoid looking too egoistic, ancient authors generally put their own view in third person as said by early writers like Medhātithi and Viśvarūpa. The first person singular was hardly in use.

It is not at all correct to say that the content of *Manu-Smṛti* is based on floating verses. One should not forget that *Manu-Smṛti* is a law book, and these laws were very much in practice. The authenticity is always needed for such books, as they cannot be changed everyday. How a lawmaker like Manu could depend on floating literature? The parallelism of thoughts should be treated as coincidence. There is no foolproof method of proving any direct borrowing of any thought from anywhere. The similarity of thoughts is natural as far as it is concerned with the reformation of the society. The very nature of the thoughts is experimental and it always has kept pace with the needs of the society.

> There is a strong presumption in favour of the practical nature of these works of *dharma* and that the legal rules contained in them must have corresponded to the laws actually enforced in the native court of justice.
>
> — Jolly, *Outline of the History of Hindu Law*, pp. 28-29, 32

The controversy regarding the authorship and the content was instigated mainly by the reference of few similar prose versions of *Manu-Smṛti* in *Vāsiṣṭha-Dharmaśāstra* and *Mahābhārata* mentioning Pracetas Manu and Svayambhuva Manu. As far as the first reason is concerned, it is very interesting to note that even Manu refers Vasiṣṭha by name (VIII.140). Manu quotes *Vāsiṣṭha* in the context of fixing the rate of interest. It seems that during the rewriting of *Manu-Smṛti* the opinion of *Vāsiṣṭha* may have been added to the main text. There may also be a possibility that there could be more than one school of law differing from each other. Manu in the case of fixing the rate of interest might have agreed with *Vāsiṣṭha* and have quoted him. But it is very difficult to comment that who is posterior to whom. There is also another possibility that both the works might have received later editions and the editors might have got a chance to quote each other. Coming to the second point about the reference of three adjectives for Manu, Kane is of the opinion:

> *Mahābhārata* seems to distinguish between Svayambhuva Manu and Pracetas Manu. The former is said to be the promulgator of Dharmaśāstra and the later of Arthaśāstra (or politics). For example, Śānti-Parva (21.12) speaks of Svayambhuva Manu and Śānti-Parva (57.43, 58.2) speaks of Pracetas as an author on Rājaśāstra or *rāja-dharma*. In some places Manu alone without any epithet is associated with *rāja-dharma* and *arthavidyā*. It is not unlikely that originally there were two distinct works, one on *dharma* and other on *Arthaśāstra* attributed to Manu. One may hazard the conjecture that the author of the *Manu-Smṛti* whoever he might have been, combined in his work the information contained in the two works on Dharmaśāstra and Arthaśāstra. — Kane in *History of Dharmaśāstra,* p. 311

This idea has to be reconsidered. In the extant *Manu-Smṛti,* the work is ascribed to Svayambhuva Manu and the six other Manus, of whom the Pracetas is not enumerated (I.62). He also has not been referred as giving any statement. Pracetas is mentioned as a son of Manu (I.35). It may also be noted that in the extant *Manu-Smṛti* Manu Svayambhuva occurs in verse VI.54 (on the vessels to be used by ascetics), VIII.124 (the part of the body where the corporal punishment has to be inflicted and exemption of the brāhmaṇas from corporal punishment), IX.158 (the twelve varieties of the sons). In addition to that, there is one more epithet to Manu; Manu Prajāpati. Manu Prajāpati is mentioned in X.78 and XII.123 (the highest *Puruṣa* is called by someone as Manu Prajāpati). In Indian literary tradition there is a practice of addressing one scholar by few names. Kauṭilya itself is an example. There may be another assumption that these words may have been used to complete the syllables of the meter of the text. At this point one thing has to be noted that Bhṛgu is also mentioned as the son of primeval Manu (*Manu-Smṛti* I.35). The entire extant *Manu-Smṛti* is presented by Bhṛgu, a pupil of Manu. Aparārka on *Yājñavalkya-Smṛti* II.96 (p. 696) quotes a verse of Bhṛgu on the ordeals in which the view of Manu is cited, which indicates that Aparārka was known to Bhṛgu in which Manu's name was referred. There is also a possibility that both Pracetas and Bhṛgu were the pupils of Manu. The Pracetas mentioned in *Mahābhārata* might be a person responsible for elaborating the *rāja-dharma* part of the original *Manu-Smṛti* and in order to maintain the line of the original work, the word Manu might have been suffixed.

Manu-Smṛti mentions many branches of Sanskrit works, but nowhere it mentions any work like *Rājanitiśāstra.* While considering the scheme of the whole text of *Manu-Smṛti* it is clear that the work is surely of a compact nature. It is not fair to say that the first and the last two chapters are interpolations. Bühler comes to the conclusion that the cosmological and philosophical portion in the first and twelfth chapters, the philosophical accounts in II.89-100, the classification of *pitaras* in III.193-201, the means of subsistence for brāhmaṇas in IV.1-24, verses 1-4 of the Vth chapter, the rules about mixed castes (X.1-7) and the duties of the castes that are repeated in X.101-31 were added at the time of versification of *Mānava-Dharmaśāstra* (SBE vol. 25, pp. LXVI-LXXIII). The first chapter, which deals with the creation and destruction of the universe and the creation of four castes, in fact, should be treated as a prologue to the whole work and the index of the whole content. Smṛtis were written to popularize the content of the four Vedas. In the beginning of the work Manu has recognized the authority of the Vedas as the source of all branches of knowledge, specially of *dharma* (II.6). Vedic literature contains lots of philosophical concepts as well. The very reason of composition of the work like *Manu-Smṛti* was to educate the common people how to lead a life by balancing *artha* and *kāma* with *dharma* and prepare them to attain the final goal of life (*mokṣa*). The last chapter, which deals with *saṁnyāsa* and *mokṣa*, is full of philosophical thoughts written for guiding the common masses towards their final goal (*mokṣa*). Kane thinks:

> Original *Manu-Smṛti* in verse had certain additions made in order to bring it in line with the changes in the general attitude of the people on several points such as those of flesh eating, *niyoga* and others.
>
> — *History of Dharmaśāstra*, p. 332

It is totally unfair to comment that *Manu-Smṛti* was intended only for kings or even for brāhmaṇas. It is also not correct to connect the work to any brāhmaṇa dynasty and to comment that *Manu-Smṛti* gives special privileges to brāhmaṇas. One should not forget that the creation of the four castes was done with the purpose of bringing harmony in the society by reminding them to stick to their own duties. In *Manu-Smṛti* both brāhmaṇas and kṣatriyas got equal importance. King being the essence of all gods, got special position in the society (*Manu-Smṛti* VII.7-10). Many strict rules were formed for the king and it was mandatory on the part of the king to follow them (VII.32-34). In the same manner, all brāhmaṇas did not get the same honour. It was must for a brāhmaṇa to be knowledgeable and well versed in Vedas (I.97, II.157). *Manu-Smṛti* itself declares its purpose of composition by stating that this work intends to remind each and every section of the society towards its duties (*MS* I.102). According to *Mitākṣarā*, Dharmaśāstras deal with all aspects of the society and, therefore, they deal with *rāja-dharma* also (*Mitākṣarā* on *Yājñavalkya-Smṛti* II.21).

The comment that the content of *Manu-Smṛti* is based on the floating literature is baseless. It is correct that many codes of conduct were in existence since the Vedic period and they were the source of *Manu-Smṛti.* Manu gave a systematic treatise covering the life of each and every person of the society. The historical parallelism should be treated as coincidence. There is no evidence to prove direct borrowing of any thought from anywhere. It is a fact that the Indian mind kept on producing thousands of great ideas for the development of the society. It is natural to have similarities between the guidelines provided by the great thinkers who formed various rules for the refinement of the society. It is difficult to believe that thousands of years ago, thousands of floating Sanskrit verses had the same content as *Manu-Smṛti* and became the basis of extant *Manu-Smṛti.*

Another question is whether *Manu-Smṛti* has gone under several recasts? It is rather unfair to say that *Manu-Smṛti* has passed through several recasts. It is a fact that *Manu-Smṛti* contains many contradictory statements. For example, Manu allows a brāhmaṇa to marry a śūdra woman (III.3). But later on he condemns this practice (III.14-19). In the same manner, at first, *niyoga* is allowed (IX.53-62). In IX.64-68 *niyoga* is criticized. The conflicting passages do not prompt the recasting of the text. There is a probability that Manu accepted prevailing laws as local laws and which he himself might have rejected. It is also possible that the author might have desired to put two opinions side by side without giving special preference to any one of those. *Nārada-Smṛti, Bṛhaspati-Smṛti* and *Vṛddha-Manu* cannot establish that *Manu-Smṛti* underwent many recasts. These Smṛtis are based on *Manu-Smṛti.* Many a time the quotations ascribed to Manu are not found in *Manu-Smṛti.* It may have many reasons. As Manu was a popular lawgiver, it was considered authentic to put any verse anywhere with the authorship of Manu. It is impossible to find any substantial evidence to prove that *Manu-Smṛti* had undergone several recasts.

Before entering into the most tedious debate on deciding the time of *Manu-Smṛti,* it will be proper to throw some light on the relation of *Manu-Smṛti* with *Mahābhārata* and *Arthaśāstra,* as these two works have maximum common themes.

Relation of Manu-Smṛti to Mahābhārata and Arthaśāstra

Mahābhārata is regarded as the encyclopaedia of all branches of knowledge. It also contains many verses related to Dharmaśāstra and *Arthaśāstra. Mahābhārata* at many places brings out the expressions like *manur-abravīt,* "the *rāja-dharma* of Manu" and "the Śāstras of Manu". Many of these references found in *Mahābhārata* are present in the extant *Manu-Smṛti* and many are not. Manu's *rāja-dharma* is well mentioned in the twelfth book of *Mahābhārata* (XII, III.35.21), where Manu is mentioned as lawgiver along with Aṅgiras, Uṣanas and others (XII.200.30). Anuśāsana-Parva refers Manu several times (47.35). Śānti-Parva speaks of two verses "sung by Manu stating his own *dharma*". One of these is same as in *Manu-Smṛti* IX.321. In another place Śānti-Parva brings out the *rāja-dharma* propounded by Manu (56.23-25). Droṇa-Parva refers *mānavī-vidyā* (7.1). Vana-Parva refers *rāja-dharmas* proclaimed by Manu (35.2.21). At one place in Anuśāsana-Parva, the author says that he is putting his own view only after hearing Manu's view (61.34-35).

These references are equally scattered all over the *parvas* of *Mahābhārata.* Apart from these, there are hundreds of verses in *Mahābhārata* bringing forth the similarity with Manu. According to Bühler, in Vana, Śānti and Anuśāsana *parvas* there are at least 260 verses, which may be considered of Manu. V.N. Mandlik (*Introduction to the Vyavahāramayūkha,* XLVII) considers that *Manu-Smṛti* has borrowed many verses from *Mahābhārata.* Bühler concludes that 12th and 13th *parvas* of *Mahābhārata* knew *Mānava-Dharmaśāstra* which was closely connected with but not identical with the present *Manu-Smṛti* (see SBE vol. 25, p. LXXIV-XCVIII). Hopkins asserts that only the 13th book of *Mahābhārata* recognizes the Śāstra declared by Manu (*Great Epics of India*, pp. 21-22). He asserts:

> References to Manu's law book are seldom verifiable in the present *Manu-Smṛti* while references in the didactic epic more often than not correspond to passages of the extant text. Hence, it may be inferred that that part of the epic which agrees most closely in its citations with our code is later than the portion which does not coincide, or, conversely, that the extant *Manu-Smṛti* was shaped into its present form between the time of the early epic and that of the didactic epic. In the first period, when Manu's Dharmaśāstra was unknown, Manu was merely a name to conjure with. The verses thus ascribed to Manu were not all put in the code when it was formed and for this reason the earlier citations are not found in the text.

Here one fact is worth mentioning that in Anuśāsana-Parva there are altogether eleven quotations from *Manu-Smṛti*, out of which only one does not correspond with *Manu-Smṛti*.

According to Kane,

> The *Mahābhārata* has nowhere been mentioned by name in *Manu-Smṛti*, though the word *itihāsa* (in plural) occurs in *Manu-Smṛti* (III.232). The *Manu-Smṛti* mentions many historical and legendary personages, about most of whom the *Mahābhārata* contains similar stories.

The following are the persons common to both *Mahābhārata* and *Manu-Smṛti*: Aṅgiras (II.151-52); Agastya (V.22); Vena, Nahuṣa, Sudās, Paijavana and Nimi (VII.41); Pṛthu, Manu, Kubera and the sons of Gādhi (VII.42); Vasiṣṭha (VIII.110); Vatsa (VIII.116); Akṣamāla and Sāraṅgī (IX.23); Dakṣa (IX.128-29); Ajigarta (X.105); Vāmadeva (X.106); Bharadvāja (X.107); Viśvāmitra (X.108); Pṛthu (IX.44). Most of these stories go back to the Vedic literature. Many of these names are familiar to *Ṛgveda* and *Aitareya Brāhmaṇa*. Manu does not state that these references have been taken from *Mahābhārata*. It also cannot be admitted that *Mahābhārata* originated all these references. It is also difficult to prove that both *Manu-Smṛti* and *Mahābhārata* collected these stories from some unknown source. There is no sense of looking for a floating connection when the Vedic background is available in an authentic form.

The content of *Mahābhārata* contains variety of thoughts, stories, religion, politics and philosophy. *Manu-Smṛti* propounds just the code of conduct needed for the welfare of the society. *Mahābhārata* is a combination of virtues and vices, while *Manu-Smṛti* teaches the great philosophy of righteousness. If we compare *Manu-Smṛti* with *Mahābhārata* it becomes clear that the civilization and laws as depicted in *Mahābhārata* are much more advanced than *Manu-Smṛti*. In Anuśāsana-Parva (XIII.90.30) the *paṅkeya*s, or the men who were invited to sit in the row at the funeral feast, were much more than in the list presented in *Manu-Smṛti* (III.184-85). The list in *Mahābhārata* includes the people entitled to sit in the row, and specified that they should be well acquainted with *itihāsa*, *bhāṣyavidas* and *vyākaraṇaratah̤* (delighted with grammar). They should also study Purāṇas and Dharmaśāstra and should take bath in the holy pool. This list is advanced in position, compared to the one held by Manu.

Mahābhārata mentions several types of arts, fine arts and different *kalā*s. Even the slave girls of Yudhiṣṭhira are said to be well versed in singing, dancing and sixty-four *kalā*s (II.61.9-10). On the contrary, Manu does not favour any type of performing art. He condemns dancing. The *kuśīlava*s (actors) have been prohibited to take part in *devapitṛ-karma* (*MS* III.155). They are also not allowed as witness in the royal court of justice (*MS* VIII.65). It seems that during Manu's period the general atmosphere was of the Vedic rituals and not of music and fine arts.

Mahābhārata describes India as a great power. The limit of their empire as geographically defined was vast. It includes all the states right from north Himalayan part of India to extreme southern part extending up to seashores. Manu has no idea of the vast empire. His ideal of a king is a very spiritual one, who has to follow the strict rules in his personal as well as public life (*MS* VII.101, 112, 123). The management of the state as described in *Mahābhārata* is also more systematic and much advanced. *Harivaṁśa* mentions Roman Denarious. The legal documents were documented as *citra-paṭa* (XV.32.20). There is a reference of rock inscription (XIII.139-43). The documentation of legal papers is not very systematic in *Manu-Smr̥ti.* It mentions only boundary made between the lands of two owners (VIII.261-26). The demarcations were done mostly by constructing ponds and by planting trees (VIII.262). *Manu-Smr̥ti* does not mention that the gifts given to priests were safeguarded by anything like copperplates as it is recorded in later Smr̥tis. The art of warfare as mentioned in *Mahābhārata* is of advanced nature. The kings knew types of *vyūhas*, which are not included in *Manu-Smr̥ti.* It mentions six types of *vyūhas* (VII.187), but does not say anything about *cakra-vyūha,* which is prominent in *Mahābhārata.* The war codes depicted in *Mahābhārata* are fully different from *Manu-Smr̥ti.* It recommends war as a last resort. One should try to conquer the enemy by *sāma* and *dāma.* The war should be the last resort (VII.198). The main theme of *Mahābhārata* is the war between Kauravas and Pāṇḍavas. The war codes are also of a practical nature and have been broken several times.

Mahābhārata shows acquaintance to advanced building construction and Vāstu-Śāstra. The elaborate description of the palaces in Hastināpura, and the creation of *lākṣāgr̥ha* show that they knew the art of architecture very well. There is a reference of a statue made of iron (XI.12.15). The iron bells were used in the temples (XII.141.32). They knew that Yavanas were strong, heroic and skilled in weapons (XIII.207.43). These elements are totally missing in *Manu-Smṛti.*

Coming down to the philosophy and religion in *Mahābhārata,* it may be said that in comparison to *Manu-Smṛti* it depicts a different wave of thoughts. *Manu-Smṛti* considers Veda a supreme authority in every respect and follows the Vedic thoughts in their full form. The six schools of Indian philosophy are unknown to *Manu-Smṛti.* The theories similar to Sāṁkhya, Yoga or even Vedānta are influenced by Upaniṣads. *Manu-Smṛti* does not put any reference to the Jaina or Buddhist philosophy. Even the Lokāyatas are not mentioned by name. *Manu-Smṛti* puts more emphasis on the science of *jñāna,* ascetic practice, *tapas, yoga* and rituals, which are recognized as older systems in *Mahābhārata. Mahābhārata* describes a Jaina priest clothed like a madman (XIV.6.18). A few references distinctly refer to the Buddhists (XIII.23.99, XIII.93.1, XII.167.46). *Mahābhārata* mentions three *pramāṇas* (*pratyakṣa* XII.269.10; *anmanā* XII.269.33; 261.9-10; *upamāna* III.31.11-33). It mentions Kapila as the founder of Sāṁkhya (XII.351, 356). It (XII.15.26) mentions Nyāya system. In XII.350.64 it is said that there are four current philosophies:

> *Jñānāni,* the Sāṁkhya, Yoga, Pāñcarātra and Pāśupatas. Hiraṇyagarbha is the teacher of Yoga, Apāntaratamas is called the teacher of Vedas; Śiva declared the Pāśupata and Viṣṇu the whole Pāñcarātra. In all these philosophies Viṣṇu is the chief god.

Nyāya also gets a place (XVIII.6-67). VIII.82.16 says about Pāśupatas. In *Mahābhārata* several forms of religion are advocated. Apart from the orthodoxy, there stands a new faith, which discards the old scripture as an authority (XII.233.20). Here it has been said:

> One who is thoroughly conversant with the Vedas may

attain brāhmaṇahood, but the devotee even by desire of wisdom surpasses the Vedas.

The Bhakti cult or the concept of personal god does not find any place in *Manu-Smṛti*, whereas *Mahābhārata* expounds the philosophy of Kṛṣṇaism (XII.345.7). Vāsudeva, an incarnation of Viṣṇu, has been described as *Parameśvara*. *Mahābhārata* recognizes many sects. The whole epic is dominated by Bhāgavata System. *Bhakti* or the grace of god gets the highest value. "The man can see Him, to whom He gives His grace. He is the chief element of salvation" (XII.337.20). Thus *Manu-Smṛti* and *Mahābhārata* in spite of many similarities (in terms of *rāja-dharma* and social codes), bear many differences. These differences were designed because of the lapse of the time. Any worth-mentioning work of a particular period is regulated by the general mode of thinking of the people of that time. The change of thinking should be treated as a natural evolution. Both *Manu-Smṛti* and *Mahābhārata* belong to two different periods. The change of the ideology introduces modernity and presents the epoch of that period.

Arthaśāstra of Kauṭilya is a great work that India has produced. It deals mainly with government and politics. It includes politics, economics, law and justice by keeping Dharmaśāstra in the background. *Arthaśāstra* literally means the science of *artha*, one of the four *puruṣārtha*s. *Arthaśāstra* of Kauṭilya deals with all aspects of an ideal governance. *Arthaśāstra* is really a branch of Dharmaśāstra as it deals with the responsibilities of the kings for whom the rules are laid down in many treatises on *dharma*. The purpose of the Śāstra as stated by Kauṭilya himself is "to prescribe means for securing and preserving power over the earth" (15.1.2). *Manu-Smṛti* II.224 refers to different views of the respective eminence of four *puruṣārtha*s. *Artha* and *kāma* supported with *dharma* may lead anyone to *mokṣa*. *Manu-Smṛti* conveys the supremacy of *dharma* and treats *Arthaśāstra* as *rāja-dharma*. It states that in the case of the conflict between Dharmaśāstra and *Arthaśāstra* the former is stronger.

These two works were written at two different times. The extant Kauṭilya quotes several individual predecessors such as Kaunapadanta, Piśuna, Bahudantiputra, Bharadvāja, Vātavyādhi and Viśālākṣa, and few schools such as Ambhiyas, Auśanasas, Pārāśaras, Bārhaspatyas and Mānavas. *Arthaśāstra* quotes verses which are often preceded with such words as *atra ślokaḥ*, thereby intimating that they are quotations from a work or works. It quotes (*Ar.* II.2) nine verses which either closely agree with Manu or state the similar ideas in similar words. (In *Ar.* II.3 it says *atra ślokaḥ* which closely agrees with extant *Manu-Smṛti* chap. VII. In II.21 of *Ar.* the prose and the verse are same as in *MS* VIII.26. *MS* VII.101 is similar to *Ar.* I.4; *Ar.* I.4 is close to *MS* VII.162; *Ar.* III.1 is same as *MS* VIII.55; *Ka.* III.7 is same as *MS* 332 ; *Ar.* I.15 can be compared with *MS* VII.105; *Ar.* III.14.27 is similar to *MS* XI.14; *Ar.* III.7.1-2 have almost the same idea and words as *MS* VIII.332; *Ar.* V.4 is close to *MS* IV.138.)

The main theme of *Manu-Smṛti* is to declare *dharma*s pertaining to the four *varṇa*s in the society and to make them adhere to their duties. Politics and governance are treated as a part of the whole scheme. Manu was more concerned with the general conduct of the human being. It seems that he had no intention to get indulged in the tricky nature of politics. He accepts the importance of wealth earned in a righteous manner. Hence he rejects all those theories which may hinder the path of *dharma*. On the contrary, *Arthaśāstra* of Kauṭilya presents the very practical and well-developed form of politics. As regards the comparison of these two great works, it may be said undoubtedly that they belong to two different ages. The interval of the time could induce many cognate changes. These changes of social codes covered all aspects of human life. *Manu-Smṛti* (III.13, later half) allows a kṣatriya to marry a woman of his own caste or vaiśya or a śūdra, but later on in III.14, it condemns it. Kauṭilya gives the relaxation (III.6.26). He not only allows a brāhmaṇa to marry a girl from other caste but advocates that in the case of a brāhmaṇa the son born of a śūdra wife should receive one-third of the deceased father's property as his share. *Arthaśāstra* of Kauṭilya appears to ridicule consulting astrology too much. In IX.4.26, it is said that, "the coveted object or goal slips from the foolish person who continuously consults the stars, for the object is auspicious or not". Kauṭilya seldom refers to the impact of *rāśi*s on human beings. While in *Manu-Smṛti* observance of the auspicious *graha* is recommended at every step (see III.43-45, 127; VII.128). Jolly argues that Kauṭilya was acquainted to *Manu-Smṛti*. It is a difficult task to comment on this point, but it may be said that in many cases the theories present in *Manu-Smṛti* have been improved or lengthened in *Arthaśāstra*. Manu is very particular about the vices of a king. He mentions many vices born of different emotions. In VII.47-48 it has been said that there are ten vices caused by lust and eight vices due to anger and a king must keep away from them. *Arthaśāstra* (VIII.3) reduces the vices due to lust to four and the vices due to anger to three, and holds a long discussion on the comparative harm caused by these vices. Manu starts the daily time-table in a brief style (VII.216.16). *Arthaśāstra* prescribes (I.19.9-24) an ideal daily timetable for kings and considers that if the king is active, his servants will also be the same. He compares administration with sacrifice (I.19.33-35).

If a man dies without a son as his successor, his mother will inherit all the properties due to him. In case the mother is also deceased, his paternal grandmother will inherit his entire properties (IX.217). Kauṭilya ignores the widow or the mother of a person as heir. Kauṭilya prescribes *niyoga* even in the case of a brāhmaṇa (III.6; I.17 about kings). Manu first accepts *niyoga* and later on rejects it (IX.57-63 and IX.64-68). Manu's view has also been supported by Bṛhaspati. *Arthaśāstra* has tried to improve Manu's idea of *niyoga* as it may have suited to that time. *Manu-Smṛti* VIII.4-7 mention that a king is entitled to look after the business of eighteen departments. Kauṭilya speaks out those eighteen titles by giving them the name of *prakīrṇaka.* Manu talks only of *nikṣepa* (VIII.179-81). Kauṭilya talks even of *upanidha* (II.64). Manu is very sure to say that (IX.1155) the son of any member of the first three *varṇa*s from a śūdra woman does not inherit his father's wealth, while *Arthaśāstra* allows such a son a share along with the sons born to a brāhmaṇa from wives of higher castes or one-third when he has no other sons (III.6.22). Manu prohibits the remarriage of the widows (V.161-65). Kauṭilya allows not only widows to remarry but also those wives whose husbands are abstained without a sufficient cause for a year or more, according to circumstances (III.4.37-38). Kauṭilya adds more points to the laws of divorce. "A wife may divorce a husband who is a traitor to the king or has become an outcaste" (III.2.48). One may divorce her husband on the ground of mutual hatred (III.3.19). Manu is very harsh to gamblers and asks the king to suppress the gamblers and to banish them (IX.221-24). Kauṭilya brings gambling under the control of the king for the purpose of detecting thieves and for getting tax to royal treasury (III.20.2). *Arthaśāstra* presents a very systematic procedure of governance. It provides for a greater development of juristic provisions than *Manu-Smṛti.* Manu deals with *kaṇṭaka-śodhana* in a very light manner, while Kauṭilya takes up this issue to full length. Manu (IX.252-53) says that a king should suppress *kaṇṭaka*s, there is hardly any detailed treatment in *Manu-Smṛti* of that topic. It does not deal with criminal matters, but just with unsocial matters. Kauṭilya has handled this matter very carefully. He says:

> A king should prevent traders, artisans, actors, mendicants, jugglers and such others people, from harming the country, as in reality, they too are thieves but are not known as thieves. —IV.1.65

Kauṭilya was a careful administrator. He recommends twenty-five departments and *adhyakṣa*s for controlling thieves. Manu prescribes banishment for the brāhmaṇas as punishment, but Kauṭilya states that there should be a branded mark on the head of the criminal brāhmaṇa. Kauṭilya considers that a stronger ruling is a must for the good administration of the country. He is in favour of using all kinds of sinister methods. In Adhikaraṇa XIV he allows unscrupulous use of poison, desperadoes, prostitutes, charms and magic for liquidating the enemy. He stands alone in recommending secret practices of poisons. Manu is far away from all these tactics. In reference to Kauṭilya, it may be said that the work itself is more systematic as it is divided in *adhikaraṇa, prakaraṇa, sūtra* and *udāharaṇa*s. Each and every idea has been explained well and is free of any contradictions. *Manu-Smṛti,* on the other hand, is not that systematic and contains many contradictions. Kauṭilya's knowledge of the alchemy and metallurgy is of advanced nature in relation to Manu. Kauṭilya exhibits a wonderful knowledge of herbs and drugs. He speaks of *rasada* (one who administers mercurial poison) and prescribes banishment for those who trade in or administer *rasa* for money in order to move away with a person secretly (IV.4.17-18). In II.13 he describes *rasa-viddha* (gold amalgamated with mercury). In II.12 he describes liquids containing gold (*rasaḥ kāñcanikaḥ*). These subjects were unknown to Manu.

Kauṭilya shows a great advancement of town planning and architectural intricacy. Apart from the fortified capital for the king, he also gives details for constructing enclosures for the gods of Vāstu-Śāstra (II.4.17-20). The construction of the temples of Śiva, Vaiśravaṇa, Aśvins, Śrī (the goddess of wealth) and Madirā (Durgā) also finds an important place in his scheme. The city gates should be presided over by Brahmā, Indra and Senāpati. The whole of the second *adhikaraṇa* is dedicated to town planning. Manu was totally unaware of these advancements.

Manu insists on *dharma*, consisting moral and spiritual good as the main goal of human life and treats *artha* (empirical enjoyment) and *kāma* (pleasure of senses) as inferior and advises to give up *artha* and *kāma* that are opposed to *dharma* (*MS* IV.176). The composition of *Arthaśāstra* was done for the benefit of the rulers. Hence, it states that "*artha* alone is supreme", for *dharma* and *kāma* depend on *artha* (I.7.6-7). Thus, though *Arthaśāstra* and *Manu-Smṛti* contain many similar theories, the principles and emphasis of both works are not identical. They represent the echoes of two different periods. Surely, *Arthaśāstra* is the outcome of a long period of diplomatic activity in the field of politics.

Time of Manu-Smṛti

The most tedious part of the study of any work is to decide its age and time. The long history of India, the lack of documentation, the endless Western theories, the multitudes of foreign invasions causing all types of destruction and disturbances are the main hindrances in reaching out to the facts. The traditions have set some milestones for deciding the date of any work; for example, the time of Buddha, Alexander's invasion, the records given by Megasthenes and the references of Greek words. All these factors are of dubious nature and create more confusion and lead to uncertainty. While discussing the date of Manu we should deal more with the external and internal evidences and will try to justify them with these factors.

The external evidences: The first available commentary on *Manu-Smṛti* is of Medhātithi, which was composed about CE 900. The extant *Manu-Smṛti* is almost the same as it was in CE 900. It proves that long before Medhātithi the work had taken its final shape. Viśvarūpa in his commentary on *Yājñavalkya-Smṛti* quotes more than 200 of verses from the beginning to the end of *Manu-Smṛti*. It is sure that Viśvarūpa had surely gone through the extant *Manu-Smṛti.* Viśvarūpa is surely a predecessor of Śaṅkarācārya. Śaṅkarācārya in his *Vedānta-Sūtra-Bhāṣya* (CE 800) himself quotes many verses from *Manu-Smṛti* [see *MS* I.5-21 (*VS* I.3.38); *MS* I.27 (*VS* IV.2.6); *MS* II.87 (*VS* III.4.38); *MS* X.4-126 (*VS* I.3.36); *MS* XII.91-106 (*VS* II.1-11)]. *Tantravārttika* of Kumārila (CE 700) has cited many verses from *Manu-Smṛti. Mṛcchakaṭika* of Śūdraka (9.39) refers the ordinances of Manu that a brāhmaṇa sinner should not be sentenced to death, but should be banished (CE 400). The inscription of Vallabhi king Dharasena (CE 571) refers the code of Manu. Śabarasvāmin (CE 571) recognizes the work of Manu. *Bṛhaspati-Smṛti* (not later than CE 500) follows *Manu-Smṛti* fully. Bṛhaspati was also aware of Bhṛgu's connection with Manu. Aśvaghoṣa (first century CE) in his *Bajrasūci* quotes *Mānavadharma*, which is available in extant *Manu-Smṛti.* The references found in *Rāmāyaṇa* and *Mahābhārata* are seen in extant *Manu-Smṛti,* and even Manu's name is mentioned in these epics (Kiṣkindhā Kāṇḍa 18.30, 18.31, 18.32; *Mbh.* Anusāśana Parva 47.34). All these evidences show that *Manu-Smṛti* was composed much prior to them all. The authority of the work indicated by all these authors proves that *Manu-Smṛti* might have assumed its popularity at least towards the third century BCE. It is also well proved that the two great epics of India had before them the work of Manu. It is not correct to say that the Smṛtis were composed later than the Dharmasūtras. Many metrical works were done along with the Sūtras. That is why there are so many similarities between Dharmasūtras and Dharmaśāstras. The Sūtra period goes back to 600 BCE.

Th. Goldstücker (1861) pointed out that Pāṇini (300 BCE) did not know of this work and no trace of it appears even in *Mahābhāṣya* of Patañjali (about 150 years later). So, the work, it indicates, was not done before the first century CE. This argument is far from satisfactory. These two grammarians were surely to concentrate on the tedious work of grammar and might not have found a proper context for referring a work on Dharmaśāstra. Hence it cannot be concluded that *Manu-Smṛti* was written after Pāṇini. Burnell argues that *Manu-Smṛti* was compiled between the first century CE and CE 500. But this theory has no base as many works composed before this period refer *Manu-Smṛti*. *Manu-Smṛti* was taken by the Indians settled in Malay Islands (Menu Kvay). This emigration started from second century CE. *Manu-Smṛti* on the other hand was much known by that time. Many Western scholars are of the view that in 300 BCE Greeks found out that the Indians had no written law (Megasthenes, Fr. XXVII). Their statement is based on the travel record placed before them by Megasthenes. He came to India later than 305 BCE. There are great infirmities in his work, *Indica*. The original work has not come down to us. Most of the discussions are based on the available fragments. The statements found in these fragments cannot be used as arguments. He stayed in India for a very short period. It is very difficult to ascertain his knowledge of Indian languages and literature. How is it possible for a person coming from another far-off country and going through the vast annals of Indian literature within a short span of time and then mentioning each and every work in his own record? Megasthenes, an ambassador in Patna court, mentions no eminent Indians by name except Sandracottos. Megasthenes has mentioned that the people in India were worshipping *tridevas* (Brahmā, Viṣṇu, Maheśa). *Manu-Smṛti* has no reference of this type. It seems that at Manu's time the concept of *trideva* was not developed. The occurrence of the words like Yavana or Kamboja can not prove that *Manu-Smṛti* was written after the invasion of Alexander.

> Yavana is an exact reproduction of the word "Ionia", which was originally a strip of the mountain coast in Asia Minor in which Miletus was (in sixth century BCE) the richest city in the Greek world.

It is possible that the Indians knew this word much prior to Alexander's arrival.

> The Greek words were known to Indians much prior to the arrival of Alexander. Pāṇini (third cenctury BCE) was acquainted with the word Yavana (Pāṇini's *Aṣṭādhyāyī* IV.1.49). The word Yavana (*Prākṛta — Yona, Yonaka*) itself is a Sanskritized form of old Persian Yauna, by which name the Ionian Greeks and later on all Greeks were designated by Persians. — *Cultural History of India*, vol. II, p. 615

In fact, there was a good trade relation between India and the Middle East countries long before the invasion of Alexander. They came to India through the way of Mesopotamia.

Another scholar holds the opinion that *Manu-Smṛti* belongs to a later period as it is in *śloka* verse, and in a very simple and modern language (see pp. 320-21 of John Peter Avery's paper, *Journal of American Society*, vol. X). The text thus closely resembles the versified forms of ritual Sūtras, the composition of which appears to have chiefly occurred in the early centuries of CE. This argument needs to be verified. The *śloka* metre was in use even long time back. The use of other metres like Āryā were in use long before 150 BCE. Pāṇini was aware of many metres (Āryā 1.1.57 and 1.2.51; Indrabajra 1.4.109; Vasantatilakā, *Vārttika* on Pā. III.2.29). The style and language of *Manu-Smṛti* are simple, but this does not mean that it is modern. The language of Upaniṣads is also simple and contains no intricacy of the compounds.

K.P. Jayaswal in his work (*Manu and Yājñavalkya,* p. 32) refers to *Manu-Smṛti* XII.100 and considers it as the sample of an aggressive brāhmaṇa spirit that arose at the time of Puṣyamitra, a king of Śuṅga dynasty. He considers that *Manu-Smṛti* was composed at that time (first century CE). This argument has no base as the high position of brāhmaṇas was continuing since the Vedic period. It is also certain that the greater part of India was in great trouble in the first century CE, and it is impossible to suppose that the work like *Manu-Smṛti,* which was surely composed in a peaceful time, could have been written then.

Bühler (SBE, vol. 25, p. cxvii) thinks that *Manu-Smṛti* was composed between second century BCE and second century CE. Many scholars agree with this date. Kane gives a very concise view. He thinks that the time of the composition of the original *Manu-Smṛti* cannot be fixed. The extant *Manu-Smṛti* is an addition to the original one, which was made some time between second century BCE to second century CE. The author goes in favour of considering *Manu-Smṛti* even being earlier than *Mahābhārata.* He also feels that even Kauṭilya, the author of *Arthaśāstra,* had a copy of *Manu-Smṛti.*

> *Arthaśāstra* is earlier than *Manu-Smṛti* though not earlier than the oldest kernel of *Manu-Smṛti.*
>
> — *History of Dharmaśāstra,* p. 208

After going through all these discussions, it seems obvious that *Manu-Smṛti* was composed much earlier than what has been mentioned by some scholars. We cannot rely on the arguments presented by different Western scholars. A society cannot run without a proper code of conduct. The social problems were in existence even during the Vedic period and due care was taken to curb them. The Brāhmanic period introduced lots of rigidity and many methods were used to protect the Vedic ritualism. It may have been the time for bringing forth the strict code of conduct. *Manu-Smṛti* was composed to show its solidarity towards the Vedas and to expand the Vedic way of living. As we go through the whole text of *Manu-Smṛti,* it becomes clear that at every step it supports the Vedic philosophy. *Manu-Smṛti* uses the word *nāstikas,* but not necessarily for Buddhas or Jainas. In the entire text of *Manu-Smṛti* the word *nāstika* has been used only a few times (II.11, III.65, IV.163, VIII.22, XI.60, XII.33). In most of the cases the word implies for the persons who do not accept the authority of the Vedas. We may witness the germs of free speculations, suggestions and scepticism even in *Ṛgveda* VII.89.3-4. The intellectual curiosity sometimes ended in revolt. When suspicion about the nature of the life on the earth arises, the belief in God gets weakened. Whenever the man is not happy with the course of his life, he starts blaming God. This leads to the disintegration of faith and declaration of independence of man. It may be treated as a reaction. It is true that the disease and the remedy appear simultaneously, and whatever the poisonous streams of error flow, there too springs up the tree of life, whose leaves have the healing effect. *Manu-Smṛti* was composed at similar time with similar purpose.

> Several vestiges show that even in the pre-Buddhistic time India proclaims of purely materialistic doctrine; and there is no doubt that those doctrines had ever afterward, as they have today, numerous secret followers.
>
> — Richard Garbe, *The Philosophy of Ancient India*, p. 25

There are ample evidences to the existence of *Bṛhaspati-Sūtra* and the Cārvākas. They tried for the removal of the Lokāyatas dogmatism and made room for speculations. This effort was not very positive and that is why it could not survive for a longer period. *Manu-Smṛti* tried to remodel its own religion, assimilating the desired notions and the morality needed for the newcomers. Surely, it was the period before Buddha. One must not forget that the morality and righteousness were the basis of Buddhism and the same principles were supported by Manu. Buddha did not breakaway completely from the traditional Indian thoughts. He tried to bring *dharma* closer to ideas of his age and the country. He was not against brāhmaṇas.

> Buddha classed the brāhmaṇas along with the Buddhist mendicants, and used the word as one of honour in reference to Buddhist *arhats* and saints.
>
> — S. Radhakrishnan, *Indian Philosophy*, vol. I, p. 361

In fact, Buddhism arose against the rigidity and showmanship of the rituals. The later Vedic period witnessed many perversions and religion was distinguished from the life. The Vedic teachings were lost in a jumbled chaos of superstitions. Buddha did not favour too much ritualism and killing of the animals for the sake of sacrifices.

> The condition of the time in which Buddha was born, the Vedas had already gained mysterious sanctity. The customs and rules codified in the laws of Manu were in force, though they had not the rigidity which they acquired at a later day.
>
> — ibid., p. 352

The internal evidences found in the text of *Manu-Smṛti* prove that at the time of the composition of the work the Vedic rituals were enjoying the prominent place in the society. Manu, at every step, has proclaimed his solidarity with the Vedic rituals. People at every stage of their lives were asked to perform the sacrificial rituals (see II.105-20; III.67-69, 181; V.145; VI.2.25-36; VII.79-80; X.1.113; XI.106, 119, 124, 130, 245; XII.70). *Manu-Smṛti* supports the killing of the animals for *yajñas* (V.23-24, 31). A brāhmaṇa may kill animals and birds for rituals. Eating of the flesh, offered to gods was permitted. These sorts of practices were common during the later Vedic period. The authoritativeness was formulated during Brāhmaṇa period (800 to 500 BCE). *Śatapatha Brāhmaṇa* states that the Vedas were revealed themselves (XI.5.81). The divine authority of the Vedas is accepted as a fact (*AitaBrā* VII.9). The Vedas were issued like breath from the self-existent (*ŚataBrā* XI.5.81). The Brāhmaṇa *granthas* were composed to formulate a system of consistent doctrine and then looked about the texts of an early age to support their position. It gave them a hold on the central facts of the life, and no philosophy could afford to discard it.

In the Brāhmaṇa *grantha*s there are frequent traces of high morals, strictness to prescribed duties towards gods, manes, seers, animals and all other lower creatures. In *Śatapatha Brāhmaṇa*, sacrifice of all things (*sarvamedha*) is thought as a means to attain spiritual freedom (XIII.7.1.1). Sacrifice is like a ship sailing heavenward; if there be a sinful priest in it, that one priest would make it to sink (*ŚataBrā* IV.2.5.10). *Āśrama-dharma*, caste system, the supremacy of the priests, the eternity of the Vedas and the types of sacrificial liturgies are supported by Brāhmaṇa *grantha*s. They framed elaborate codes of laws to obey the rules to be followed during sacrificial performances. The ideals of marriage as described in *Manu-Smṛti* are similar to those of Brāhmaṇa *grantha*s (see *Āpastamba Mantra Brāhmaṇa* I.3.14; *AitaBrā* 3.3.8; *ŚataBrā* V.2.1.10). The duties of a *brahmacārī* prescribed by Manu are inspired by Brāhmaṇa *grantha*s (see *MS* II.119; *ŚataBrā* XI.3.31). The offering of the animal flesh to certain guests was also recommended in *Aitareya Brāhmaṇa* I.15. The concept of atonement was developed in Brāhmaṇa *grantha*s (see *MS* XI.45; *AitaBrā* 7.28). The name of Nārāyaṇa also occurs in *Śatapatha Brāhmaṇa*. The theory of the creation also took a different shape; *Taittirīya Brāhmaṇa* says, "formerly nothing existed, neither heaven nor atmosphere nor earth". "Prajāpati himself toiled and created living beings" (*ŚataBrā* I.1.3). All these thoughts have been well incorporated in *Manu-Smṛti*. The ideals of marriage as described in *Manu-Smṛti* are very close to Brāhmaṇa *grantha*s (see *Āpastamba Mantra Brāhmaṇa* I.3.4.A). It is apparent that *Manu-Smṛti* was composed at the time when the doctrines enunciated in Brāhmaṇa *grantha*s were estimated very high. This time was surely much prior to Buddha.

The antiquity of *Manu-Smṛti* is well reflected in the philosophical ideas of *Manu-Smṛti*. It is well proved that all the schools of Indian philosophy got their final systematic form after Buddha.

> The progress of the philosophy is generally due to powerful attack on a historical tradition when men feel themselves compelled to go-back on their steps and raise once more the fundamental questions which their father had disposed of by the older schemes.
>
> — Radhakrisnan, *Indian Philosophy*, p. 17

It was the time when Indian thinkers secured *ātmavidyā* or philosophy by *ānvikṣikī* or the science of inquiry. *Manu-Smṛti* VII.43 says that a king must study *ānvikṣikī*. Scripture should be well supported by logic. Manu holds that those who are misled by logic and disregard the Vedas deserve excommunication (II.12). Kauṭilya (300 BCE) points out that *ānvikṣikī* is a distinct branch of study over and above *trivedas*, *vārtā* and *daṇḍanīti* (I.2). The term *ānvikṣikī* was used in 600 BCE and by the end of the first century BCE, the term was replaced by the term *darśana* (see *Mahābhārata* Śānti-Parva 10.45; *Bhāgavata Purāṇa* VIII.14.10). It seems that though during Manu's time this science of logic was introduced, it was not above the Vedas. It was the starting point for the development of other philosophical thoughts. Manu does not mention the name of any school of Indian philosophy. Manu has taken the Vedic testimony in a very strict manner while other branches of philosophy have taken it in a liberal spirit. The shifting of this ideology might have taken several centuries. The different schools of thoughts have handled and fashioned the Vedic thought in their own way, which Manu could not afford. Surely, it was the time prior to the birth of systematic philosophy.

Among the different schools of Indian philosophies Sāṁkhya, Vedānta and Yoga were growing through many generations even before Buddha. The early sacred literature of Jainas mentions the systems of Vaiśeṣika, Buddhism, Sāṁkhya and Lokāyata (Weber's *Sanskrit Literature*, p. 236). There is abundant evidence, both in Hindu and Buddhist works, of unquestionable antiquity and authenticity of Sāṁkhya and Yoga systems having been current before the time of Buddha (Rajendra Lal Mitra, *Yoga-Sūtra*, p. xvi). Buddhist legends mention Kapila as one of the predecessors of Buddha (see Garbe's *Sāṁkhyapravacana-Sūtra*, *vr̥tti*, p. 3). *Manu-Smr̥ti* does not mention Sāṁkhya as a philosophical system, but it follows the identical thoughts. The account of creation given in the first chapter, the acceptance of three sources of knowledge (XII.105) and the detailed description of three *guṇa*s are closer to Sāṁkhya system. The type of Sāṁkhya which has been included in *Manu-Smr̥ti* is the development of the legitimate thoughts of the Upaniṣads. The theory of the creation as described in *Manu-Smr̥ti* reflects the idea projected in Puruṣa-Sūkta and Hiraṇyagarbha-Sūkta of *R̥gveda*. It should not be confused with Sāṁkhya philosophy. *Manu-Smr̥ti* does not mention Nyāya philosophy. These points also suggest the pre-existence of *Manu-Smr̥ti*.

The whole discussion pertaining to the time of *Manu-Smr̥ti* may be concluded in following manner:

1. The original *Manu-Smr̥ti* was written at the time when the contents of Brāhmaṇa texts were more popular and Upaniṣadic philosophy was gaining momentum.
2. *Manu-Smr̥ti* tried to bring a balance between the thoughts described in Brāhmaṇa *grantha*s and Upaniṣads.
3. It was probably the time before Buddha as Buddha has criticized the killing of the animals during the Vedic sacrifices, which is supported by *Manu-Smr̥ti*. The ethics prescribed by Buddhism finds its seed in *Manu-Smr̥ti*.

4. The original *Manu-Smṛti* was re-written several times. The addition of new theories and exclusion of few verses cannot be ruled out. The exclusion of several verses may have also happened due to scriber's mistake. The extant *Manu-Smṛti* was written before the invasion of Alexander. The writer of *Arthaśāstra* was familiar with the contents of *Manu-Smṛti.*
5. *Manu-Smṛti* was written much before the birth of systematic philosophy, which was started only after Buddha.

The Content of Manu-Smṛti

Manu-Smṛti contains twelve chapters and 2,694 *anuṣṭubh* couplets. The opening chapter describes the origin of the world, creation of the beings, the origin of *Manu-Smṛti* and the epochs of the *yugas*. It also brings out the four classes of people and their respective *dharmas*. The second chapter deals with the main subject matter. It reveals the nature of *dharma,* from where these have originated and how to practise them. The text of this chapter describes the *dharma* of *caturvarṇa,* and *saṁskāras* performed at different stages of human life from birth to death. The third chapter deals with the observances of the householders, their role in the society and their duties towards family members. The subject has been discussed at length. The fourth chapter starts with the day-to-day life of human beings. The chapter also speaks of women and their *dharma,* their position in the family and the privileges given to them. The fifth chapter deals with the questions related to birth and death, rites to be performed after the death of people of different age groups, eatables for twice-born, sacrificial animals and duties of women. The sixth chapter denotes the life of *vānaprasthas* and *saṁnyāsa,* the third and fourth stages of human life. The seventh and eighth chapters bring out a detailed account of *rāja-dharma,* diplomacy and art of statecraft during war and peace. Public administration, legal procedures, civil and criminal disputes, formation of different governing bodies, punishment, trade and commerce and taxation are the main subjects of these chapters. The ninth chapter opens with the detailed duties of women, their importance in the family and rights in relation to inheritance. The later part of this chapter discusses the remaining issues pertaining to *rāja-dharma*. In the closing part of this chapter, some light has been thrown on the duties of vaiśyas and śūdras. In chapter ten there is a discussion on mixed castes emerging through the intermixing of four castes. *Āpad-dharma* has also been included in this chapter. The main subject matter of the eleventh chapter is to bring out the details of minor and major types of expiation (*prāyaścitta*). The last chapter (chapter 12) of *Manu-Smr̥ti* touches the philosophical heights. It speaks of the theory of *karma*, the journey of the soul, the reason for high and low birth of all creatures, the impact of the good or bad deeds and how to improve the *karma*. The subjects like self-realization, attainment of *niḥśreyas* and doubtful matters related to *dharma* have also been brought out.

Thus starting from the concept of *dharma* the content of *Manu-Smr̥ti* extends up to each and every sphere of social life and conveys the messages of a well-disciplined life for the betterment of the society and State as such.

Commentaries on Manu-Smr̥ti

The earliest existing commentary available is *Manu-Bhāṣya* of Medhātithi. He was the son of Vīrasvāmin and he lived around CE 900. According to Kane, he might have flourished between CE 825 and 900. Vijñāneśvera, the author of *Mitākṣarā*, has quoted him several times (see Ernst Hass, *Catalogue of Sanskrit and Pali Books in British Museum Library*, pp. 86-87). Many Western scholars have agreed with it. But by judging the antiquity and popularity of *Manu-Smr̥ti* Medhātithi cannot be considered as the first commentator. In his work he himself often quotes the passages and explanations given by other commentators prior to him. At many places he uses the phrases like *aney* (VII.139) or *aney tu vyacakṣate* (III.271-74). But he has not somehow mentioned the name of any of his predecessors. He none the less refers to the ancient expositors of Manu (V.127). He also discusses various readings at several places (VIII.53, 119; IV.99, 185, 229). He notes that the order of the verses was traditionally different. It seems that at the time of Medhātithi some scattered commentaries written by unknown authors were available. It may also be presumed that by that time few commentaries might have been lost because of the continued foreign invasions and political turmoil. Most probably, Medhātithi was the native of south India. While elaborating the word *kutapa* (III.234) he says, *udiceṣu kambale iti prasiddha*. One may also come across many similar names to his or to his father's name in Cāḷukya inscriptions. Kane thinks that he belonged to north India, as he knew many things related to north (see *Manu-Smṛti* VII.32; VIII.42, 400, the monopoly of the sale of elephants and saffron in Kashmir). His work is commendable and unparalleled. Varadarāja in his *Vyavahāra Nirṇaya* calls him *asahāya* (peerless). He receives many attributes for his monumental work, which no one can do easily.

Many of his successors have adopted his views and style of expression. His interpretations and explanations have been well accepted by later commentators. He commented on the same *Manu-Smṛti* as we have now. Unfortunately, the manuscript is not easily available in its complete form. Many scholars may find his work often diffused, tedious and obscure. But at the same time it is the most authentic work and is useful for syphoning out the subsequent interpolations. It seems that in Medhātithi's commentary many of the verses do not exist which were brought in the text in few other later commentaries. It is rather difficult to know the source of his commentary. He quotes several verses from his own work called *Smṛtiviveka*. While comparing this commentary with other commentaries it can be noticed that Medhātithi has followed the Mīmāṁsā system for putting his explanations on Manu's verses. He interprets on the basis of Jaimini's Sūtras and mentions several terms like *vidhi* and *arthavāda*. He also uses many *nyāya*s for explaining Manu's statements (*guṇalopa ca mukhyasya nyāya*, II.102; *brāhmaṇaparibrājaka nyāya*, I.22; *kākatālīya nyāya* I.22; *viśvajīta nyāya*, II.2). Medhātithi mentions Asahāya, Kumārila Bhaṭṭa and Śaṅkara, thus he cannot be placed before CE 820. *Mitākṣarā* makes a mention of Medhātithi, which means he should belong to a period earlier than CE 1050. Bhaṭṭa Lollaṭa (CE 1150) also refers Medhātithi. Therefore his time may be fixed sometime between CE 825 to 900.

Another commentary written on *Manu-Smṛti* is of Govindarāja. Bühler discovered the manuscript of this work and it belongs to the Maharashtra government. It is now available everywhere in India. Rav Shahib Mandalika published the manuscript of this work. Jolly has published a portion of it in *Manuteekasangraha*. In his commentary, Govindarāja has mentioned his other work named *Smṛtimañjarī*. The author is mentioned in *Kalā-Viveka* (p. 304) and Jeemutavana's *Vyavahāra-Mātṛkā* (p. 342). Kullūka, the famous commentator of *Manu-Smṛti*, was highly influenced by Govindarāja's commentary. He has tried to bring out many more explanations, which are not available in Medhātithi's commentary. Many a time he differs with Medhātithi. Kullūka in his commentary has presented the contrary opinions of both. Kullūka says that Govindarāja has given two different meanings of the word *ugra*. Ugra is a son of kṣatriya, born of a śūdra wife (see *MS* IV.212; *MS* X.9). He does not agree with Govindarāja on *MS* III.285, while on *MS* III.178 Kullūka agrees with both Medhātithi and Govindarāja (Kullūka differs from

Govindarāja on *MS* I.5, 8; II.122-27; III.50, 53, 127, 129, 191, 284-85; V.16, 51, 72, 84, 104; VI.14, 79). The colophons at the end of Govindarāja's commentary on *Manu-Smṛti* describe him as the son of Bhaṭṭa-Mādhava. *Smṛtimañjarī* gives the information that he was the grandson of Nārāyaṇa and lived on the banks of holy Ganges. The first verse of the commentary states that he had received the Śāstra of Manu in an unbroken tradition of teacher and pupil and had examined all previous commentaries on Manu. His commentary is very concise. Bühler and Burnell have assigned Govindarāja to twelfth or thirteenth century CE. Kane puts him somewhere between CE 1000 and 1110.

The next famous commentary on *Manu-Smṛti* is of Mādhava-Sāyana. He lived in the fourteenth century CE. The manuscript of this work is available at many private collections.

The most famous commentary on *Manu-Smṛti* is that of Kullūka Bhaṭṭa. It is a *vṛtti* called *Mānavārtha-Muktāvalī.* The most authentic edition of this work is Nirnaya Sagara edition, published in 1909. The commentary is very concise and is of analytical nature. He has taken lots of his material from Medhātithi and has brought out a critical and clear study of *Manu-Smṛti.* But many a time he also points out Medhātithi's mistakes (I.71, 103; II.101). According to his own statement, he was a native of Benares. His time may be fixed to sixteenth or seventeenth century CE. This commentary is well recognized and has been referred by most of the scholars working on *Manu-Smṛti.*

The commentator Nārāyaṇa has been referred by Bhaṭṭojī in his commentary on *Caturviṁśatimata* (vide p. 61 of the Benares Sanskrit Series edition). It was written in CE 1479. Nārāyaṇa has also been quoted by Rāyamukuṭa in CE 1431. The commentary refers to the explanation given by Govindarāja on *Manu-Smṛti* VIII.123. His another work, *Kāmadhenu-Dīpikā,* discusses in detail *prāyaścitta*s for various sins. He also deliberates on the topic of flesh eating at some length (*Manu-Smṛti* V.56). He also wrote a book, *Śuddhi-Dīpikā*, dealing with *aśauca* in detail and *mahāpātaka*s (*MS* XI.209). He refers to a *mālākāra*, the author of a lexicon. He is later than Govindarāja and flourished between CE 1100 and 1300.

According to T.R. Cintamani (1943, *AIOC*, vol. II, pp. 352-60), there exists a manuscript containing a fragment of Bhāruci's commentary on *Manu-Smṛti*, bearing the title *Manuśāstra-Vivaraṇa*. It seems that even Medhātithi borrowed few explanations from him (see *MS* VII.13). Medhātithi mentions the names of Asahāya, Bhāruci and Yajavana (II.109; IV.162; IX.141, 147).

Raghavananda wrote a brief commentary on *Manu-Smṛti* named *Mānavārtha-Candrikā*. He follows Kullūka in every respect. He mentions the names of many commentators except Mādhava-Sāyana. It seems that he was a native of south India. A copy of the manuscript is in Paris Library and was used by Loiseleur Des Longchamps for his edition of *Manu-Smṛti*.

Jolly in his edition of *Nārada-Smṛti* has incorporated a portion of *Bhāṣya* of Asahāya as revised by Kalyāṇa Bhaṭṭa on the encouragement of Keśava Bhaṭṭa. Vivadaratnākara quotes *Manu-Smṛti* IX.165 with Asahāya's explanation. It also quotes him on *Manu-Smṛti* IX.198 that the special rule related to *strī-dhana*, mentioned by Manu, refers to a kṣatriya woman who has a brāhmaṇa co-wife (see p. 578). Medhātithi also mentions the name of Asahāya on *Manu-Smṛti* VIII.155 in Mandalika's edition.

There is a commentary on *Manu-Smṛti* written by Nandanācārya. It is a part of Tanjore Manuscripts (see p. 126 of Tanjore catalogue). He was a native of south India. The text is in modern style; first time it was published in 1813. Kullūka on *Manu-Smṛti* VIII.184 states that Bhojadeva arranged few verses of *Manu-Smṛti* and suggests him as a commentator.

He also mentions a commentator named Dharaneedhar and says that he was later than Medhātithi (see Kullūka on *Manu-Smṛti* V.50). Ramachandra has also written commentaries on *Manu-Smṛti*. Mandalika has published most of the commentaries. Jolly has also published (in 1885 for Bengal Asiatic Society) extracts of all these commentaries (except Kullūka's and Ramachandra's).

The most authentic translation in English was done by Sir William Jones, which appeared in 1794. It was indeed a highly successful attempt and was highly appreciated by the scholars like Theodor Goldstücker and Monier-Williams. The author has followed Kullūka's work. According to some scholars, it is diffused and rhetorical. Sir William Jones has converted the materialistic Sāṁkhya system of the text into metaphysical deism. But in fact during Manu's period the Indian System of Philosophy was not very clear. Since that time many translations of *Manu-Smṛti* came into existence, but they could not do real justice to the text and were unable to bring out the proper analysis of Manu's theories. The commentary of Sir G.C. Haughton was published in 1825. Haughton's edition of Sir William Jones' translation was reprinted in Madras (1863) and by Grady in London (1869). Loiseleur Deslon Champs commentary appeared in 1856 in French and it was very close to that of Sir William Jones. J. Muir has written the model translations of many passages of the text in his "Sanskrit Text" and "Metrical Translation from the Sanskrit". Franz Johaentgen in "Ueber das Gesetzbuch des Manu" (1863) has discussed many topics related to *Manu-Smṛti*. E.W. Hopkins (Leipzig, 1881) has discussed few important subjects of *Manu-Smṛti*. Bühler and Jolly have contributed much to the study of *Manu-Smṛti*. They brought out the translations of many Smṛtis. Burnell's translation of *Manu-Smṛti* opens up many new vistas for further study of the text.

Rav Shahib Mandalika has done the great task of publishing

many commentaries on *Manu-Smṛti.* Ganganath Jha's translation with *Bhāṣya* of Medhātithi on *Manu-Smṛti* has added a new chapter to the tradition of commentaries on *Manu-Smṛti.* Written in two volumes the work is based on several MSS of *Manu-Smṛti* and was published in 1932-39 in Gayakwad Oriental Series.

K.P. Jayaswal brought out a comparative study named *Manu and Yājñavalkya* (Calcutta, 1930).

Few Other Works on Manu

Motwani, Kewal, 1958, *Manu Dharmaśāstra*, Madras: Ganesh & Company.

Sternbach, L., 1974, *Mānavadharmaśāstra*, Varanasi: All India Kashiraj Trust.

Doniger, Wendy and Brian K. Smith, 1991, *The Laws of Manu*, New Delhi: Penguin Books India.

1

Dharma and Manu-Smṛti

Meaning of the Word Dharma

THE word *dharma* occupies an important and venerable place in Indian writings. It will not be an exaggeration to state that this word has become the nucleus of Indian thinking and Indian philosophy. Right from the Vedic period till the modern times, this word passed through several stages and was used in different senses. The dictionaries of different languages have brought out various meanings of the word *dharma*, such as ordinance, usage, duty, right, justice, morality, virtue, religion, good work and conduct.

The oldest scripture *Ṛgveda* takes it as an adjective or as a noun, sometimes in masculine and sometimes in neuter gender (*ṚV* I.187.1; X.21.3). In *Ṛgveda* the word *dharma* has been used at least sixty times independently. In *Ṛgveda* also, the word *dharma* has been used in different senses. The word itself is derived from the root *dhṛ* (which means to uphold, to support, to nourish). *Ṛgveda* has used this word with the sense of "upholder", "sustainer" or "supporter". At many places the word has been used along with the words like *ṛta*, *satya* and *vrata*, bringing out the sense of "order or ordinances". In many cases, the word expresses the meaning of "religious rites, or the ancient law, fixed principles, conduct and regulation" (*ṚV* IV.53.3; III.17.1; V.63.7; X.56.3). In *Aitareya Brāhmaṇa* the word has been used in an abstract sense; "the whole body of religious rite" (*AitaBrā* VII.7). In Upaniṣads the word *dharma* is treated as equivalent to *satya* (*BṛUp* I.4.14). *Mahābhārata* personifies *dharma* as a deity. *Bhagavad-Gītā* uses the word with the sense of duty: "do your own duty (*dharma*)" (*BhG* III.35). Jaimini has treated *dharma* as a "desirable goal, instructed by Vedic injunctive" (*Pūrva-Mīmāṁsā-Sūtra* I.1-2). Many others have defined *dharma* as something "from which results the happiness". Now it is clear that the word *dharma* has passed through different stages of meanings and later on, the meaning got consolidated to the sense of the "privileges", "duties" and "obligations" of a person and his conduct as a member in a particular stage of life or of a particular caste. While going through all the meanings of the word *dharma*, one thing is quite clear that the main sense of the word is "truth" or what "ought to be". This meaning got extended from time to time, depending on the context of the usages. In Vedas the word is used as an attribute to different gods or in reference to sacrificial rites. The meaning of this word took an abstract form in Upaniṣads and adopted a practical approach in Dharmaśāstras.

Dharmasūtras and Dharmaśāstras emphasize the elaborated and expanded meaning of *dharma*. The word has retained all those senses as denoted in early literatures. But at the same time it also involved the concrete and pragmatic expositions. Depending on the circumstances, the word was brought closer to the community and became a part of the life of every person for uplifting his material, moral and spiritual endeavours. *Dharma* became a tool of inducing values and virtues to common man for forming a better society.

The opening chapter of *Manu-Smṛti* tells that the sages requested Manu to impart *dharma* for all *varṇa*s. According to *Manu-Smṛti:*

> *Dharma* has been practised by learned people for leading a moral life, the life which is free from hatred and partiality and is accepted by their hearts. —II.1-2

The concept of *dharma,* perpetuated by Manu, covers a wide range of senses related to the practical life of human beings. It is rather impossible to be free of desire. But the desire must attain a proper direction and should be fulfilled in a detached manner (*MS* II.3-4). Manu has extracted the very essence of all those senses of the word *dharma* that were visualized by his predecessors (*MS* II.7.10, 12). Manu treated this word as a concept which had a wider range. It was intensely practical and utilitarian. Manu's main anxiety was to enhance the moral and spiritual life of each and every individual and to create a righteous society. His concept of *dharma* embraces all those constituents, which are needed for making a perfect individual or a perfect civilization at large. No society can think of achieving happiness and prosperity as long as each member of that group is not aware of his conduct and duties towards his fellow members. An individual is an integral part of the society. Therefore, no one should be contended just with his own pleasure; he has to think about the pleasure and pain of others. Manu introduced the concept of *dharma* in relation to an individual and society as well. *Dharma* became the basic part of the scheme of life, as it guided a man to lead a successful life in the society.

Changing Form of Dharma in the Vedas, Upaniṣads and Brāhmaṇas

Manu-Smṛti has made a remarkable attempt for elaborating the different aspects of *dharma* and also has focused on their importance in worldly life and even life after death. It is an extraordinary synthesis of all those principles attached to the concept of *dharma* enunciated by Vedas, Upaniṣads and Brāhmaṇas. This concept provides a scheme of self-realization by making a man capable enough to judge his own vices. The scheme is deterrent to evils and is the promoter of virtues. It gave a new track for the cultural evolution of mankind and for manifesting an organized society. *Dharma* reminds a man that he is a manifestation of the Supreme and tends to go back again to Him. But before that he has to justify his birth through his good deeds. *Dharma* leads a man to perform good deeds. *Dharma* should be treated as a base of man's physical, mental and spiritual existence.

The main aim of *Manu-Smṛti* was to impart the unique nature of *dharma* in its wider sense and to give *dharma* a simpler and practical horizon. Manu has accepted *dharma* as a supreme power and personified it as a deity.

> It is a majestic bull and does the fulfilment of everyone's desire. Therefore *dharma* has to be taken care at every cost.
>
> — *MS* VIII.16

Dharma should be treated as the might or inner power, which may kindle one to move on the right path. The divinity of *dharma* reflects its immense potentiality and abstract nature.

> It is immortal and accompanies the soul even after the destruction of the mortal body. — *MS* VIII.17

Manu's concept of *dharma* is associated with the philosophy of *karma*.

According to *Manu-Smṛti:*

> God created *dharma* and *adharma* for judging the *karma*, performed by the human being, in a logical manner.
>
> — MS I.26

Dharma became the qualifying standard for determining the status of a mortal. It is imperative that a man has to follow certain norms or code of conduct throughout, in every sphere of his life. *Manu-Smṛti* is concerned in imparting instructions for all stages of the life and to all the sections of the community. The four stages of the life and the four sections of the community were designed to convey the message of *dharma* in a systematic and effective manner.

> The *āśrama-dharma* was related to the different stages of human life and the *dharma* guiding the path for different sections of the society was taken as *varṇa-dharma*.
>
> — *MS* I.102

Medhātithi, commenting on Manu, says that the author dilates upon *dharma* as fivefold, e.g. *varṇa-dharma, āśrama-dharma, varṇāśrama-dharma, naimittika-dharma* (such as *prāyaścitta*) and *guṇa-dharma* (the duty of the king). Apart from these *dharmas*, Manu has also propounded *sādhāraṇa-dharma* — duties common to all, such as *ahiṁsā, dayā* and other virtues. Manu has comprehended the concept of *dharma* under these titles.

The division of the society into four classes and assigning to each of them their *dharma* were done for functional convenience of the society. The uniqueness of this system is undeniable. It was introduced in a natural way. The four classes were fully regulated by their *dharmas*. Manu has not allowed any member of any class to defy the prescribed *dharma*. He claims that the composition of the division of the society is done only with the purpose of instructing them the *dharmas*. Manu has created a definite line of demarcation between these four classes through their *dharmas*. No one was allowed to cross the line until or unless it becomes unavoidable. Manu gives more emphasis on the practice of *ācāra*:

> The established usages or fixed rules for the conduct in life were handed down from generation to generation by well-disciplined members of the community. — *MS* II.20

> The *ācāra*, recommended by the Vedas, is the highest *dharma* and the twice-born must follow that. — *MS* I.108

The main aim of *dharma* is to improve the quality of life. Hence, it is essential to practise *dharma*.

> Practically, it is not a very easy task and, that is why it is considered as the root of all types of penance.
>
> — *MS* I.109-10

Nature of Dharma

Manu's concept of *dharma* is of practical nature. It is a consolidated scheme, which has been practised by the great people:

> The ideal conduct of those great men becomes an example for other people, as it inspires them to move on the same path. — *MS* II.20

The *varṇa-dharma,* as enunciated by Manu, is the very base for the survival of the Indian way of life till today. It was the scheme of the division of labour, which becomes necessary for achieving the proficiency and perfection in work. The vocational specialization may contribute much towards the refinement of the work.

> The main duty of the brahmaṇa is to study and to teach Vedas, to perform sacrifices and to help others for performing the rituals and to give and take the charity. — *MS* I.88-89

> The kṣatriyas should protect the people, should donate the wealth freely, should perform sacrifices, should study the Vedas and should be detached to worldly life. — *MS* I.89

> The job of rearing the animals, charity, studying the Vedas, commerce, trade and agriculture should be done by the vaiśyas. — *MS* I.90

> The śūdras were allotted the responsibility of serving the other three *varṇas*. — *MS* I.91

Special Features of Dharma

This scheme provides a definite place to every section of people in the community. The *dharma* allotted to each section eliminates the confusion and perplexity of the common people and may inspire them to do their jobs in a perfect manner. The clear distinction of the *dharmas* will check the undesirable interference of one section with the other and that will avert the anarchy. A particular group of the society may contribute more effectively to the society by abiding to its *dharma* in a true manner. This was the doctrine of *sva-dharma* and it was the strong basis of the *varṇa-dharma*. The *dharma* was more rigorous for the people of higher *varṇa*s in comparison to the *dharma*s of lower *varṇa*s.

> There is no sin for śūdras. It depends on them to follow the *dharma* or not. — *MS* X.126

The distinction of the *dharma*s for different *varṇa*s provided ample scope for the people to perform their duties in the best possible manner, as they know that by not following their allotted *dharma* they would be downgraded. The arrangement of the *varṇa-dharma* gave chance to everyone to improve himself through the *karma*. *Dharma* in the form of code of conduct gave guidance to every *varṇa* for inducing harmony in the community. According to *Manu-Smṛti*, there is no fifth *varṇa*.

> All the mixed castes have been included in the fourth *varṇa* and were instructed to follow the *dharma* of fourth *varṇa*.
> — *MS* X.4

Capability, efficiency and dedication towards the allotted *dharma* were the main criteria for judging the standard of the people of different *varṇa*s.

Dharmas Pertaining to Four Āśramas of Human Life

The division of the life of an individual into four stages and assigning a distinct *dharma* to each stage were meant for providing a well-planned and systematic scheme of life to every one. It may be considered as a timetable to set up the routine for the different phases of life. The *dharma*s prescribed for the four stages of life gave much scope to everyone to do his jobs with full concentration. *Upanayana* (initiation) was considered as the most important *saṁskāra* for entering the first stage of the life (*brahmacarya*). It was a preparation for following the difficult *dharma*s of the student life. A student may concentrate more towards his study by restraining his senses. The code of conduct assigned for student life and the atmosphere at *gurukula* would be beneficial and relevant for all ages to come (see *MS* II.95-98). Manu prescribes:

> A student not obeying the *dharma* of the student life should be banished like a śūdra. — *MS* II.103

Teachers too had to impart the knowledge to the students in the prescribed manner.

> A teacher must not teach at a place lacking in *dharma*, wealth or service. It will be like putting a seed in a barren field.
> — *MS* II.158

It was the main *dharma* of a student to be respectful to his teacher.

> A student, who salutes his teacher every day, and is having reverence towards him, enjoys longevity, knowledge and fame. — *MS* II.121

The *dharma*s of *brahmacarya* stage were helpful for making a student competent to lead a good life in future. The service of the teacher, father and mother was considered the greatest *dharma* of a student (*MS* II.225-29).

After *brahmacārī* stage a person was allowed to enter the *gṛhastha āśrama*. It was the phase of life for paying back the debt towards family and society. Manu had glorified this stage of life immensely. The *dharma*s allotted to this stage were directly related to the welfare of the society and own family members. *Manu-Smṛti* brings out a picture of a disciplined and responsible householder. This stage of the life was meant for performing good deeds.

> The *gṛhastha āśrama* shelters everyone in the same manner as the wind takes care of all creatures. This stage is the most important one, as it gives chance to the people to have an application of the knowledge procured by him earlier.
>
> —*Manu-Smṛti* III.77-78

At the second stage of the life a person has to take care of the students and the old people.

> Among all four stages of the life *gṛhastha āśrama* is the most praiseworthy and noble one, as at this stage the people follow the rules instructed by Vedas and Smṛtis, and nurture other three *āśramas*. As all the rivers seek their asylum at the ocean bed, all the *āśramas* get sheltered by *gṛhastha āśrama.*
>
> —*Manu-Smṛti* VI.89-90

The high ideals of *dharma* prescribed for this stage enabled the people to dedicate their lives for others.

Manu has also considered the institution of marriage as an instrument for taking care of *dharma* and has considered it as an opportunity for discharging the ordained duty. Through this institution one may sublimate the most vital aspect of the human life. It is also a *dharma* to ensure the purity of the line and to eliminate the defects of the line.

> A marriage should take place between the same castes and there should be a proper match.
>
> It is totally improper to marry someone just with the desire of satisfying the lust. —*MS* III.5 and 12

Manu-Smṛti prescribes eight types of marriage, but considers that only *brāhma, daiva, ārṣa* and *prajāpati* types of marriages are in accordance with *dharma* or virtuous conduct (*Manu-Smṛti* III.39-40). In fact, Manu was in favour of maintaining a real congenial married life. The happy domestic life may motivate the family to discharge its duties optimally.

> In the family where the wife is satisfied with husband and the husband is contended with wife, prosperity comes itself.
>
> — *MS* III.60

During household life one has to abide with all those *dharma*s related to sacrifices and rites, the debt to sages and debt to *pitṛs*. They too have to take care of the guests. The whole code prescribed for householders is highly appreciable. It provides a life free of hatred, greed and passion.

> A person has to take care of his own, but at the same time one should earn his livelihood without harming anyone else. — *MS* IV.2

*Dharma*s ordained for householders were to teach humanism and fellow feeling for nurturing an ideal society. It is based on the principle of "live and let others live". Manu lays due emphasis on the adherence to *dharma*s ordained for the different stages of life. The *dharma*s for the four stages of life were designed in accordance with the need, psychology and aptitude of the people at different ages. The *dharma*s of first two stages focused on the welfare of the society and the family. But after certain age, when a person has fulfilled his duties towards family and society, he has to think for his own spiritual elevation. The attachment towards life is a natural phenomenon, but it has to be within a limit. The later two stages of life are concerned with the life of retirement. After reaching this stage of the life, a person becomes more mature, disciplined and free from sins and attachment. He may realize the reality of life in a better manner. He may recognize the nature of that great Reality as the cause of the creation.

> The world has been created by self-manifestation and the transcendent reality which is the soul of everything.
>
> — *MS* I.8
>
> The body is not the physical entity but a habitation of the Supreme Self. — *MS* I.17-18

Men are born according to their *karmas*. *Mokṣa* (the final goal of the life) can only be achieved by getting rid of the bondage of *karma*. Manu says:

> It is only after discharging the three debts that one should direct one's mind towards *mokṣa*; to do otherwise is sinful.
> — *MS* VI.35, 37

A person may concentrate on the deeper philosophy of the life only after pacifying his desires. The success of life depends on the desired coordination of the four stages of life. In other words, it may be said that *dharma*s prescribed for the four stages of life are interwoven. They should not be taken in isolation. *Dharma*s related to the first two stages of life are connected with the worldly life, while *dharma*s prescribed for the other two correspond to a detached life. Manu's plan of life provides ample scope to everyone to act in accordance with his physical and mental capability. Once a person realizes that now his children are in a position to take care of the household and his own physical condition is deteriorating, he should leave the house and go to the forest.

> In *vānaprastha* a man must lead a life of continence and abstinence from sense-enjoyment. — *MS* VI.2-3

It is the age for self-study and introspection.

> With a subdued personality a person should focus more on his personal virtues like kind-heartedness, forgiveness and friendliness to all creatures. — *MS* VI.4-5

A detached person belongs to every member of the society. On the whole, *vānaprastha* is a stage of life when the outwardly activities of a person should cease and he should begin with the inner spiritual quest.

Manu's idea of spiritual quest is based on the austerities, as it teaches to control the senses and to maintain the mental equilibrium. *Saṁnyāsa*, the final stage of the life should totally be dedicated to spiritual concerns. At this stage a person should withdraw himself fully from the world and should prepare himself for the other world. A *saṁnyāsī* knows the emptiness of the life, its joy and its sorrow. Now he should meditate on the Reality and should preserve his equanimity unaffected. His morality has to reach to its highest point. A *saṁnyāsī* does not belong to anyone and nothing belongs to him.

> Therefore, he should keep on moving from place to place. He takes into himself, the sacrificial fire and moves out of his habitation. — *MS* VI.33-34
>
> His aim must be to attain immortality, and with the control of senses, extinction of pleasure and pain, and non-violence towards all creatures, he may reach to his goal. — *MS* VI.60
>
> Austerity can purify a person by destroying his sins. — *MS* VI.31

A detached person is free from all types of fears, as he has surrendered himself to the Supreme.

> He neither greets the life nor does he applaud the death, he, just like a faithful servant, waits for his Master's command. — *MS* VI.45

Mokṣa is a personal gain and can be achieved only through personal efforts.

> Therefore, a *saṁnyāsī* should move alone. No one has deserted him and he has not renounced anyone. — *MS* VI.42
>
> He has to know the Self within himself. Every action is motivated by His power and without Him everything will be futile.
>
> A *saṁnyāsī* is never tempted to *adharma* as he is seeing the *ātman* everywhere. — *MS* VI.74-82

The first two stages of the life are meant for *pravṛtti* (activity), but the later two stages of the life are designed for *nivṛtti*.

> A *saṁnyāsī* performs the desired actions without attachment, and it helps him to be liberated. — *MS* VI.81

Life should be a balanced combination of attachments and detachments. The stage of *saṁnyāsa* is the high time to analyse the subjects related to birth, life, relation of man with *Brahman* and death.

> It becomes the *dharma* of a *saṁnyāsī* to ponder on the nature of the *karma* and its consequences. He must also think about the ways of improving the *karmas*. — *MS* XII.89-90

Manu has stressed the need of following *dharma* in true sense.

> Wearing just the garb of a *saṁnyāsī* is not going to serve the purpose. — *MS* VI.66

Saṁnyāsa-dharmas are meant for lifting a person to the highest point in human life. Manu's intention was to drive each and every being to this height. The views of Manu pertaining to *dharmas* of a *saṁnyāsī* are the outcome of his philosophical thoughts. He has incorporated the philosophy of *karma* and *Jñāna* in his codes and has shown the way it could be implemented in the day-to-day life of human beings. The observance of *dharmas* may enable a man to move on the right track and not to be misguided. The knowledge of the reality of the world, life and death and life after death will help a person to take the life in its proper perspective. *Dharmas* are the voice of the Supreme. At the stage of *saṁnyāsa* a person is very close to *ātma-bodha*.

> It gives him pleasure in this world and provides him the chance to attain the final emancipation. — *MS* VI.85-86

While analysing the *dharmas* prescribed for the different stages of life, it becomes quite apparent that Manu has laid more emphasis on higher morality. These were needed for uplifting the life of an individual and for the betterment of the society. *Dharmas* were not just the codes of conduct, but they were also the means of recognizing the importance of virtues and their implementation in the life.

Practical Approach to Dharma

Manu is often criticized for prescribing the rigid *dharma*s and their mechanical nature. The critics say that the adherence to these *dharma*s is not practical. Manu himself has realized this fact, as is clear from his contention that it is impossible to get a pure man. It indicates that he was aware of the inconsistency of the human nature. He also knew that sometimes the rigidity of the *dharma*s might affect the life of an individual. Manu introduces few exceptional *dharma*s by moving outside the range of the ordained *dharma*s. He gave due recognition to the customs peculiar to places, to classes, and to families. These were the communities outside the pale of four main *varṇa*s.

> The primeval laws of countries, of castes (*jāti*), of families, and the rules concerning heretics and of different companies of the traders should also get proper recognition.
>
> — *MS* I.118

Manu wanted that local *dharma*s, whether they agree with existing laws or not, should be taken in account:

> A king who is administering justice as well as consolidating his kingdom in the conquered area is to see that the local customs are safeguarded and are maintained. — *MS* VIII.3

> The allotment of *dharma*s should be in accordance with *jāti, deśa, kula* and *śreṇī*. — *MS* VIII.41, 46

The customary *dharma*s (laws) are made on the basis of the requirements of the people of that group or society. Manu wanted to maintain a balance between traditional *dharma*s and customary *dharma*s. *Manu-Smṛti* makes a provision by declaring that the practice of a *dharma* may also depend on a person and the situation. The life is more important than anything else and it has to be protected at every cost. According to Manu, the concept of *dharma* could be flexible allowing certain modifications with the time and age. Thus it was permissible to make the desired alternative to the existing *dharma* for the sake of a good cause. It is the doctrine of *yuga-dharma*, which permits the adaptation and adjustment of new *dharma*s to the existing *dharma*s, and provides chance to compromise with the prevailing situation.

Nature of Āpad, Prāyaścitta and Sādhāraṇa Dharma

Manu-Smṛti introduces a new category of *dharma* known as *āpad-dharma*. Under this relaxation all four castes had the liberty to change their prescribed profession in order to save their lives.

> A vaiśya may take up the job of a śūdra in an unfavourable condition and once the situation is improved, he may come back to his own profession. — *MS* X.98

> A śūdra may do the work of an artisan if he is not in a position to maintain the livelihood of his family members. — *MS* X.100

> In the case of emergency a brāhmaṇa may go to any house for getting some help without considering caste. — *MS* X.102

> A teacher may teach an undeserving student or may accept donation from anyone. — *MS* X.103

> If the life of a brāhmaṇa is on stake, he may eat anything, whatever he gets. He should not think about the nature of food. — *MS* X.104

The provisions of concessions and relaxations in performing *dharma*s are the example of the concept of the realism and liberalism adopted by *Manu-Smṛti*. Any action, done for the survival, cannot be treated as a sin. It is the practical approach to *dharma*.

Prāyaścitta (penance or atonement) *dharma* is one of the most remarkable concepts promulgated by Manu. It is a provision, which gives a chance to the sinner to punish him by himself. The highest attainment of a man cannot be achieved until or unless a person realizes his mistakes and tries to change himself. *Prāyaścitta* is a particular kind of *naimittika* (casual) act. It is an act enjoined in a sacred precept as the means of removing the sins. Manu has defined it as "penance or vow or the combination of the both" (*MS* XI.47). Manu has prepared an elaborate scheme of *prāyaścitta-dharma* (see Chap. 8), which is meant for eliminating all sins from the society. Manu visualized that inflicting a harsh punishment to a sinner may not be as effective as to give him a chance to go for *prāyaścitta*. Manu states:

> Atonement has to be done by a person who has done a sin unknowingly, but it may also be performed even for an intentional act of sin on the strength of the Vedic text.
>
> — *MS* XI.44

Manu has taken the support of earlier authorities for determining the scope of atonement. It has covered the widest possible range of offences.

> A man who commits a prescribed act, or performs a blamable one, or cleaves a sensual enjoyment, must perform a penance.
>
> — *MS* XI.47

This *dharma* has been extended to all castes and every member of the society. It has been considered a more powerful force than even injunctions. Now a question arises whether the act of atonement may remove the sins and may change a sinner to a pure man.

> The penance does remove the effect of the sins, but at the same time, non-performance of the atonement in each case creates an extra sin. — *MS* XI.229

It may be correct to think that atonement is not capable of washing out the sins completely. But at least one has to support the view that the act of atonement will check the recurrence of sins.

Manu's concept of *dharma* was fully based on the moral and ethical aspects of life. Apart from all these specialized *dharmas* prescribed for different stages of human life or group of people, he also conceived the idea of *sādhāraṇa-dharma* which is meant for each and every member of the society for all the time. It was the universal application of personal ethics and virtues. A person cannot accept the importance of any code until or unless he does not possess the common virtues. These were the *dharmas* related to social life and humanity. Human being must have faith in humanity. The humanity consists of the virtues like

> contentment, mental restraints, forgiveness, endurance, control of senses, truthfulness, purity, wisdom, knowledge and free from anger. — *MS* VI.92

A man because of his ignorance and sense of ego receives radical moral failure. The prospective nature of all these common *dharmas* governs the universe with order and regularity. It covers the wider connotation of values, morals, virtues, ethical norms and duties. A man must possess the capacity of distinguishing between right and wrong. Every action should be done with proper contemplation. The common *dharmas* teach a man to incorporate in himself the virtues and to avoid vices. The virtuous actions may serve to bridge the gap between man as an individual and man as a component of the society. Manu considers contentment as the highest *dharma*.

> The presence of contentment provides pleasure, but its absence may cause grief. — *MS* IV.12

> A person, not following the norms of common *dharmas*, will be abused by everyone and will suffer in many ways.
> — *MS* IV.157

> A person desirous of obtaining heaven should not torment any creature and should try to accumulate *dharma* in the same manner as the white ant slowly and slowly erects the mud wall.
> — *MS* IV.238

> He, whose speech and thoughts are pure and under control, attains the highest spiritual fruit. One should not touch the sore spot of others, should not intend harm and should not utter the unwholesome word which will make another shudder.
> — *MS* II.160

Manu advised people to stay away from the crooked and deceitful livelihood. In order to lead a happy life one should avoid hatred, vanity, pride, anger and harshness. Of the two sets of the observances — *yama*s and *niyama*s — the former is more important. The *yama*s are continence, compassion, contemplation, truth, non-attachment, non-violence, sweetness of behaviour and self-control.

One may win heaven by being soft and subdued (*MS* IV.11). The personal merits matter more than any other qualification.

> A brāhmaṇa reaches the highest goal by muttering prayers, whether he performs other rites or neglects them, it may not matter much; he who is friendly to all the creatures is declared to be a true brāhmaṇa.

A person must have the sense of sacrificing something for others without thinking of his own pleasure. Manu insists:

> Everyone must go for selfless charity. The charity should be given with reverence.
> — *MS* IV.234-35

It is a social *dharma* based on the ethical virtues of *dayā, tyāga* and *samatā*. *Manu* was in favour of a society free of discrimination.

> It is the duty of the affluent group to take care of the needy persons. — *MS* IV.226

It benefits both the giver and the receiver. *Dāna* brings harmony to the society allowing for a fair distribution of the riches.

The personal cleanliness (*śauca*) has also been considered as an important *sāmānya-dharma*. It also covers the health and personal hygiene. It is an indispensable socio-ethical virtue. It advocates for a healthy life. An impure body cannot conceive the pure thoughts. In the same manner a healthy surrounding is needed for a trouble-free life.

> Every day, only after having bath with pure water, a person should proceed for other activities. — *MS* II.176

> After certain age one should take bath three times in a day. — *MS* II.51-52

> A food should only be taken after purifying the mouth by sipping water and then turning the face towards the east. His meal will procure long life, if a person eats facing the east. — *MS* II.53

> After eating the food one should first sip the water thrice; next wipe the mouth twice; and lastly, should touch with water the cavities of the head. — *MS* II.60

> Manu prescribes small diet for a healthy life. "No one should eat the left-over food. One should also be careful about eating in between the two meal-times; over-eating should be avoided; one must not go anywhere without having purified himself after meal. — *MS* II.57

> Excessive eating is prejudicial to health, to fame and to bliss in the heaven; it prevents the acquisition of spiritual merits. — *MS* IV.62-63

*Dharma*s related to personal cleanliness were framed to enhance the physical and mental health of human beings; as one may lead a righteous life only with good health and sound mind.

Role of Rituals and Yajñas in Human Life

Manu has included some daily rites under *dharma*. These rites are of special significance. The performance of the five daily-*yajña*s has a social and humanitarian bearing; for example, the *nṛ-yajña* signifies that one should entertain the guests.

> The person, who does not take care of father, guests, gods and servants, is as good as dead. — *MS* III.72

Bhūta-yajña is meant to show gratification towards all living beings.

> The householder should offer food to animals, insects and plants. — *MS* III.93-94

> Serving all the creatures is the easiest way to reach heaven. — *MS* III.95

Manu has brought out the scientific significance of putting oblation to the fire.

> The oblation, which has been put in the fire in a prescribed manner, goes to the sun; the sun brings rain; the rain helps the crops grow, and the grains are needed for the survival of all creatures. — *MS* III.76

Pitṛ-yajña provides an opportunity to a person to show his gratitude towards his ancestors.

> Every householder must perform *śrāddha* and should feed at least one person. — *MS* III.83-84

These concepts express the intricate beliefs, sentiments and the knowledge of the people about the nature of the universe, of human life, the life after death and rebirth. Every action of the life was kept under the purview of *dharma*.

Importance of Four Puruṣārthas

Dharma was governed by the four ends of life. The four *puruṣārtha*s were considered as the aims of human endeavour. *Dharma* became the most prominent one, as it may keep the balance of *artha* and *kāma* and finally may lead to *mokṣa*. *Artha* and *kāma* regulated by *dharma* may surely bring happiness to life and may give the longest possible course of progress.

> Some declare that the chief good consists in the acquisition of spiritual merit and wealth, others place it in the gratification of desire and the acquisition of wealth, others in the acquisition of spiritual merit alone, and some say that acquisition of wealth alone is the chief good, but the correct decision is that it consists of aggregate of all these three. —*MS* II.224

Manu persists that there should be a balanced pursuit of *trivarga*. The second stage of life (*gṛhastha āśrama*) allows to enjoy *artha* and *kāma* in accordance with *dharma*. However, the first and last two stages of life have no scope for *artha* and *kāma*. *Dharma* will not allow the enjoyment of *artha* and *kāma* beyond limit, and the excess of any enjoyment leads to misery and unpleasant end. It is the most practical and prudent approach towards life. On the other hand, a desire fulfilled in restricted manner brings happiness. The human desire has no end. The desires multiply very fast and its elasticity keeps on increasing every moment. It is also certain that no one may be fully satisfied at any point. Dissatisfaction causes grief and a grieved person loses his mental ability. A wise and prudent approach towards *artha* and *kāma* will help a person realize the facts of life in a proper perspective. The realization of truth induces bliss and joy. The scheme of four *puruṣārtha*s should be treated as the key to happiness as it teaches a person to enjoy the worldly life in a balanced manner. It keeps a man away from undesirable and useless indulgence. It opens the vista of detached enjoyment of life.

Manu has interpreted *dharma* as *satya*, duty, virtue, merit, law, tradition and even punishment. These meanings have been associated with various aspects of human life and bring forth a complete ideology for ethical and moral progress of the society. Manu has taken the life of a human being in a very positive manner. A person must have some purpose to live and for that he has to follow certain ideology. In this world, the creatures of different types and grades are mutually linked up. No one can think of having an independent existence and self-sufficiency. Every action performed by a man is going to have some impact on his fellow men. Pleasure and happiness of an individual have no meaning unless and until he is in a position to contribute to the well-being of another life also. An individual is an integral part of the society. Every person owes a duty to himself and to those around him. There should not be any conflict between individual and social duty. Therefore, a person has to bring out his best abilities and has to rise up to the highest degree. *Dharma* makes a person capable of realizing his virtues and to use them in best possible manner.

Manu's concept of *dharma* deals with all the aspects of a virtuous life and shows the way to acquire the fullest stature. It covers a wider range of action that a person performs in his individual and social life everyday. It caters to the welfare of each and every member of the society at every stage of life. The allotment of *dharma*s for different *varṇa*s, different stages of life, for various professions, and for all other aspects of life provides a definite guideline to lead a successful life. *Dharma* is a perennial source of gaining perfection of *karma* and divine bliss. The two categories of *dharma* — *viśeṣa* and *sādhāraṇa* — are complementary to each other. The former includes the possession of certain qualities and actions needed for a particular stage of life or for a profession. The latter is the practical application of certain absolute human virtues by an individual at every point of time in one's life. *Sādhāraṇa-dharmas* bear universal scope and are of eternal nature. In fact, the proper implementation of *viśeṣa-dharma* needs the strong foundation of *sādhāraṇa-dharmas*.

Manu was aware of human psychology. Generally, people are prone to violate the codes of conduct. The rigidity of the rules alone will compel everyone to remain on the track of *dharma*. Manu always cites illustrations to demonstrate the consequences of obeying or disobeying *dharmas*. These illustrations are mostly taken from Vedas, making the whole description more effective. Manu induces uniqueness to the conception by adding many relaxations.

> One should speak the truth but without giving offence, although one should never compromise with truth for being nice. — *MS* IV.138

> *Dharma* should not be accumulated at the cost of troubling others. — *MS* IV.176

> *Dharma*, which ends unhappily, should be abandoned. *Dharma* should be used for the welfare of the world.
> — *MS* II.159

The Sources of Dharma

The concept of *dharma* as propounded by Manu is fully based on the Vedic ideology. In fact, all Dharmasūtras and Dharmaśāstras consider Vedas as the source of *dharma*. *Manu-Smṛti* lays down five different sources of *dharma:*

> The whole Veda is the foremost source of *dharma;* and next the tradition and practice of those that know it; and further the usages of virtuous men; and lastly, the self-satisfaction.
> — *MS* II.6

This statement depicts that Vedas were the main sources of *dharma*. The Smṛtis and customs follow the path shown by

Vedas. It is a well-known fact that Vedas do not instruct the subjects related to *dharma* in a direct manner. Vedas do not include the topics discussed by Dharmasūtras or Dharmaśāstras. But one may come across the scattered references very close to the subject matter of Dharmasūtras and Dharmaśāstras. At this point, one should not forget that Vedas also present the picture of the society of that time, and no society can move on without introducing certain codes of conduct. *Manu-Smṛti* also deals mainly with social codes. Hence, getting some ideas from Vedas and incorporating them in *Manu-Smṛti* should be taken as a natural phenomenon. P.V. Kane has brought out about fifty Vedic passages that refer to topics such as marriage, the forms of marriage, the different kinds of sons, adoption of a son, distribution of property, inheritance, *śrāddha* and *strī-dharma* (*History of Dharmaśāstra*, vol. 1, part 1, p. 7). These references are mostly associated with the evocations rendered to different gods. The brotherless maidens' difficulty in getting husbands has been made clear by several Vedic passages. "Like a woman growing old in her parents house, I pray to thee as Bhaga from the seat common to all". This reference also may be found at many places in the Vedic literature (*ṚV* I.124.7; IV.5.5; *AV* I.17.1; *Nirukta* III.4-5). *Manu-Smṛti* has also included this rule.

> A person should not marry a brotherless maiden or a daughter of an unknown father. In such cases the daughter has to go for *putrikā-dharma*. —*MS* III.11

According to *putrikā-dharma*, a girl, being an appointed daughter, has to take care of her parents and that a son born of such girl has to perform the *śrāddha* of his maternal grandparents. Under such cases the wife and the son both will be more attached to maternal side and may not do the required service to own family members.

The reference of different types of marriage is seen in the

Vedic literature. *Manu-Smṛti* mentions eight types of marriage, but gives preference to *brāhma* type of marriage. "The virtuous son born of brāhmaṇa marriage may rescue himself and his ancestors even from the hell." This concept has also been revealed in Sūtra literature (*GauDhSū* IV.4; *ĀpaDhSū* II.5, 11, 17; *BhauDhSū* I.11.2). The references of *āsurī* marriage and *gāndharva* marriage do also find place in the Vedic literature. A passage of *Maitrāyaṇīya Saṁhitā* (I.10-11) depicts that in the case of *āsurī* marriage the wife is purchased by her husband. *Manu-Smṛti* has condemned *āsurī* marriage. "One should not go for *āsurī* marriage, as it does not induce happiness." *Ṛgveda* mentions *gāndharva* marriage as follows:

> When a bride is fine looking and is well adorned, she seeks by herself her friend among men. — *ṚV* X.27.12

The importance of *aurasa* and *kṣetraja* sons was even noticed by the Vedic sages.

> A son born of another husband of the wife, or another person though very pleasing, should not be taken in adoption.
> — *ṚV* VII.4.8

Manu expresses similar view:

> Only *aurasa* son is having the right of inheriting father's property. — *MS* IX.162-63

The son born of a properly married woman was known as *aurasa* son. *Taittirīya Saṁhitā* VI.3.10.5 brings out the concept of three debts. Manu says, "A son is responsible of rescuing his ancestors from the hell" (*MS* IX.183). The introduction of eleven types of sons was done with the purpose of continuing the tradition of *śrāddha* (see *MS* IX.180). In *Aitareya Brāhmaṇa* the story of Śunaḥśepa suggests the provision of adopting a son (VI.3.10.5). Śunaḥśepa was adopted by Viśvāmitra in his own family. In *Manu-Smṛti* it has been said:

> In an emergency, a son adopted from the same caste is known as *dattaka putra*. — *MS* IX.168

Taittirīya Saṁhitā VII.1.8.1 tells the story of Atri who gave his only son in adoption to *aurasa*. There is an indication of *kṣetraja* son in *Ṛgveda*:

> What invites you Aśvins in his house to bed as a widow does to her brother-in-law or a young damsel to her lover.
> — *ṚV* X.40.2

It could be interpreted that during the period of *Ṛgveda* too, the practice of *niyoga* was, perhaps, in existence. Manu says that "a son born through *niyoga* is *kṣetraja* son". *Taittirīya Saṁhitā* VIII.3 recommends that the eldest son should inherit father's property. *Manu-Smṛti* also gives more importance to the eldest son:

> A father becomes free of *pitṛ-ṛṇa* after the birth of first son; the first son is entitled to inherit father's wealth.
> — *MS* IX.106-07

Vedic literature admires studenthood. *Śatapatha Brāhmaṇa* suggests the duties of a student:

> A student should not drink and should offer *samidhā* (sacrificial sticks) to fire every evening. — *ŚatBra* XI.3.31

According to *Manu-Smṛti*:

> A student must place fuel on the sacred fire, let him abstain from wine, honey, meat, perfume, garland and substance used for flavouring the food. — *MS* II.176-77

Śatapatha Brāhmaṇa declares king and learned brāhmaṇas as the upholder of sacred ordinance. Manu too agrees with this idea *MS* V.4.4-5:

> A king must discuss the administrative matters with learned brāhmaṇas. — *MS* VIII.1.11.20

Śatapatha Brāhmaṇa speaks of Vedic study as *yajña*, and *Taittirīya Āraṇyaka* 2.10 mentions five *yajñas*. *Manu-Smṛti* also describes five *yajña*s in detail. It considers the study of Vedas as a *yajña*, which has to be performed by the people of all castes and throughout the life. The human virtues have been eulogized everywhere in the Vedic literature. *Ṛgveda* X.117.6 condemns a selfish man who only caters for himself. Later on, Manu elaborated the same moral in a very convincing manner:

> It is the duty of all *varṇa*s not to trouble any person, to speak truth, and not to grab other's wealth in an unjust manner.
> — *MS* X.63

> All these references are sufficient to prove that *Manu-Smṛti* and all other Dharmaśāstras got lots of their subject matter from the Vedic literature. Hence, it will not be incorrect to say that Manu has extended many concepts that were already propounded in the Vedic literature.

The scattered statements related to the various aspects of *dharma* were transformed into systematic treatises. The virtuous conduct of those people who knew the essence of the Vedas in depth should also be treated as the source of *dharma*. These codes or sacred laws were taught by the people well-versed in Vedas. Manu says:

> The learned people followed all these rules in their own life, and later on, their high character served as an example for the rest of the people. — *MS* II.20

Manu has emphasized much on the fact that the learned people have scrutinized well all those laws ordained in Vedas with the eye of knowledge. *Dharma*s propounded in *Manu-Smṛti* were fully in accordance with the Vedic texts:

> For that man who obeys the law prescribed in the revealed text and in the sacred tradition gains fame in this world and unsurpassable bliss after death. — *MS* II.9

> The customs handed down in successions among the four chief castes and the mixed race of that country are the conducts of a virtuous man. —*MS* II.18

Vedas and Smṛtis move together in every respect:

> Vedas and Smṛtis are the revealed canon for those who wish to understand *dharma*, and their views are traditionally regarded as valid law. —*MS* II.13

Manu has asked the wise people to stay away from atheists and scorners of the Vedas (*MS* II.11).

Manu has also considered "self-satisfaction" as the source of *dharma*. The "self-satisfaction" refers to the consent or approval of high-minded people for any of him actions (*MS* II.12). The consent of virtuous men must be considered as an authority in such cases which cannot be settled by other authorities. Virtuous people do not pursue worldly objects and do not go for the acquisition of wealth, and to the gratification of their desires. Therefore, they can perceive different situations in proper perspective. Their expression of satisfaction in the matter may be equally authentic. The contradiction of two laws can be analysed by the wise people.

> When the two sacred laws are conflicting, and both are held to be law; both laws are considered valid laws. —*MS* II.14

It prompts that the conflicting laws were meant for different situations. A wise man has to choose the relevant one depending on the situation. Manu has laid much emphasis on the good traditions as the source of *dharma*. That is why *Manu-Smṛti* suggests that "noble people should stay in the regions where the traditions are well observed" (II.22-25).

2

Human Values and Manu-Smṛti

Meaning of the Word "Value"

THE word "value" means "worth", "fair" or "intrinsic worth of goodness". Values may be treated as criteria of regarding anything useful or estimable:

> Values are something superadded upon the other qualities of objects by the mind, in order to express their relation to its purpose and acts.
>
> — *Encyclopedia of Religion and Ethics*, vol. 12

Plato considers values as:

> The good and the culmination of the ideal world and as the principle which was to unify, systematize and organize all other fellows.

The meaning of this word becomes quite specific when it is prefixed with the word "human". The human values are changing considerably in this material world. But the inner spiritual side of human beings has not changed much. The old primitive passions are still dominating in human life. The material ambitions have overpowered the interest of humanity. We are losing our passion to know our real nature and are getting absorbed in a fake dramatic life. It has become more pathetic in the context of a great country like India. Indian thoughts have paved the path of humanity and have provided the extraordinary mass of material for the refinement of mankind which has hardly an equal in any part of the world.

Indian Concept of Values

The great philosophies provided by Vedas and Upaniṣads are interesting and instructive from the cultural point of view. They contain all ingredients to influence the spiritual life of the whole world. Spiritual experience has been regarded as the foundation stone of Indian belief system. The *brahma-vidyā* taught by Upaniṣads is the science of Self. *Brahman* is the Self of the universe and the universe is the manifestation of *Brahman*. The whole creation is unified in *Brahman*. It is a fact that the material development can never provide a permanent satisfaction as it induces competition, craze and crime. It drives us away from desired virtues and values that are very much needed for the sustenance of a healthy society. Indian thought stands on its own legs and has guided all other sciences. It is in a position to reach to the origin of problems the universe faces and then may offer some positive solutions. Indian minds have always pondered over the origin of mankind. Indian thought prompts harmony between God and man. According to Indian thought, human being is born with the light of Self and thus possesses the power of illumining everything. We cannot feel His presence within ourselves as our experiences are limited by time and space. Our mind cannot go beyond a certain limit.

The Supreme has manifested Himself as creation and has provided us the enormous energy to do a lot of good things in our lives. Man is the most intelligent creation on earth as he possesses the power of thinking. He is having the power of analysing things and may discriminate between right and wrong. Man lives with so many other creatures but his actions are totally different from them. The man, as a rational creature, may take constructive decisions for improving his life. However, owing to his ignorance and sense of ego he ignores this reality and the level of morality tends to decline. The life on earth is a gift to him given by God for bringing self-perfection. This perfection can only be achieved by doing the assigned duties with utmost sincerity. The fulfilment of the duties leads to a good moral life and diverts the non-divine elements to divine spirit.

Concept of "Ṛta" in Manu-Smṛti

The detachment from self and attachment to God are the very foundation of human values. Virtuous are those who may cooperate in the divine scheme. Indian thinkers introduced the law of *karma* for creating a moral world. According to the theory of *karma*, a man reaps whatever he sows. "We reap what we sow" (*BṛUp* III.2.13). Every little action done in one's life decides his future. It is through our deeds that we relate ourselves to the rest of the world. No one can bypass the law of *karma*. The beginningless and endless chain of births and deaths is caused by *karma*. We can be free of *karma* only by following the path of values and virtues. The law of *karma* stands as an order in the world. Though the man is born bound to *karma*, he may reform his future by understanding the Vedic *ṛta* (the right order). *Ṛta*, by its law binding nature, governs the universe and keeps everything in order. *Ṛta* is the root of all ultimate values, and man, by understanding it, may reform his future. *Ṛta* provides righteousness to the social, moral and religious life of a person. The righteous deeds illumine the whole world. In order to attain that height, one has to inculcate certain values. "Disorder or falsehood is the opposite of *Ṛta*" (*ṚV* VII.56.12). Usually, we take this falsehood as the main goal of the life and get deceived every time.

In order to make the Vedic concept of *ṛta* more purposeful and potential, Manu transforms this concept into *dharma*. Hence, *dharma* covers the wider connotation of values. *Dharma* is the expression of spiritual impulse to perfection. *Dharma* can be taken as justice, righteousness, or the regulation of life. It makes a man enjoy the best of human life. It is the Supreme Power that governs each and every action performed by a man. It is implanted in every heart. This impulse has the power of making anyone as perfect as God. Manu has conceptualized a real broad spectrum for *dharma*. He says:

> *Dharma* embraces the whole life and determines one's duties as an individual and as a member of the society.
>
> — *MS* IV.156, 242

Significance of Values in Human Actions

Dharma is in no way different from values. A man is not born just for himself. After taking birth he becomes the responsible member of the society. The whole value system has been charted by keeping in mind the welfare of the society at large. While doing any action one must think whether it is going to be good to the society or not. By bringing values in practice, one may develop the self-restraint. Values generate virtues. A virtuous man leads a comfortable life and provides comfort to everyone else. He is in no way different from God. The virtues overcome the weaknesses and make a man fearless. Strength, fearlessness and freedom are the main essence of value system prescribed by Manu. Vices are always associated with human beings. Manu's concept of value system is based on human psychology. Man is born with desires and that keep on increasing. Desires are transformed into different actions. But all actions are not pure. Impure actions are the result of confusion and illusion generated in human mind. The confused state of mind causes ignorance and man moves away from reality. The false ego dominates and the person starts thinking only about himself. He becomes the victim of various types of vices. The long line of seers realized the reality of a perfect and happy life and brought out the means of procuring that. The seers wanted to lead human beings from ignorance to knowledge. No one likes the darkness of ignorance. The vices represent darkness and the virtues immortal light. Discernment is really needed to follow all these traditions.

> Vedas are the main source of *dharma*. The remembrance of the great Vedic seers, the conduct of great men and self-satisfaction are the other sources of *dharma*. —*MS* II.6

A person cannot adhere to the preaching of great importance unless and until his mind is ready to absorb that. A man must have the power of analysing every action done by others and should know how to catch hold of good deeds and should discard the undesirable deeds. A person becomes perfect only after correcting his deficiencies. By balancing the inner tendencies one may have the divine qualities. The easiest way is to follow the good conduct shown by great personalities.

> The great people born in this country have instructed the whole mankind through their own mode of conduct.
> —*MS* II.20

The great people have made the distinction between *dharma* and non-*dharma*. Their conduct may be treated as the concrete example to follow. The great people come to us with a series of good deeds and inspire us to do the same. The value system stated through different sources becomes the norm for the society for moulding the behavioural pattern of its members. The desired level of good behaviour of a society is very much needed for the progress of any country.

Manu could realize the need of the perfect society and he was also aware of the methods of managing the vast society. A person passes through few phases in his life. The demand of each phase of life is different. Man's role in the welfare of the society also keeps on changing. Every person cannot do everything needed for the smooth running of the society. Thus it became necessary to divide the phases of life and to allot the duties for different phases. The determination of the duties was done to procure the best output of actions performed in that particular phase of life. The performance of allotted duties was considered as value or virtue. Manu concretized the concept of *āśrama-dharma* (*dharma* pertaining to four *āśramas*, viz. *brahmacarya*, *gṛhastha*, *vānaprastha* and *saṁnyāsa*) so that the members of the society may cultivate different values in different phases of life in a very clear manner. It was a rigid time-table for organizing the whole life in a better way. These four stages of life are more concerned with the individual aspect of human life. Society is the sum total of individuals. Every member of the society has to adhere to value system. The guidelines given for different stages of life are responsible for the ethical and moral growth of a person, and to prepare him slowly towards four *puruṣārthas* (*dharma*, *artha*, *kāma* and *mokṣa*). Through these four steps, man can gradually purify himself from earthly taints and prepare himself for spiritual home.

The first stage of life is of *brahmacārī* (studenthood). It is an innocent and tender stage. The training given at this stage is going to be continued for the rest of the life. It is the best time to practise self-control and discipline.

> Having restrained a host of senses and also by subduing the mind, without troubling the mind, by asceticism a person attains all objects. — *MS* I.110

A good conduct is the prerequisite for the performance of every work. Concentration of the mind is very much needed for bringing perfection to any work and it cannot be achieved without controlling the senses.

> A man, who neither thrills nor recoils after hearing, touching, seeing, tasting or smelling anything, is known as a man who has conquered the senses. — *MS* II.98

The modesty in behaviour is the real showcase of ones personality. A student must learn to respect his elders.

> One may thrive for long life, knowledge, fame and strength by greeting older people. — *MS* II.121

> The mother deserves the highest respect as she is the first teacher of a child. —*MS* II.133

Manu has regarded mother as the best teacher. She is the best one to lay the foundation of values in a child.

> A teacher is more important than ten instructors and a father more important than a hundred teachers, but a mother is more than a thousand fathers. —*MS* II.145

> A student must have a sense of trust in his teacher and elders. He should pay respect to his teacher as from him only he is receiving the spiritual, empirical and Vedic knowledge. —*MS* II.117

> A teacher should impose discipline in the student in a very amicable manner. He also has to be modest and disciplined. A teacher is not supposed to cause any type of injury to the student. By using sweet and low speech a teacher should arouse the desire for knowledge. A student must be taught what is best for him. —*MS* II.159

A teacher must treat the students just like his own sons. He should not be malicious to others in thoughts or actions. The values cannot be imposed. Manu advocates the idea of the self-realization of values. A young student watches his teacher's ideal conduct. He gets inspired and tries to do the same.

> A teacher must not distress the student in spite of being himself grieved. —*MS* II.161

Restraining the cluster of sensory power may improve the conduct of both student and teacher. The dedication and reverence towards the teacher will be beneficial for a student in his studies (*MS* II.192-94). Manu has given a long list of values for students to follow. All these values are related to different virtues which a student must possess. Paying respect to his teacher is the first lesson of developing the sense of reverence to others. In other words it may be said that a student must imbibe all virtues needed for his future life.

The stage of *gṛhastha* (householder) is an important phase of life. It is the stage for performing *karmas* for justifying the human birth and for improving the next birth. It is the time to enjoy the earthly life in a befitting manner. At the same time, a householder has to uphold the social codes and values. A householder has already procured a rigorous training of maintaining the level of virtues. He is aware of his duties. It is the time for taking care of *artha* and *kāma*. A householder has to move in two different directions simultaneously. Thus he should know how to strike a balance between *artha, kāma* and *dharma*. His desires and actions must have their base in wisdom. Thus the first thing he has to do is to continue with his desired conduct and should take care of the society. It is the time for him to demonstrate his good conduct for the welfare of others. Manu has dictated an elaborate scheme of virtues for householders. A householder gets a chance to earn money, name and fame. It is very natural for him to get misguided and fall for mundane illusions. This situation may invite many vices and may divert a person from his aim.

> One should make his living by taking up a profession which causes no harm, or very little harm to any other living beings, except in extremity. — *MS* IV.2

Greed is the biggest vice. It makes a person selfish and he wants to grab everything without thinking about others. The non-availability of desired object initiates anger and an angry person becomes insane. In order to get rid of this chain of vices one has to restrain himself at the very beginning.

A person must go for a lawful profession.

> A person should think only about a minimal subsistence. The best person is he who accumulates food only for a single day. — *MS* IV.2-8

The commodities are limited and thus hoarding may cause others to suffer. Manu seems to believe in a socialistic pattern of society. The equal distribution of the wealth may solve many problems occurring in the society. The excess of desire is the root of all types of miseries as it may invite unknown troubles.

> In order to be happy a man must maintain a perfect contentment and should remain self-controlled; for contentment is the very root of happiness, and the opposite of contentment is the root of all unhappiness. — *MS* IV.12

Ācāra, the proper conduct, is really needed for the welfare of a society. Manu has given much emphasis on *ācāra*. The good conduct shown by a person may elevate his own personality and even become beneficial for others. It is like a lamp illumining everyone.

> A person should always engage himself tirelessly in good conduct appropriate to his own innate activities that have been thoroughly set down in the revealed canon and tradition and that is the very root of religion.
> — *MS* IV.155-56

The good conduct is a moral-boosting attribute. A person with good conduct develops self-confidence and always remains cheerful.

> From good conduct one may obtain longevity, good progeny, incorruptible wealth and may destroy his bad marks. On the contrary, a person with bad conduct becomes the object of reproach among people; he is always ill and has an unhappy fortune and a short life. — *MS* IV.157-58

A man of good conduct even without any distinguishing mark lives for 100 years. Good conduct is a multitude of certain virtues. These virtues have a direct impact on the social life of a man. No one in the world is praised for his wealth and power unless he is in a position to use them for helping others. For helping others in any manner one has to subdue his own ego and needs. He also has to broaden his outlook and has to come closer to humanity. As a human being, it is mandatory to possess the human values. Indian tradition has equipped people with a long list of values needed for a person to be recognized as human being. All these values have been regarded as *dharma*. That is why Manu kept on reminding human beings to study diligently Vedas and Dharmaśāstras. A person should regularly take into consideration the teachings that rapidly promote increased intelligence, wealth and welfare. The wealth cannot be ignored as it is very much needed for the survival. But it should be earned and spent in an intelligent and fair manner. The wealth earned through undesirable sources may make a man ill and sad. Manu considers him an unreligious one. Such a person may thrive for some time, may have good fortune or may conquer his enemies but finally, he and his roots are annihilated.

> An unreligious man, a man whose wealth is dishonestly gained, or a sadist does not achieve happiness here on this earth. — *MS* IV.170

Truth, religion and proper occupation help a person to cultivate virtues.

These things can be learnt by following the path shown by father, grandfather or good men. These people had practical experience of life and one should feel obliged to them. Performing the sacrifices for gods, disembodied spirit, manes and ancestors teaches a person the sense of sacrificing for others. It is best to give someone the most precious object. Giving something to someone without any selfish motive is known as *dāna*. It is the outcome of sacrifice. It is the result of absence of hatred (*adveṣa*), lust (*lobha*) and absence of delusion (*amoha*). It has to be supported by purity of motive and humility.

> Charity should always be given with faith. — *MS* IV.227

> A man should always fulfil the duty of giving gifts, offerings and rewards, placing them in the proper receptacles with contented disposition, to the best of his ability. — *MS* IV.228

> A man should donate everything whatever he himself is using for his own comfort. — *MS* IV.229-37

> Both who receives with honour and he who gives with honour, go to heaven, in the opposite case they go to hell. — *MS* IV.235

The act of *dāna* makes a person happy and healthy. The repeated action of *dāna* will generate a fellow feeling in a person. He will feel that he belongs to everyone and all people belong to him. But *dāna* should be given to a worthy person and even should be taken from a virtuous person. A violent, greedy, proud, restless and fraudulent person is not entitled either to give or to receive charity. One has to be careful of "an exploiter, obsessed with the pursuit of his own self-interest, a hypocrite and falsely humble" (*MS* IV.196). Manu advises to restrain the speech, arms and stomach. These three parts of the body are the main sources for distracting a person from the path of truth. The uncontrolled speech pushes a person into many types of problems. Arms represent the demonstration of undue power. Stomach is the centre of greed and lust. The blind use of these three breeds vices. The uncontrolled speech is the outcome of misbalanced mental state. Under the influence of this state, a person loses his reasoning capacity and speaks without thinking the fallout of his words. His ego dominates and he becomes self-centred. He speaks lies and tries to convince others. The vice of *anṛta* causes many problems for others.

> The untruth statement makes the fruits of sacrifice and *tapa* (inner heat) slip away. — *MS* IV.237

Manu's Practical Approach to Value System

Manu's approach towards value system is of practical nature. His main motive is to create a harmonious society. Keeping this in view, sometimes he gives options to deviate from truth.

> One must speak truth, but one should speak what is pleasant, one should not speak unpleasant truth.
>
> — *MS* IV.138

A proud person considers himself the mightiest and very easily becomes violent and causes harm to others.

Violence is the biggest enemy to the society. It has brought many great civilizations to ashes. It has to be stopped at any cost.

> A resolute, gentle, controlled, non-violent man who does not associate with greedy people, whose ways are not cruel, wins heaven. — *MS* IV.246

A violent person never remains happy as he becomes destructive and negative.

> By refraining from oppressing any person, one should gradually pile up religious merits just as an ant piles up the anthill. — *MS* IV.238

Lobha (greed) generates harmful vices. It is the outcome of dissatisfaction. A greedy person wants to snatch away everything from everyone. He may go for any cruel act just to satisfy his greed.

Atithi satkāra has a special place in the value system presented by Manu.

> A householder must honour the guest to the best of his ability. The guests have to be offered seat, food, water, fruits and bed. — *MS* IV.29

The guest is like God and one should feel privileged to welcome the guest. He should be served the food first. The host must have a conversation with him in a very pleasant manner and should offer him all comforts. By doing so, one may come out of the narrowness of the mind and may develop tolerance towards others. One may also learn to share his possessions with others. That is really needed to live in the society in a peaceful manner. Materialism provokes vices and spirituality generates merits. Materialism is the main cause of the vices such as, hatred, selfishness, false pride, anger, cruelty and fraud, whereas the spirituality is the fountainhead of all virtues. It prompts a person to peep within, and to ponder over the subjects that are beyond sensual perception. It corrects the narrow-mindedness of materialism and makes a man plain, truthful, simple, straight and pious.

Righteousness is an expression of divine spirit. Human values teach us how to lead our lives perfectly in the spirit, and how to strive for a socio-spiritual reformation of the community. It does not mean that one has to despise body, life and mind, as they are also the instruments for carving the life of spirit. Spirit and life have to move together, and this togetherness provides positive energy for the realization of truth and to understand the reality of illusions which most of us possess. The value system recommended by Manu does not prohibit normal family life or simple enjoyments. *Kāma* has been denounced but marriage has been considered sacrament for producing offspring and to get free of *pitṛ-ṛṇa*. *Patnī-dharma*, *pati-dharma* and *mātṛ-dharma* also have to be followed in a desired manner. The family relations have to be maintained. These duties were prescribed to ease the family conflicts, but not at the cost of society. One should know the limits. The passions need to be regulated and should be used for a good cause. The excess of attachment may create a hindrance on the path of duties. Life has to be enjoyed with detached attitude and with purity of mind. Wisdom is needed to perform every action. There must be a balance between desire and action. The desire must travel in right direction.

Manu could determine the values for different stages of life by keeping in mind the psychology and requirement of that particular age. There is a difference of attitude between young and old people. Their role in the society also varies. A person gets opportunity to enjoy the life for a certain period of time. But after crossing certain age one must change the pattern of life for his own comfort and peace. *Vānaprastha*, the third stage of life, is considered as a stage of human life when a person has already enjoyed the life and is free from family responsibilities.

> When a householder sees that he is wrinkled and grey, and is having grandchildren, then he should take himself to wilderness. — *MS* VI.2

His role in the society has also to be changed. It is the stage when a person must prepare himself finally for entering in the world that is free of all sorts of attachment. It is the preparatory period for last stage of life, i.e. *saṁnyāsa*. The values assigned for this period have to prepare him for a different type of life.

> *Tapas*, non-attachment, meditation, indifference towards all emotions and austerity are the main duties prescribed for a person who has completed his studentship and has fulfilled the duties of a householder. — *MS* VI.36

Values pertaining to *vānaprastha* are in continuity to the values prescribed for the first two stages of human life. At this stage a person has to practise those virtues in an upgraded and rigid manner. As a free person, he has to take the task of improving himself seriously with full concentration. The seriousness towards observing the virtues like detachment and penance will provide him the mental freedom and give him a chance to think about something, which he has not thought of before.

> Going forth from his house, silent, furnished with pure things regardless of object of desires presented to him, he should move to forest. —*MS* VI.3

At this stage a person is a member of a wider family with extended responsibility. The restriction of emotions, physical needs and feelings will help him to toil for everyone.

> As controlled, friendly and mentally composed, he should always be a giver and a non-taker, compassionate to all living beings. —*MS* VI.8

He may think many things in a new perspective and reach new dimensions. The purity of mind, body and action helps a person to locate the subtleness of the Supreme Self and its inherence in the body. At this stage a person is mature enough to move on his own. His mental faculty is in perfect condition and his decisions are correct.

> He should go quietly alone without having a companion for the sake of his perfection, with mind fixed on *Brahman*, neither being forsaken by anyone. —*MS* VI.31

The loneliness of the forest provides a person the perfect atmosphere to realize the vastness of the nature and the creator and his own negligible existence. It is the state of self-realization, asceticism and renunciation. These practices transform a person and make him virtuous. Virtues are needed for transcendental purposes leading a man to peace and purity giving him the clear vision of the Supreme. Such a person is free of sorrow and fear and is exalted in the world of ultimate reality.

> Such a person does not cause even an atom of danger for any living creature. —*MS* VI.39

The values prescribed for the fourth stage of life — *saṁnyāsa* — were the extension of the previous values prescribed for *vānaprastha*. The rigorous practice of penance, total detachment from empirical life, self-realization and mental freedom transform a person totally. After reaching this stage of life a person should think only about his own renunciation.

> After spending the third part of his life in the forest, a person may abandon all attachments and wander as an ascetic for the fourth part of his lifespan. — *MS* VI.33

Freedom of mind desired for the stage of *saṁnyāsa* can never be achieved unless and until a man has performed the duties allotted for the first three stages of life. There is no provision of skipping the sequence of allotted codes. The anxiety created by not doing the due tasks will not allow the mind to feel free. The mental tension will keep on bothering from time to time and the person may suffer from a sense of guilt.

> When a man has studied Vedas in accordance with the rules and begotten sons in accordance with his duty and performed sacrifices according to his ability, he may set his mind and heart on *mokṣa*. — *MS* VI.37

The study of Vedas and performance of sacrifices are meaningless without having the virtues of kindness and sympathy for others. The personal reward of *mokṣa* (renunciation) cannot be achieved without working for the community. It is the notion of give and take. The first three stages of life are just like an examination which everyone has to clear. Freedom is the reward for the successful completion of the first three stages of life.

> When a man expounds Vedas, promises safety to all living beings and leaves his house to wander as an ascetic, he wins the world made of brilliant energy. — *MS* VI.40

A free person does not bother for earthly pleasures. He has understood the reality of all types of enjoyments. He has reached the very source or root of all enjoyments. There will be no danger for him as he has stopped thinking of life and death.

> He should not welcome dying, nor should he welcome life, but should wait for the right time just as a servant waits for the orders of his master. — *MS* VI.45

> He should endure hard words and never despise anyone, nor become enemy to anyone for the sake of his body. — *MS* VI.48

A *saṁnyāsī* lives in his own world. He never gets influenced by his surroundings. He is like a lotus leaf. He has experienced the consequences of being indulged in the pool of desires. He has achieved the purity of mind and body. His sparkling personality may influence anyone as it is purified by truth. The materialism does not blemish him.

> He should not be sad when he does not get anything nor delighted when he gets something, but takes only for his daily sustenance. His vital breath has transcended from the attachment of material things. — *MS* VI.58

It is the high time for a person to take an account of his previous deeds, their faults and results. There is still some time to rectify the mistakes. He may remember the people suffering from diseases and should also analyse the reasons behind that. Even at this stage he must think for other creatures.

> To protect the living creatures, he should watch the ground constantly as he walks, by night or day. — *MS* VI.69

It is the best time for a *saṁnyāsī* to go for higher thinking and meditation. He may ponder over difficult subjects like the destination of lower self, its relation to higher soul, the creation of the universe and the final journey of a man. *Tapas* performed by a person provides him the vision (*samyak darśana*) to understand the truth.

> A man who has the ability to see correctly is not bound by the effect of his past actions, but the man who lacks the vision is caught up in the cycle of transmigration. — *MS* VI.74

The concept of *āśrama-dharma* propounded by Manu is a concrete example of the social management. The four social orders (brāhmaṇa, kṣatriya, vaiśya, śūdra) are the four sections of the society. The values recommended for these orders were based on the concept of eternal *dharma* and were inspired by spiritual ideals prescribed by the Vedas. Manu has dreamt of an ideal society where every individual is ready to follow the path of morality and spirituality. The duties allotted to different sections of the society were representing different value systems desired for the proper functioning of that particular section. The main purpose for adhering to *varṇa-dharma* was to remind common people the importance of four *puruṣārtha*s and how to attain *mokṣa* by following the path of *karma*. That is why Manu emphasized that the people of all sections should take up their allotted duties as *dharma* and should perform those duties with maximum care. Manu wanted that all these four sections of the society should be trained in a genuine manner for the performance of their duties. The moralities which have to be practised by these orders should be inspired by inner conviction and not by compulsion. It was a real ideal situation when every individual was considered equally responsible for the welfare of the society by contributing his own share. The value system for different sections of the society was designed in such a manner that it may not conflict with each other and the society may be benefitted by their combined efforts. The code of conduct assigned to four *varṇa*s was in accordance with their training and qualification. The lack of efficiency or slackness while performing the assigned duties was considered as sin and the persons committing this kind of sin were subjected to harsh punishment. It is good that no one violates the code of conduct. But the non-observance of value system or situation when someone is undermining the social causes has to be dealt with strictly. Manu accorded brāhmaṇas a primacy in social orders. He was personified as *dharma* himself not because he belongs to the brāhmaṇa clan, but because of his righteous character.

> Like a wooden elephant, like a leathern deer, so is a brāhmaṇa who has not perused Vedas; these three carry their names only. — *MS* II.157

The values like controlling the senses, truthfulness, dutifulness, non-violence, kindness and fairness of the conduct have to be observed by all sections of the society. These virtues are needed for all types of jobs. Kṣatriyas, who were the ruling caste and were equipped with high powers, were responsible for preserving justice and order in the society, but they too were not allowed to violate *dharma*.

> A king must view all affairs with justice and should restrain his lust and anger. — *MS* VIII.44

> If a ruler is just and caring, his people hasten towards him like a river towards the sea. — *MS* VIII.175

Vaiśyas were responsible to take care of trade and to supply commodities needed by the people. They also were not permitted to be engrossed fully in mundane pursuits disregarding the public interest and moral values.

> The other vaiśyas should not commit corporal or any other type of injury, should speak the truth, should not steal, should maintain the purity, should restrain the senses and should be free of vices. — *MS* IX.332-33

In a society everyone cannot perform everything. Thus it becomes necessary to introduce the division of labour. Any system based on the code of conduct and governed by value system may contribute to the progress and happiness of the society.

Value as an Instrument for Improving the Quality of Life

Apart from these values, Manu has also prescribed another set of values needed for everyone. It is remarkable that the profound observations and thinking of Indian sages were never restricted to a particular religion, country, caste or belief. It was painted on a vast canvas having a variety of colours representing each and every creature born in the universe. It was very much handled with universal significance and was made for the welfare of the whole mankind. Thus, it never will lose its relevance as long as the history of mankind goes on.

The other set of values was meant for enriching the general conduct of human beings, and this represented the universal value system. It is based on truth, and truth can never be changed. The synthetic vision of Manu seems to comprehend the vast, impersonal and general value system needed for the spiritual growth of the whole world. In it, the whole world is presented as one single being of incomparable vastness, animated by one spirit. One may realize this truth by exercizing or by practising certain virtues in his day-to-day life. The seeker has to pass through certain essential conditions for achieving the goal. The final goal of life is to achieve the freedom from life and death or immortality. The balanced enjoyment of *dharma, artha* and *kāma* may liberate a man from the bondage of life and death. The right employment of the intelligence makes a person understand the truth. The virtues like tranquillity, self-restraint, renunciation, patience, peace of mind and faith make a man fit to live in an ideal society. A person has to come out of his personal cocoon and should be ready to lose everything for the sake of others. Manu draws a very clear dividing line between right and wrong. The norms of moral actions are also well decided. The tenfold laws pertaining to *dharma* have to be observed by everyone. One must follow the strict mental discipline and should train his mind to achieve the end or to reach to the eternal. The tenfold *dharmas* are "patience, forgiveness, self-control, not stealing, purity, mastery of sensory power, wisdom, learning, truth and control of anger" (*MS* VI.92). The preservation of spirit is patience. A composed and kind-hearted man does not care to the harms inflicted by others. Human love is another form of loving God. Everyone has come to the earth for the sake of the Eternal. Self-control achieved through *dhyāna* may help a person concentrate on difficult subjects and withdraw him from undesirable actions. One has to be satisfied with his own possessions. The habit of stealing is an outcome of greed and laziness. One must try to remain happy with whatever he himself is possessing. A person should know the difference between true and false desires. One must be free from the tyranny of greed and lust. Lust is an animal desire and impulsive craving. One has to denounce it. The purity of body and mind is needed for exercizing all virtues. The pure mind will not allow any impurity of thought to enter it. The pure body may keep a person healthy. A pure mind may cherish the feelings of *maitrī* and *karuṇā*, cheerfulness, selflessness, love and compassion for everyone. Wisdom is the highest activity of human mind and it takes a person closer to Reality. It eliminates the illusions and provides the power of estimating the real worth of anything. Ignorance caused by illusion is the main cause of all vices. Wisdom clears the dust of illusion and makes the mind shine. It also provides the power of analysing the difference between right and wrong and a person may identify the truth. Anger is the result of too much of attachment. The unavailability of the desired object triggers anger resulting in many other vices. The control of anger makes a man calm and peaceful. A peaceful man is always gentle and modest to others. The behaviour of a person towards others depends very much on his inner mental condition. The fairness or gentleness can be expected only from a cool and composed person. An angry man loses his power of thinking and does many things that are harmful to others. A composed person remains happy and makes others also happy.

According to Indian thought, a righteous man is not he who retires to a lonely cave of a mountain and moves away from his social responsibility, but he who decides to stay in the society and loves the worldly objects as the representative of God. One's own soul is not more precious than the souls of all others put together. Man's every common duty done in the favour of community helps him in realizing the Self. One has to transcend from his narrow individuality and should identify himself for greater purposes. The vices may make a person flourish for a short period but not for ever. A person with vices may have a disastrous end as he hampers the cause of so many other people. The world is not for committing sin; it is a pathway to the divine bliss and goodness. These were the messages conveyed by the value system presented by Manu.

Relevance of Manu's Idea of Human Values in Modern Life

Manu-Smṛti highlights human values that are based on the justice and truth. *Satya* and *dharma* are interchangeable. The combination of these two becomes righteousness. The main reason for the perversion of the society is the lack of righteousness. Everyone wants to behave in his own way and forgets the interests of other people. This situation generates discrimination and injustice. The proper induction of righteousness may check the moral degradation of the society and may improve the social conduct of an individual. Modern society is passing through a stage of utter confusion regarding the nature of morality. The disharmony is resulting in several types of socio-political, religious and economic problems. The real harmony can only be achieved by inducing *dharma* and ethical values. Theories related to human values are fast losing their ground. The conflicts between individuals and the society are becoming rampant. Every one of us possesses a pure and noble heart. Despite this, we move away from our original nature and indulge ourselves in all kinds of evils. Man is the combination of divine and non-divine elements which make him vulnerable to evils. One must eliminate the non-divine elements not by destroying them but by suffusing them with divine spirit. The real problem challenging the harmony of the society arises when a person gets too much attached to worldly possession and in order to protect them he causes problems for others. The growing economic, political and dangerous religious rivalries are adding fuel to the fire. People are busy with the present and have undermined their future self. The absence of values has made the society unjust, and an unjust society can never secure justice. People have lost their faith in judiciary. The frustration caused by social discrimination may push many people away from the path of rectitude. Everyone is busy in serving his own interest without being concerned about others. The gap between the rich and poor is widening. The corruption has engulfed the whole system and has become the normal pattern of the society. The community feeling has lost its value and sense of humanity is diminishing slowly. It is not an ideal situation and needs to be improved at any cost. The first necessary step to achieve this end is to improve the relation between an individual and the community. It can only be improved by reviving the importance of human values. A rational man has to integrate himself to the eternity of the past to enjoy a meaningful present and ensure a bright future for his progeny. The past is like the root of a tree providing nourishment to the present and even to the future. It reminds us of the great heritage and inspires us to make endeavour for shaping the present and it kindles the light for us to move forward tirelessly.

Indian philosophy has not made any difference between human values and religion. In fact, religion makes a person practise the values and broadens the mind to understand the reality of human existence. Religion takes a person beyond empirical perceptions and provides strength to lead a worldly life with righteousness. The deep-rooted selfishness and unlimited desires keep on creating confusion in the human mind and we start interpreting religion as the property of a small group. Religion becomes a tool for the demonstration of pride and supremacy. People have started practising religion in a very superficial manner and that too for personal benefits. Fanaticism spoils the significance of religion. Religion, as a matter of fact, induces the spirit of divine nature. It marches on the track of value-oriented dogma and teaches us to root out pride, resentment, lust, etc. It fills us with the tender feeling of love and compassion for everyone, and that helps unite people.

The modern generation is exposed too much to science and technology. They do not accept any ideas without having a scientific and logical background. In order to revive the old practice of human values, we need to present the whole treasure of thoughts in a scientific manner. We have to make them realize the reasons behind the problems that have been creeping in the present-day society and are troubling everyone. We have to move step by step to bring back the past glory. Everyone possesses the capacity of rising to his full divine stature and his potential can be realized if one strives for it. Human being is the most precious creature on the earth and his brain contains the immense power to think and to perform the most tedious tasks. Unfortunately, we are generally lazy in extending our mental efficiency and have developed a tendency to leave everything to destiny. Any problem coming up in any form is termed as fate or luck. We do not try to reach out to the root cause of the problems and do not try hard to get some genuine solution. There is a high demand for getting some readymade answers for solving every problem. But it is not a desirable method. Our old scriptures are having the right solutions needed to solve many of the modern problems. We are unaware of many good and useful things preserved in our old tradition. A person takes birth with some purpose and should fulfil it in the best possible manner. We are supposed to demonstrate our best ability for the sake of ourselves and even for others.

> Life is a great festival to which we are invited, and thus we might show *tapas* (self-renunciation), *dāna* (charity), *ārjava* (right dealings), non-injury to life and *satya-vacana* (truthfulness). — *ChāUp* III.17.4; *TaitUp* I.9

Importance of Human Values for Maintaining Global Harmony

The importance of leading a righteous life based on values has been repeated in all great Indian scriptures. It is not just a theoretical pronouncement. Our great sages have demonstrated practically by practising all those theories in their own lives. Their success and achievements are a great source of inspiration for all of us. It is not a fiction, but a simple method of teaching the role of values in our day-to-day life. These moral stories are based on the personal experiences of seers who wanted to share the gist of all those with the coming generations. The mere knowledge of something is not going to be sufficient. One has to reach to the nucleus of all virtues. The messages related to *dharma* given by our genius ancestors are meant for the welfare of one and all. It is rather impossible and will also not be fair to interpret the word *dharma* (religion).

The word *dharma* covers a vast arena. It covers all attributes needed for an ideal society. The morality taught by Indian tradition touches all the points that have the potential to rectify the shortcomings of the modern life. Our tradition gave us the valuable concept of pluralism. The whole universe is the manifestation of single Supreme Consciousness. The concept is not only unique but also very catchy and carries a lot of meaning which can be of much importance to the modern world. Pluralism is a beautiful word carrying much of insight. Pluralism is about eliminating the vices like hatred and jealousy and to extend love, mercy and sympathy to all creatures. We have to broaden our outlook and have to cross the geographical, cultural and religious boundaries. The essence of pluralism is, "live and let live" (*MS* VII.41; VIII.271). It should never be limited to just a slogan. The politicization of these words has to be checked. The unique concepts enshrined in Indian scriptures have already provided us the light to come out of darkness. We have to accept that light and should try to walk on the path in right earnest. Amidst the din and bustle of strife and struggle, hatred and jealousy in our daily lives, one can still try to be a potent voice to bring about the right change. We have to reduce the human sufferings and that will be possible only by examining and improving our own conduct and behaviour. It has been said in *Manu-Smṛti*:

> By mastering our own body and sense-organs, we may listen the righteous command of the Self or consciousness and this may lead us to the right path. — *MS* XII.83

Self-discipline is the key to all virtues, as it strengthens the good impulses and weakens the bad ones. The methodical impact of will-power makes everything possible.

The temporal relevance of human values also has to be kept in view. We have to cope up with the fast-changing social life and the varying attitude of different societies. Flexibility is needed for making anything more practical. Manu has always advised to maintain a balance between spirituality and social necessity. Manu has given us many options in conduct for any emergencies, which are collectively referred to as as *āpad-dharma*. The existence of life has to be saved at all costs as the self is the embodiment of the great Self. Thus Manu sometimes allows a relaxation in value system. But at the same time he advocates that *dharma* has to be protected by all means. According to Manu,

> One should always adhere to *dharma* as it helps a person cross the dark and difficult situations in this world.
>
> — *MS* IV.242

3

Manu's Treatment of Brāhmaṇas

Ethos of Indian Culture

THE culture of India, including its philosophy, religion, ethics and social customs, has blossomed from the soil of spirituality. Righteousness and release (*mokṣa*) are the main goals of the Indian way of life. There has been continuous development of the Indian thought process that has taught the common people the very purpose of their life on the earth. The unbroken succession of great spiritual leaders has kept on reminding the people to maintain the path of surrender and sublimation and has tried to transform the society by bringing about necessary reforms. Our sages have not wasted their energies on empirical problems of daily life, but have meditated on the deeper problems of human existence. This philosophy has always held an independent and prominent position in the life of every individual and has guided their every action. The worldly life was considered as an invitation for practising a moral and dutiful life. The law of *karma* compelled every person to conserve the moral energy. One may improve his next birth by performing virtuous deeds. Virtue alone is the best possession for a man. An individual has to bear the responsibility of taking care of the other members of the society by maintaining the values in his every action. Thus the demonstration of the virtues became the main criterion of the social life.

Nature of the Class Division of the Society during Vedic Period

In order to achieve the desired level of efficiency and to ensure the better productivity it became necessary to divide the society into few groups or classes. In the Vedic period *karma* determined the class. Every person was free to migrate from one class to another class depending on the change of his *karma*. In *Ṛgveda* there is a reference of a poet whose father was a physician and maternal grandfather was a stonecutter (*ṚV* III.43.5, IX.112.3). In *Bṛhadāraṇyaka Upaniṣad* there is a narration of the dialogue between two characters, Balāki, the teacher, and Ajātaśatru, the king of Varanasi. The teacher was not in a position to explain the nature of *Brahman* correctly to the king and was defeated by the king. At last the brāhmaṇa teacher becomes the student and Ajātaśatru, a kṣatriya, becomes the teacher (*BṛUp* 2.1.15). Satyakāma Jābāli, whose family details were unknown, was accepted by Gautama as a pupil (*ChāUp* IV.4-5). Viśvāmitra, the son of Gādhi, was originally a kṣatriya and was the king of Kānyakubja. Later on, he became *brahmarṣi.* All these examples reveal that a person was free to move from one class to another depending on his position and profession. The division of class was based on the virtues possessed by a man and not on his birth and lineage. It was considered that a man becomes virtuous by the virtuous actions performed by him. The concept of class system came into existence on the basis of talent or virtues possessed by a group of people.

Classes and Castes during Smṛti Period and Justification for the Change

The group which was more spiritual, deeply ethical, less materialist and efficient to guide the rest of the society was placed on the top. It is the correct genesis of the class which was known as brāhmaṇa. The word brāhmaṇa is derived from the word *brahma* suffixed with *ṇa*, which means "the one who knows *Brahman*". Thus, the class known as brāhmaṇa was engaged in the higher knowledge and was entitled to study and teach the Vedas. Because of the multiplicity of their virtues they were granted many privileges. The several provisions of common laws made for other classes were not applicable to Brāhmaṇas.

If we go through the history of Dharmaśāstra, the literature containing the ancient laws, we find that from the period of *Baudhāyana-Smṛti* (sixth centuary BCE), the brāhmaṇas were considered the authority of the knowledge pertaining to *Brahman*, capable of teaching *dharma* and the symbol of dutifulness.

Manu has also followed the concept of four classes of the society and has determined the code of conduct for different classes. He also has defined the nature of the four classes and has proclaimed their functions. There must be a balanced and proper coordination of the duties performed by different groups of the society. The desired development of the society depends on the collective effort made by the different groups of the community. Thus, it becomes the responsibility of every group to take care of its assigned duties. Manu wanted to stipulate the code of conduct for all time to come. He has brought in the element of human psychology which keeps on changing from time to time. Manu had a great faith in the guidelines given by the ancestors and was of the belief that everyone should make the best use of it. The prescribed codes of conduct for different groups are of a rigid nature, but at the same time these contain flexibility needed for emergencies. The rigidity of the code of conduct is needed, so that people may not even dare to think of deviating from the path of their duties. The flexibility of the code of conduct makes the whole system more vibrant and practical. In order to give a divine tinge to his classification Manu has accepted the old theory of the creation of four classes as propounded by *Ṛgveda* (see Puruṣa-Sūkta X.90.12).

> For the prosperity of the universe the cosmic Puruṣa created brāhmaṇa from his mouth; rulers from his arms; vaiśyas from his thighs and śūdras from his feet. —*MS* I.31

God has thus created four classes out of his own limbs for performing different jobs needed for the survival of universe. The human body consists of different limbs with the purpose of doing different jobs and the survival of the body depends on the total activities performed by different limbs. All limbs of the body are of equal importance. The difference is only of the jobs performed by those limbs. The loss or malfunctioning of any of the limbs may affect the whole body. It is the same in the case of the society. The four classes are just like the limbs of the society, working in perfect harmony for the welfare of the whole body — the society.

The useful functioning of the whole body depends on the job done by different limbs separately. The sluggishness shown by any part of the body may make the whole body unproductive. So is the case with the society where each and every group has to perform its assigned role in a perfect manner, failing which the society will be thrown out of gear and may crumble. The society is just like a band of musicians, where artists play different instruments individually with perfection and produce a combined rhythmic sound. Similarly the four groups or classes of society may strengthen it by performing their duties in the desired manner.

Before moving to the point of Manu's treatment of brāhmaṇas, one thing should be made clear that Manu belonged to the age of social evolution which was much different from the Vedic period. The civilization was stretching rapidly and new concepts related to customs and conventions were also taking shape. Perhaps, the glorified traditions of Vedas were being undermined. There was a need for re-establishing the Vedic value system, considering that as an authority. Manu wanted to make the best use of the ancient codes and their usages which prevailed during the Vedic period. He wanted to make the whole social system more systematic and effective. Perhaps it was the demand of the time to divide the society into a few groups and to standardize the definition of those groups. Manu thought to combine law and *dharma* for the betterment of the society and thus, it became necessary to assign definite duties for different groups of the society. He also realized that there must be a group whose character and conduct should serve as a guideline to the rest of the society. This group of people must possess certain qualities and qualifications to command the respect and reverence of everyone living in the community.

> Brahmā himself has emitted brāhmaṇa from his mouth, through *tapa*, to convey the offerings to gods and ancestors, and to guard this whole creation. —*MS* I.94

Place of Brāhmaṇas in the Society

Brāhmaṇa was placed at the top in the society because of his super intelligence. Manu considered Vedas the treasure of the knowledge pertaining to *Brahman*. This higher knowledge can only be grasped by intelligent people. The knowledge of *Brahman* was considered as the highest achievement of the life and the group of people engaged in pursuit of the higher knowledge was known as brāhmaṇas.

> The brāhmaṇa is the lord of the whole creation, because he is eldest and because he maintains Vedas. —*MS* I.93

Manu's another conviction was that *dharma* in terms of justice and duty should be the base of the society. He was very clear for according the title of brāhmaṇa to any person. There were certain duties and conduct assigned for a brāhmaṇa and the one who fulfilled those required criteria can alone be classified as brāhmaṇa.

> A brāhmaṇa should engage himself in the teaching and learning of Vedas, sacrificing for himself, sacrificing for others and giving and receiving charity. —*MS* I.88

These jobs required a different bent of mind and couldn't be done in a perfect manner by everyone. Maṇu allotted all these jobs only to brāhmaṇas with a notion that the brāhmaṇas are the custodians of the intellectual and spiritual traditions of the Indian heritage. Brāhmaṇas were given the difficult task of guiding the whole society and for that they had to be perfect in every respect.

> The very birth of a brāhmaṇa is the eternal physical form of *dharma*; because he is born for the sake of *dharma* and is fit to become one with the Ultimate Reality. —*MS* I.98

In other words it may be said that brāhmaṇas, through their conduct, have to present themselves as the most ideal example before others. That is why, while mentioning the desired qualification for brāhmaṇas, Manu becomes very stern and brings out the most difficult ordinances for them.

> Among brāhmaṇas the learned ones are the best, among learned men the best are those who understand their obligations; among those who understand their obligations, those who fulfil them; but the best are those who understand Vedas. —*MS* I.97

Conditions for Getting Brāhmaṇahood

The most essential qualification for a brāhmaṇa was to be well versed in Vedas. He should also be capable enough to assert firmly the Vedic thoughts to others.

> A brāhmaṇa who from adherence to rationalism despises the Śruti and its tradition, he, an infidel blamer of Vedas, is to be banished by virtuous people. —*MS* II.11

The training on studying Vedas and understanding the hidden

meaning of Vedas were given to brāhmaṇas at a very early age. Their conduct and behaviour had to be up to the mark and they had to lead a very simple and tough life.

> *Ācāra* (good conduct) is the highest *dharma* mentioned in Vedas and is approved by traditions, therefore, a prudent brāhmaṇa has to concentrate on it. — *MS* I.108

The brāhmaṇahood was the main criterion for a brāhmaṇa which included all codes prescribed for a brāhmaṇa. Mere birth in a brāhmaṇa family was not sufficient enough for achieving the status of a brāhmaṇa.

> A brāhmaṇa who has fallen away from the conduct desired for a brāhmaṇa will not get the fruit of the Vedas, but if he is attached to it, he enjoys the full fruit. — *MS* I.109

Vedas are the real source of *dharma*, and the knowledge of *dharma* improves the conduct and the proper conduct is the root of *tapa* (austerity). *Tapa* creates an inner heat which is needed to understand the reality of the world and after understanding the reality of the world the whole vision of a person gets changed. A brāhmaṇa must have all these qualities as he is the guardian of the community. Manu asserts that the duties proclaimed for a brāhmaṇa were already enshrined in Vedas. The virtue of unselfishness was a much desired quality for a brāhmaṇa as this virtue is the root of all other virtues. A brāhmaṇa can never look after the society without possessing virtues. The virtues may help a person to get rid of the ego and may develop the sense of love and friendship towards everyone. It was a must for a brāhmaṇa to be self-contented and self-restrained, otherwise he cannot develop a fellow feeling towards others.

> A brāhmaṇa, even if being in the state of physical distress, should not strike others and should not be malicious to any person in thought or by action. — *MS* II.161

He should remain unaffected be it the state of pleasure or sorrow.

> A brāhmaṇa should always be alarmed by adulation as if it is poison and should always desire scorns like ambrosia.
> — *MS* II.162

A person with wisdom knows that there is no loss by being abused by someone or there is no gain by receiving respect from someone. A scorned person sleeps happily, awakes happily and leaves the world happily. On the contrary, the man who scorns, never remains happy. A brāhmaṇa has to perform the deeper austerity to reach to this state of mind. It is a difficult path and needs great effort. Only a person with purified mind may move on this path. The detachment towards the worldly life is much needed for a brāhmaṇa. He only should concentrate on his duties without thinking much of other things around him. The seniority comes not through age or through having grey hair, it comes through the conduct shown by a person to others. Brāhmaṇas were also supposed to use their superior knowledge in practice.

> The seniority of a brāhmaṇa comes through knowledge and wisdom. — *MS* II.155

A brāhmaṇa, without knowledge, has no right to be called a brāhmaṇa.

> A brāhmaṇa, without knowledge is like an elephant made of wood, like a deer made of leather, these three bear nothing but their names. — *MS* II.157

Thus, it is very clear that brāhmaṇas represented a special group of the society, because of their unique character, because of their knowledge and because of their wisdom. They were the people who had already reached the climax of the penance and were in a position to offer the same to the rest of the society. The social contribution rendered by brāhmaṇas was based on the fairness and justice and that is how they were known as the guardians of the society. A person with ego or lust cannot provide a selfless service to the society.

While discussing the privileges granted to brāhmaṇas, we often forget the severe conditions laid down by Manu for brāhmaṇahood. In fact, the brāhmaṇas had to observe lots of restrictions even during the second stage of life as the householders. He was not allowed to marry someone of low caste. For a brāhmaṇa, marriage was considered as the most sacred institution, as even after marriage he had to take care of the society.

> A brāhmaṇa, marrying a casteless or of lower caste out of infatuation surely brings quickly his family and descendants to the condition of śūdras. — *MS* III.15

> A brāhmaṇa having taken a śūdra wife goes to hell; if he begets a son from her, he loses the status of brāhmaṇa. — *MS* III.17

All these restrictions were imposed on brāhmaṇas for saving their Brāhmanic character. A brāhmaṇa is known for his character and after losing his character he has no right to be called a brāhmaṇa. A wrong marriage may have a bad impact on the prescribed duties of a brāhmaṇa and may spoil his whole career. Marrying a woman of low caste will surely affect the atmosphere which a brāhmaṇa needs for his academic pursuit as the wife may not have the same wavelength and she may create hindrance in fulfilling the allotted jobs. The daily routine of a brāhmaṇa householder has to be different and difficult in comparison to other classes of the society. He has to perform his daily sacred duties including five sacrifices strictly.

> A brāhmaṇa should make *utsarga* of Vedas outside the village in the month of Pauṣa or on the first day of the bright fortnight of Māgha in the forenoon. — *MS* IV.25.96

Utsarga is a ceremony performed on completing the annual course of Vedic study. It indicates that the brāhmaṇas were supposed to continue the study of Vedas without any break. Not only that, they have to follow all formalities needed for the study of Vedas. They have to maintain the mental and physical purity and have to study Vedas with full concentration.

> A brāhmaṇa should strenuously avoid two occasions for the recital of Vedic *mantras*, viz. when the place for recital is impure or he himself is defiled. — *MS* IV.127

The purity of the mind is very much needed for the recital of Vedas and that cannot be procured without clean body and clean surroundings. It was the duty of a householder brāhmaṇa to maintain the purity of the environment. The study of Vedas was necessary at every step of his life as the Vedas gave the needed direction for the smooth sailing of life. Brāhmaṇas, only after studying the Vedas tirelessly, can give proper direction to the society.

> A brāhmaṇa, who does not study the Vedas throughout his life, is quenched like a grass in the fire. — *MS* III.168

A brāhmaṇa as a householder has to perform the duties of multifarious nature. He has to look after his family and has to follow the duties prescribed for the householder; has to study Vedas and even has to perform the sacrifices. At the same time he was also required to earn his livelihood. It was not an easy life and it needed much of mental and physical effort. Failing in any of these duties, he was considered a sinner.

> A brāhmaṇa can never seek *mokṣa* (final emancipation) without studying Vedas, without extending progeny and without performing the sacrifices. — *MS* VI.37

A brāhmaṇa has no right or freedom to enter in the territory of another order without fulfilling the conditions assigned for the previous order.

> A brāhmaṇa, who has discharged his three debts, who steadfastly practises the tenfold law, has duly heard Upaniṣads may become a *saṁnyāsī* (renouncer). — *MS* VI.94

The ten points of the duty are patience, forgiveness, self-control, not stealing, purification, mastery of the sensory powers, wisdom, learning, truth and lack of anger. The detached life was very much needed for a brāhmaṇa and the systematic process of tenfold law helped him to be detached to the worldly life. Therefore, it is amply clear that the brāhmaṇas were put under severe restrictions and had to possess a variety of qualities. They were regarded as the masters of the society and were supposed to look after the community in every sphere. It was the group of most intelligent, dedicated and efficient people. They were entirely different than the other three groups of the society because of their very special qualities.

Special Privileges Given to Brāhmaṇas in Dharmaśāstras and Manu-Smṛti

Under such circumstances it is not illogical that a person leading a detached life, bearing several types of restrictions and possessing a high degree of spiritual knowledge is allowed to enjoy certain privileges and is considered superior to others. This supremacy was never granted at random. The brāhmaṇas were allotted the most tedious assignment of being the guardians of the society and were given the charge of teaching *dharma* and righteousness to the whole society because of their intelligence and spiritual lifestyle. The privileges accorded to them should be considered as the humble reward for their virtuous life which they cultivated through severe penance and renunciation. Throughout their life they served the society in a selfless manner and imparted the precious knowledge to others. According to a reference found in *Manu-Smṛti*,

> The teacher has to impart the knowledge to his students till his death. He has no right to deny that to the seeker of the knowledge. — II.243

Manu was fair enough to proclaim that:

> Whatever exists in the universe is all the property of the brāhmaṇa and he is entitled to have it all by his superiority and eminence. — *MS* I.100

Giving right to the whole property to brāhmaṇa has a special significance. A detached and self-restrained brāhmaṇa, even being the master of the whole property, will never be involved in it, but at the same time he can be the honest custodian and will be ready to share that with everyone. Manu granted the permission of studying and teaching Vedas only to learned brāhmaṇa because only intelligent and prudent will be able to assimilate and interpret the deep and symbolic meanings of the Vedic text. A person with ordinary intelligence may not be able to grasp the complexity of the Vedic knowledge and may interpret that in a faulty manner. Manu did emphasize the importance of learning Vedas, because he trusted Vedas and considered that only the knowledge of Vedas could shape and improve the conduct of any person. Even among brāhmaṇas the ones who knew the essence of Vedas and brought that in practice, were considered the best. Manu gave more importance to the practical aspect of the knowledge than of the theoretical one. The observance of the duties in a keen manner is the very practical approach to Vedic knowledge. Brāhmaṇas were given the charge of preaching *dharma* to the society because they were well versed in Vedic studies and were able to follow the instructions related to *dharma*. Manu thought that only brāhmaṇas could protect Vedas because of their righteous conduct. The birth of a brāhmaṇa is a perpetual incarnation of *dharma* and he is the only protector of higher knowledge contained in Vedas. Brāhmaṇas, because of the power of their penance and meditation, were capable of getting the gist of *parā-vidyā* (the knowledge of *Brahman*). They were also capable of visualizing many things beyond sensual perception through intuition. That was the reason of their supremacy among others.

> When a brāhmaṇa is born, he is born above the world, the chief of all creatures. — *MS* I.99

Brāhmaṇa was considered the head of the society because of his virtues and that is why he received honour and respect from all corners.

Role of Brahmaṇas in Elevating the Society

The biggest treasure of a brāhmaṇa is his ideal conduct. His conduct is worth enough of inspiring everyone and for improving the conduct of those who come in his contact. By the virtue of his great character he is capable of examining justly the good or bad qualities of others. The mental age of a brāhmaṇa will always be higher than the person of the same age belonging to any other group of the society. The mental age is the degree of a person's mental development expressed as an age at which the same degree is attained by an average person. A brāhmaṇa is known because of his mental development and not because of his physical age.

> Now one should consider a ten-year-old brāhmaṇa and hundred-year-old kṣatriya as father and son; but of them the brāhmaṇa is the father. — *MS* II.135

The similar expression is also found in the fifth canto of *Kumārasambhava* of Kālidāsa: *na dharmavr̥ddheṣu vayaḥ samīkṣyate* (age is no bar for an intelligent person).

> A man does not become old by the virtue of his grey hair; the knowledge acquired by him makes him old even at an young age. — *MS* II.156

Brāhmaṇa was respected for his knowledge which he kept on imparting to everyone without any discrimination. He used to take care of his students more than a father or mother.

> The teacher, who fills the pupil's two ears with knowledge which never goes in vain, should be known as his father and mother. — *MS* II.144

The teacher has been considered as the second mother for a student because he provides to his student the empirical, Vedic and spiritual knowledge simultaneously.

> The mother and father produce a child through mutual desire and bring him to the existence. But the birth given by a teacher in accordance with proper rituals is the real birth free from old age and death. — *MS* II.147-48

Manu clearly mentions:

> Wealth, kingship, age, actions and learning are the basis of respect, but the highest respect one may achieve is through *vidyā*. — *MS* II.136

There were two categories of teachers:

> The teacher who teaches the selected portion of Vedas to make a living is known as *upādhyāya* (instructor), but the one who teaches his students in accordance with rules and feeds the students is called *ācārya*. — *MS* II.141-42

The teachers who teach without expecting any return from the students have been considered the most respectful. The supremacy and venerableness offered to brāhmaṇas were rightfully earned by them. There was no scope for them to think about their own livelihood or for accumulating wealth. They were required to surrender their whole life for the sake of the welfare of the society. They were created for *niṣkāma-karma*.

Manu's social philosophy was based on progress of each

and every person living in a community. He wanted to make everyone perfect in the term of conduct and behaviour. But everyone cannot have the equal mastery over the Vedic knowledge, and they needed someone to guide them earnestly and provide them a strong base. Manu considered brāhmaṇas as the strong base or pillar of the society. As such it became mandatory to provide several benefits to brāhmaṇas for the maintenance of the pillar. He might have realized that only the learned brāhmaṇas might serve the purpose of the solid pillar.

Reasons for Granting Special Privileges to Brahmaṇas and Their Nature

The privileges given to the brāhmaṇas should be taken as an incentive given to them with the intention of recognizing their great contribution towards the desired progress of the society. It is very natural to reward a hardworking and sincere person and it exists very much in tradition. Manu did not give any special favour to brāhmaṇas. They were given special status and the highest security throughout their life and no one had the right to ignore or insult them.

> One should never injure a teacher and a brāhmaṇa. A learned man should never threaten a brāhmaṇa. No one should beat a brāhmaṇa even with a blade of grass and should not cause the blood to flow from the body of a brāhmaṇa. —*MS* IV.167

> As many grains of dust are absorbed as the blood coagulates on the ground, for that many years, the man who caused the bloodshed will be eaten up by violent animals in the next world. —*MS* IV.168

> The brāhmaṇas were supposed to remain away from any type of fighting or violence. They had to be free of all sorts of viciousness and wickedness. Even a brāhmaṇa should not raise a finger against another brāhmaṇa.

> Even if a brāhmaṇa merely assaulted another brāhmaṇa out of desire to slay him, abides 100 years in hell *tāmisra* (darkness). — *MS* IV.165

> If any person hurls cruel words on a priest, his tongue should be cut off; if someone mentions his name or caste maliciously, a red hot iron nail of ten-fingers long should be thrust into his ears; if he instructs the priest about his duties, hot oil should be poured into his mouth and ears. — *MS* VIII.270-73

A brāhmaṇa is a harmless person and it will never be proper to harm a harmless person. The harmless person has to be protected from all sides.

Role of Brāhmaṇas in Governance and Administration

Manu always was in favour of a lawful state and emphasized much on justice and truthfulness in the administration. The formation of laws, their implementation, bringing amendments from time to time and the protection of laws can only be done by the wise and learned people. Only such persons can avoid the undesired consequences and may provide justice to everyone. Manu had much faith in the guidelines related to law and justice provided by Vedas and for that the help of learned people was very much needed. Vedas have prescribed spirituality in administration and only brāhmaṇas were well versed in Vedas. The administration was in the hands of the ruling class. In order to induce spirituality into administration the king had to seek the help of brāhmaṇas. The king was not free to take any decision without being assisted by brāhmaṇas.

> The king having risen early, should revere brāhmaṇas learned in the three Vedas, the knower of all *vidyās*, the knower of science, ethics and politics, and wise. He should stand firm in the decisions taken by them. — *MS* VII.37

In this verse the word *vṛddha* means those who have read the scriptures thoroughly and *viduṣa* means those who understand the treatises on polity. Because of these qualities the brāhmaṇas were considered as the best and the most suitable consuls for the king. In the matters like war and peace, for improving the condition of the kingdom, the accumulation of wealth and the protection and preservation of the acquired territory, the king needs the opinion of a wise and clear-minded person and for that a king must have an experienced advisor.

> The king should always serve unpolluted old priests who know Vedas; a person who serves such persons is even respected by ogress. — *MS* VII.38

> The brāhmaṇas are the incarnation of humility and the king must learn this virtue from them. — *MS* VII.39

Humility (*vinaya*) encompasses many virtues including discipline and good manners. The king has to be humble before a priest as he is much higher than the king in the field of wisdom. The king needs the quality of foresightedness possessed by a brāhmaṇa. Brāhmaṇas played an important role in the administration only because of their vivid knowledge of different subjects.

> A king must acquire the knowledge of three Vedas, the knowledge of the eternal science of politics, the methods of punishment, the knowledge of philosophy and the knowledge of soul. — *MS* VII.43

All this knowledge can only be received from a learned person like a brāhmaṇa. It was a must for a king to appoint a few learned brāhmaṇas among the group of ministers.

> The king must discuss the most important concerns of sixfold policy (*sandhi* or peace or alliance, *vigraha* or war, *yāna* or march or expedition, *āsana* or halt, *saṁśraya* or seeking shelter and *dvaidhibhāva* or duplicity) with a learned and distinguished brāhmaṇa. — *MS* VII.58

These were the most tedious parts of the governance and a king had to handle them with much care. Brāhmaṇas, because of their high intelligence level and analytical capacity, would surely be giving the right advice. The brāhmaṇas were also needed for the domestic rituals of the king.

> The king must appoint a domestic priest to perform the domestic rituals and daily sacrifices. — *MS* VII.78

> The king should perform sacrifices for religious purposes and should offer gifts, goods for daily use and money to Brāhmaṇas. — *MS* VII.79

Manu has put lots of restrictions on a brāhmaṇa. He has to lead a worldly life with minimum subsistence without thinking much for the normal enjoyments enjoyed by other groups of the society. At the same time he was in-charge of varieties of activities and was required to do everything with total perfection. Therefore, it was the duty of the king to take care of his day-to-day needs.

> A king should be reverent to the brāhmaṇas, returning from their *guru*'s family. — *MS* VII.82

The king had to revere the *vipra* coming back after finishing their education by giving them money, and that money, dispersed among brāhmaṇas, was regarded as a kind of royal investment.

> The money given to priests cannot be taken away by thieves or enemies and it is never destroyed. Therefore, the king should deposit his incorruptible treasure with brāhmaṇas. — *MS* VII.83

The money offered to brāhmaṇas was the safest one as they would never misuse that and would render an unparallel service to every one. Manu gave very special preference to the wealth given to the priests and considered that even better than putting oblation in the fire.

> What is offered as an oblation in the mouth of a brāhmaṇa is better than the daily fire sacrifices, it is never split, dropped or destroyed. —*MS* VII.84

In the scheme designed by Manu, the Vedic scholars were kept on the top and were considered the most worthy recipients for receiving the endless rewards.

The king had to seek the help of brāhmaṇa at every step of the governance. This recognition of a brāhmaṇa was because of his thinking power. He could set his mind on any given topic brilliantly and might draw a definite conclusion. The brāhmaṇas had a special place even in the court of justice.

> A king who wishes to hear legal cases should enter the courtroom modestly accompanied by brāhmaṇas.
> —*MS* VIII.1

The law and justice must be handled by honest and fearless persons, and brāhmaṇas were possessing these qualities. Apart from these virtues, they also studied the *ānvīkṣikī* (the logical philosophy) and were the makers of law treatises.

> The priest should enter the high court flanked with three judges, and seated or standing, he should hear the cases.
> —*MS* VIII.10

The court of law governs the whole system related to governance and keeps everyone in order. The small error in the implementation of law and justice may create a big problem for the ruler. Therefore, the ruler must have good people to help him.

> When the three priests who know Vedas and the learned one, appointed by the king, sit in proclaiming judgement, that place is known as the court of Brahmā. —*MS* VIII.11

There were few categories of brāhmaṇas, but among them the best were those who were practising renunciation in their life. Even the brāhmaṇas of inferior categories were considered better than śūdras.

> A brāhmaṇa who makes his living only by his birth as a priest, or who merely says that he is a priest, may, at the king's pleasure, explain justice, but never a śūdra.
>
> — *MS* VIII.20

It is a rare reference in *Manu-Smṛti,* which mentions in a very distinct manner the hereditary character of brāhmaṇas. But one should not forget that during Smṛti period due to the growth of population, the fluidity from class to class created problems. Thus, it became necessary to draw a definite line between different groups of the society, for which, the birth became the criterion for deciding the caste. It was believed that the marriage selection and vocational specialization would contribute much towards the refinement of the progeny. Therefore, the birth of a child in a brāhmaṇa line became the testimony of the child's brāhmaṇahood. Even among brāhmaṇas, all were not strictly adhering to the rules and regulations formed for them. They were considered as the inferior type of brāhmaṇas. Manu could not agree that the mere birth of a child in a brāhmaṇa line was sufficient enough to make him a brāhmaṇa; he must fulfil the conditions of acquiring knowledge and wisdom. The privileges were granted only to wise brāhmaṇas.

> A wise brāhmaṇa, finding a treasure which has been previously hidden away, may take the possession of it even without leaving anything for the king, as he is the lord of all. — *MS* VIII.37

> If a king discovers any ancient treasure hid in the ground, after giving half to the priest, he can store the other half in the royal treasury. — *MS* VIII.38

In fact, the king needed the genuine people as ministers and advisors. The decentralization of the power among capable people was very much needed for an ideal governance of the state. At the same time the affairs of different departments had to be supervised from time to time by qualified and honest experts.

> When the king is not in position to inspect the affairs related to different departments, he should appoint a learned brāhmaṇa for the inspection of the state affairs. —*MS* VIII.9

Manu's concept of governance was totally based on the real practice of *dharma*. The presence of brāhmaṇa in the governance was just to protect *dharma*. All members of the government were supposed to follow the path of *dharma* in a strict manner for the sake of the country. The priests, because of their right conduct and because of being the incarnation of *dharma,* were considered the leaders of the administration and it was their duty to inspire others involved in the governance to practise righteousness.

It cannot be denied that Manu gave extra importance to brāhmaṇas. They were considered the leaders of each and every affair related to the welfare of the society. They got lots of financial support from different corners of the society, as they did not possess anything of their own. No one was allowed to utter a single word against them and they commanded the highest respect of the common people. But it should not be interpreted in a negative manner. Manu's treatment of brāhmaṇa is an example of ethical consciousness and juristic fairness. The main concern of Manu was to establish an ideal and lawful society. He did not spare any person from the clutches of the law. Exploiting the law for giving someone favour may cause injustice to others. Thus, everyone has to be treated in a similar manner. The severe laws of punishment presented in *Manu-Smṛti* were designed for everyone. A brāhmaṇa was praised and adorned as long as he was able to maintain his noble character and wisdom. Failing in that duty he too had to face all those humiliations, insults and punishments prescribed for others. The bad action committed by any person in the society may disturb the tranquillity of the common people. Manu was very critical of a brāhmaṇa who was proud and tried to empower someone because of his position.

> A brāhmaṇa who does not know how to give a greeting in reply to a greeting should not be greeted, he is just like a śūdra. — *MS* II.126

This reference clears the doubt that distinction between a brāhmaṇa and śūdra was not just because of their birth. A brāhmaṇa, behaving in an undesired manner, is just like a śūdra. In a society everyone has equal right to the dignity, and one should not hurt anyone without any particular reason. Violence had no place in the pious life of a brāhmaṇa, because this evil may wash out all other virtues and may ruin someone's life then and there. A brāhmaṇa had to lead a very calm and composed life and should not have caused injury, either physical or mental, to any creature. Manu prescribed more severe punishments for brāhmaṇas involved in any type of violence. A brāhmaṇa is more learned, trained and knowledgeable than any other person of the community. He is an awakened person and is capable of analysing the pros and cons of every action. At the same time he is the maker of law and knows the impact of breaking law. The crime committed by him becomes more serious, because it may give a wrong signal to other people of the society. A brāhmaṇa cannot cause even verbal injury to anyone. The verbal injury may cause the same impact as the physical injury. A person causing verbal injury must be punished without the consideration of his caste. A brāhmaṇa causing verbal injury to any person has to suffer severe punishment:

> A brāhmaṇa who defames a ruler should be fined fifty *paṇa*s; for a commoner the fine is half of the fifty and for śūdras it is only twelve *paṇa*s. — *MS* VIII.268

A brāhmaṇa is never allowed to be aggressive to anyone. He is known for his humble and gentle behaviour and by becoming violent, he is destroying his name and fame. Thus he is committing double crime and has to pay more penalty than others. Manu has given much power to this group, but has never allowed it to misuse the power.

Manu is quite emphatic in respect of punishment. A person, not adhering to his desired conduct and is breaking the law is a criminal regardless of his caste. No one should cross the limit of prescribed norms. The person crossing the limit and disturbing the society has to be punished.

> If a father, teacher, or domestic priest fails to attend their duties, they should not go unpunished by the king.
>
> — *MS* VIII.335

It was the doctrine of *sva-dharma*, the very basis of *caturvarṇa*.

Severe Punishment Prescribed for Brāhmaṇas

Every class had to follow the assigned duties without crossing its defined limits and without interfering with the duties allotted to the other groups. The king, being the supreme power, had to keep an eye on the jobs performed by different classes and had the power to punish anyone deviating from the duties. The brāhmaṇas were not the exception, and they were also kept under severe vigilance. A brāhmaṇa engaged in any type of theft was required to pay the heavier fine in comparison to other castes.

> A priest has to pay the fine for the theft sixty-four times more than the value of the stolen object or even hundred times more, because he knows about the virtues and the vices. — *MS* VIII.338

The job of teaching Vedas was done by brāhmaṇas free of cost. They were entitled to get some gifts from the students, depending on their will, but the teacher had no right to compel the students to pay remuneration. The teacher cannot take the property or the wealth of any student by force.

> A priest, who, by sacrificing for someone or even by teaching someone the Vedas, tries to get the property from the hands of the student on his own, is just like a thief and has to be punished like a thief. — *MS* VIII.340

The crime of theft was considered as a very serious one and was dealt strictly. A brāhmaṇa was not allowed to leave the allotted work of sacrifice without finishing that.

> If an officiating priest chosen for a sacrifice abandons his work due to his illness, he should be given the gift in proportion of the work done by him. If the priest does not finish the allotted work even after receiving the gift, the job can be given to someone else, and the amount of gift already given should be taken back. — *MS* VIII.206-07

Though brāhmaṇas had a high status in the court of justice, they were not allowed to give false witness.

> A brāhmaṇa, giving false witness, has to be banished.
> — *MS* VIII.123

Manu has strongly condemned all sorts of violence. Even the people of the high class were required to be non-violent and should not cause physical injury to any member of the community. Keeping or using of weapons was restricted and no one was allowed to use the weapon without any substantial reason.

> A brāhmaṇa can take up weapons when their duties are being obstructed and when the time has brought calamity upon them. They can use the weapons for self-defence, in a struggle for the sacrificial gifts or in order to protect women or priests, or those who have not done anything wrong.
> — *MS* VIII.348-49

Many a time the robbers prevented the brāhmaṇas from

offering sacrifices and fulfilling other religious duties. They could also use weapons during foreign invasions or for saving their own or others' property or for saving their cows and other belongings, specially, during the war. Manu has not recommended the capital punishment for brāhmaṇas and has considered it the most heinous sin and even unpardonable crime. It reflects the high ethical, moral, rational and juristic values of the Indian tradition. But in case a brāhmaṇa becomes *ātatāyī*, he is permitted to be killed. If a brāhmaṇa becomes *ātatāyī* and stretches his bow to take someone's life or endeavours to kill someone, he does not deserve mercy from any corner.

> One should surely kill anyone without hesitation, attacking him with a weapon in his hand, even if he is a *guru*, child, an old man or a brāhmaṇa who is very learned.
>
> — *MS* VIII.350

An *ātatāyī* brāhmaṇa is no more a brāhmaṇa and is not entitled to get any privileges. Such a person may be very dangerous for the community and needs to be destroyed. Terrorism was considered the most serious offence as it creates a terror among people and ruins the calm atmosphere of the society.

> There is no sin or stain at all for a killer in slaying a man who has a weapon in his hand. The *ātatāyī* can be killed openly or even secretly. It is the *ātatāyī*, who has raged the anger of the person involved. — *MS* VIII.351

"Openly" means that killing the *ātatāyī* in an open fight with weapon and "secretly" conveys the notion that a violent brāhmaṇa may be killed even by poison or by any magic spell. Manu has recommended the slaying of the *ātatāyī* brāhmaṇa even without heading for the judicial procedure, because he is a violent person and may harm any person at any time. There is no sense of keeping him alive for a longer period. The killing of the *ātatāyī* brāhmaṇa is an exceptional concept in the history of Dharmaśāstra and reveals the untouched aspect of socio-legal aspect of the Indian thought. The immunity of the brāhmaṇas from the capital punishment was because of their utility to the society. It is for this reason only that they were put on the top of the social hierarchy. The killing of the *ātatāyī* brāhmaṇa reflects the juristic fairness conceived by Manu.

Ātatāyī Brāhmaṇas

In order to understand the concept of the *ātatāyī* brāhmaṇa in *Manu-Smṛti* at length it becomes necessary to know the real etymology of the word *ātatāyī*. The word is derived from the root *ātan*; to stretch a bow for shooting. But this word has been used in the context of murderous assault. *Vāsiṣṭha-Dharmaśāstra* provides the definition of *ātatāyī* as

> An incendiary, a poisoner, one armed with a weapon, a robber, one who wrests the field or carries away someone's wife are called *ātatāyī*. —III.15, 18

Any unlawful act coupled with violence which may endanger the life of the victim is the basis for declaring a person as *ātatāyī*. Manu has condensed the definition of *ātatāyī* given by Vasiṣṭha and it has been followed by other lawgivers later on. Manu has concentrated on the point of "the intention to kill with a weapon" for declaring a brāhmaṇa as *ātatāyī*. A brāhmaṇa was not allowed even to touch the weapon without any serious reason. If he is raising a weapon towards someone without any genuine reason, surely he is having some bad intention in his mind. It means that he is deviating from his high ethical standards and impeccable integrity that make him a brāhmaṇa. As such *ātatāyī* brāhmaṇas were totally different than the normal brāhmaṇas. It was a different class itself and was not supposed to get any protection under the cover of class privilege. Character and conduct were the most important elements in the determination of class. Manu gave uppermost attention on the aspect of violence, and the class aspect became secondary. He treated *ātatāyī* brāhmaṇas at par with other *ātatāyī*s. Thus, killing an *ātatāyī* brāhmaṇa was not considered a sin. Manu took this point very seriously as he believed in the administration of justice, and evil intention shown by any person was a crime. He had a very clear vision of brāhmaṇa-*dharma* and *niyama-dharma* (see *MS* I.93 and X.3).

Analysis of the Whole Concept Related to Brāhmaṇas

The above analysis reflects that the system of *varṇāśrama* established by Manu was a perfect one in many respects. It is a fact that in a society every person is not equally intelligent and talented. One may notice the difference of efficiency for doing any work and the style of working. The individual differences cannot be ignored. At the same time there is a difference of aptitude, and liking and disliking. Thus, one cannot expect that every person will be fit to perform every work and it becomes necessary to distribute the work in accordance with the mental, physical and acquired capability of a person. At the same time it also has to be observed that whether the person responsible for undertaking the work is serious towards his work or not. All these elements affect the nature of the distribution of the work. The most important jobs will be given to most intelligent people. The job, requiring the physical strength, will surely be given to mighty people. The jobs related to finance and trade will be given to the people who are really interested in that type of work. The people, who are not capable of doing many things because of certain reasons, have to support the other groups of people already engaged in different works. The people with high intelligence are much in need and they get more privileges and occupy the highest post. Thus, the grade or the class or status or authority is ranked one above the other and hierarchical system is introduced in a very natural way. This was the genesis of the order or classes created by Manu in *Manu-Smṛti*. That is why Manu accorded the highest position to brāhmaṇas. Never, it was because of the birth in the line of brāhmaṇa.

Manu kept on reminding at every step that one might achieve the status of a brāhmaṇa because of brāhmaṇahood. This status was accorded to them because of their good conduct, noble character, super intelligence, virtues and unique role in the society. Brāhmaṇas were much exalted by Manu, but never, it was baseless. Their privileges were always balanced by the enormities of their duties. One should not forget the role of a brāhmaṇa in constructing a righteous society and for monitoring the conduct individually. Any person looking after others in a selfless manner may command the respect and reverence of the community. People do not mind the privileges given to a worthy or deserving person. Brāhmaṇas commanded the respect because of their service to common people. It is totally wrong to say that Manu did a special favour to brāhmaṇas. He prescribed the most tedious codes for brāhmaṇas and made it almost compulsory for them to follow those rules strictly.

Brāhmaṇas were kept on the top of the hierarchy not without reasons. It was very much needed for the society to work under the leadership of a learned brāhmaṇa. A society cannot run smoothly without the element of hierarchy. There should be someone to act as a superior one and to guide others at every step. In the absence of a definite leader no one will listen to others and every one will act as a leader. This situation may create commotion and conflict. In a situation of the conflict people will listen only to a trusted and genuine person. The trust can only be developed through noble deeds and the leader must have that quality. The job of learning can only be done by intelligent people and intelligence is needed for every work. But everyone cannot be equally intelligent. In such a situation the intelligent people are much in demand for the performance of different jobs. Brāhmaṇas became important because of their mental wealth which they acquired through penance. So there is no question of having a grudge against brāhmaṇas.

As we turn the pages of the world history, we may notice the elements of hierarchy in every civilization. The Roman history witnesses the worst type of hierarchy in which the slaves had no power and were forced to live like animals. The Greeks and Spartans had the similar system, where the power was confined to very few people and others were treated in a cruel manner. The Egyptian civilization also maintained the tradition of ranking in administration. The whole of Europe is known for its feudal system where a few people were the owners of the vast property. Christianity also mentions the ninefold celestial hierarchy where the angel is known as of the lowest order. However, the class hierarchy envisaged in *Manu-Smṛti* is of a very different nature as people belonging to the four classes were all given due importance and led a harmonious life. Even in the modern society, the hierarchy is very much in existence. There are prescribed qualifications for every post. The top jobs are always given to most competent and intelligent people. There is a tier system in every department. The high officials are given more facilities in comparison to the officials holding low ranks. The modern age is the age of superspecialization where people go for narrow specialization and acquire competence and expertise in given specialized fields, and that enhances their competitive power to a great extent. People also prefer to consult the specialists in different fields and consider them more efficient than others. There is a concept of creamy layer, the more enlightened or empowered section of the people in a particular group of the society. At present, there are more classes within the society than what was created by Manu. This is a natural process of social evolution.

Manu knew that common people cannot manage the affairs of the society properly in the absence of a worthy leader. But at the same time, he also wanted to maintain the Vedic tradition and Vedic concept of *dharma*. He was of the firm opinion that only Vedic tradition might keep the people on track. The brāhmaṇas were well versed and specialized in Vedic concepts. Other groups of the society did not know much about Vedic rituals, traditions and philosophy. Apart from this, brāhmaṇas, because of their disciplined life, good conduct, morality, spirituality and righteousness, were contributing immensely towards an inclusive development of the society. They first made themselves perfect and then guided others to become perfect. They tried to arouse the inward impulses of the people and showed them the way to lead to the truth. They even tried to safeguard the ethical principles propounded in Vedas. They followed the idealism prescribed in Vedas and made it available for the daily use of the mankind. The brāhmaṇas never looked themselves as innovators, but only the restorers of the old traditions. The vast Indian literature is the solid testimony to the great contribution made by brāhmaṇas towards the development of Indian society and culture. The brāhmaṇas had distinguished themselves in various ways and, that is why, they were categorized as superior to the people belonging to other classes. They commanded honour and respect, and enjoyed certain privileges because they deserved all that. Manu has not done any special favour to the brāhmaṇas, the only thing he has done is that he has highlighted the intellectual pre-eminence of the brāhmaṇas and through that he has demonstrated that the spiritual leaders may give directions to the rulers for ideal governance. His concept of brāhmaṇas is not remote from the accepted norm of giving more importance and privileges to the distinguished intellectuals. Brāhmaṇahood is the most essential criterion for a brāhmaṇa.

That is why Manu is quite critical of brāhmaṇas who move away from the desired path of their duties and indulge in wrong deeds, and he brings them down to the lowest status. An objective analysis of Manu's codes related to brāhmaṇas reflects that his treatment of brāhmaṇas is not only rational but also judicious and transparent. One can very well appreciate the concept if he is in a position to capture the prevailing socio-cultural ethos and Manu's spirit.

4

Rāja-dharma and Manu-Smṛti

Evidences of Monarchy in Vedas and Dharmaśāstras

INDIA was under monarchy for a very long period. Vedas, Upaniṣads, Brāhmaṇa *granthas* and the two great epics — *Rāmāyaṇa* and *Mahābhārata* — highlight the glory of the monarchs and justify their importance. They mention good monarchs as well as bad monarchs. All these scriptures prescribed very precise guidelines, which were mandatory for a king to follow. The sincerity of practising those prescribed norms became the standard for judging a king. The parallel word for king or monarch, which is often used in Indian literature, is *rājan*. The word *rājan* is derived from the root *rañj*, meaning "to please" or "to satisfy". *Rājan*, therefore, is one who is capable of satisfying his subjects in every manner. Keeping this philosophy in view, it was considered necessary for a king to possess the qualities that may induce happiness among the subjects.

Dharmasūtras and Dharmaśāstras took a lead in pinpointing the special qualifications of a king. These scriptures, while enumerating the duties (*dharmas*) of the four *varṇas*, elaborated *rāja-dharma* in detail. The duties of the king became the legitimate part of Dharmaśāstras as he being a kṣatriya was second in the line of four classes of the society. The question arises, why does a society need to have someone to rule or to govern? The answer is very simple, as all men in a society do not possess those virtues, needed for a harmonious society, there should be someone to regulate the undesirable elements that create disturbances in the community. The person who is entitled to govern or to regulate the society should be endowed with higher virtues. *Rāja-dharma*, as proclaimed in different Śāstras and Smṛtis, brings out the codes of governance in a very vivid manner.

The Origin of the King

The polity and conduct of a king have been discussed in *Manu-Smṛti* in a detailed manner. In fact, the codes pertaining to a king prescribed in *Manu-Smṛti* served as the model for the later literature. According to *Manu-Smṛti*, kṣatriyas are entitled to rule the state. They are supposed to govern the country in a just manner and to protect the citizens. While discussing the origin of the king, Manu says:

> God created the king to regulate the injustice and irregularities taking place everywhere in the world. The king was created with the essence of gods like Indra, Pavana, Yama, Sūrya, Agni, Varuṇa, Candra and Kubera.
>
> — *MS* VII.3-4

Nature of Kingship

A king should be bright and full of energy like the sun, as swift as wind and should be capable of delivering justice like Yama and Varuṇa. *Manu-Smṛti* treated the gods of the Vedic literature who were the basic elements of the creation, as models for the kings. A king must have the power of all those gods. It proves that a person who is given the power to rule the country should not be an ordinary man. That is why, *Manu-Smṛti* declares:

> King is the incarnation of all gods, therefore a king even in his childhood should be given due respect. — *MS* VII.8

> A person, dishonouring the king out of ignorance, will be ruined instantly. — *MS* VII.9

The best ruler must have the ability of developing both trust and fear among his subjects. He has to be tactful to face the different situations. He must have a multifarious personality and an intelligent mind.

> Before doing anything he has to analyse all the pros and cons, the prevailing situation, time, his own capacity and the likely result of the action. — *MS* VII.10

A king must have the power of taking correct decisions with accurate foresightedness.

> A king may listen to the advice given by different ministers separately, but at last based on those advices, he should do what exactly is needed. — *MS* VII.56-57

In the context of four classes of the society, the word *dharma* has been used to denote duties allotted to different groups. The concept of *rāja-dharma* as presented in *Manu-Smṛti* is totally based on the ideology of *dharma*, which got modified from time to time depending on the changing need of the society. According to *Manu-Smṛti*:

> King, his ministers, kingdom, capital, treasury, army, and ally are the seven constituents of the state and the king is the caretaker of all these. — IX.294-96

> All these parts are equally important and are complementary to each other. — IX.297

A successful planning and coordination of all these components are needed for the proper functioning and development of the state. The primary duty of a king is to strengthen the internal as well as external security. No state can flourish well if the security is on stake. King is the guardian of the society.

> It is his earnest duty to look after the welfare of the four classes. He has been created for this job. No one in the country should feel helpless at any time. — *MS* VII.35

> A king has to take care of fatherless, immature children, students, orphans, the chaste ladies, widows and sick women. — *MS* VIII.28

The internal disturbances may cause dissatisfaction among the people and the enemies may exploit the situation. It is the job of the king to distinguish between good and bad people. He must have the information about the undesirable elements, those who are moving away from the path of *dharma* and violating the codes. For proper development of the state and for the happiness of the common people the king should take deterrent measures against evil-minded people. The king has every right to use the tool of *daṇḍa* to control the bad elements of the society. Punishment is an effective instrument for the king to control the people moving on the wrong path.

> The fear of the punishment makes people happy as they do not deviate from their duties. In an ideal state each and every person must be in a position to enjoy his rights.
> — *MS* VII.15

> The fear of the punishment may not allow anyone to exploit the weaker sections; if the king fails to punish the offenders, the powerful would roast the weak, like fish in the pit.
> — *MS* VII.20

The fundamental idea behind it was to create terror in the minds of all criminals by the example of swift and harsh punishment.

Qualifications Desired for a King

A successful king is bound to maintain the socialistic pattern of the society. A king must have certain qualities for inflicting punishment in a proper manner. However, he has no right to misuse his power.

> The king is created by Brahmā to protect the people of all *varṇa*s and *āśrama*s. — *MS* VII.35

> It is desirable for the king to have profound knowledge of science, law, logic, philosophy, trade, commerce, administration, diplomacy, *ātmavidyā* (spiritual knowlege) and of common human behaviour. — *MS* VII.43

The power of inflicting punishment has to be given only to that king, who has subdued his senses and is free of lust and greed:

> Only a self-restrained king may control and govern the subjects. A king should apply himself to the conquest of his organs, for one, whose organs are conquered, is able to bring the people under control. — *MS* VII.44

> Greed is the root of many vices. In the same manner the vices like anger, lust and jealousy are capable of destroying anyone's wisdom. The king has to stay away from all these vices. — *MS* VII.45-46

A king has to punish the culprits and anti-social elements without discrimination and in a fair manner.

> A king has to stay away from the vices like hunting, gambling, day-dreaming, controversies, womanizing, pride, covetousness, lust for song and dance, wandering aimlessly. — *MS* VII.47

A king has to be totally devoted to the service of the people. His indulgence with any other thing may distract him from the path of duty. In consequence, the public has to suffer and the whole kingdom will be in trouble.

> A king may be ruined along with his family members, who suppresses his subjects, because of not being able of discriminating between the right and the wrong. — *MS* VII.111-12

The king should always think seriously for the welfare of his people.

> The king from whose kingdom enemies carry-off his subjects

> screaming, and he and his ministers remain silent onlookers, is as good as dead. — *MS* VII.143-44

The progress of the country depends on the effort put together by each and every citizen and for that everyone has to take his duties seriously.

> A king is responsible to alloting duties to different people according to their caste, country, status and family. — *MS* VIII.41

There will not be any dispute in the society if every one performs his duties diligently. While inflicting punishment the king has to be wise and careful. Justice should be the only basis of the punishment.

> A righteous king punishes even a brāhmaṇa who moves away from his duties and becomes *ātatāyī.* — *MS* VIII.350

> The punishment given in an unjust manner will defame the king and will push him to hell after his death. — *MS* VIII.313

It is a natural phenomenon that many people get tempted to violate the code of conduct for some reason or the other. These people will keep on repeating the same crime unless and until they are not checked. The punishment may give them some lessons to improve themselves.

> Sinful people, after being punished by the king may realize their mistakes and may become pure. — *MS* VIII.318

Criminals have to be handled in a strict manner. In fact, the glory and fame of a king depended on how far he was able to maintain the law and order in the country.

> A king may enjoy the pleasure of *Indraloka* by restraining bad elements in his kingdom. The king, who is successful in checking the crimes, gets fame and becomes a monarch among other kings. — *MS* VIII.386-87

Construction of Durgas

During Manu's time, the main challenge before the king was to face the attacks and threats planned by the enemy kingdoms far and near. Kings always had to keep themselves fully equipped to go for a war. It was a constant affair for ambitious kings to increase their army and force for extending their territories and to protect the subjects from the invaders. The preparations against the external security, therefore, became the major task of the rulers.

The first important step towards setting the external security is to fortify the kingdom strongly.

> The king should dwell at a place which must have fertile land, wise men, prudent ministers, resources for employment, free of disease and terrorism and should be beautiful with fruits, flowers and creepers.
>
> — *MS* VII.69, 76

Manu-Smṛti recommends few types of castles for the safety of the kingdom.

> A king should construct the township inside any of six *durgas* (*dhanudurga, mahidurga, jaladurga, vṛkṣadurga, nṛdurga, giridurga*). Out of these six *durgas*, *giridurga* is the best because of certain reasons. Therefore, the king should stay in *giridurga*. The enemies cannot harm the king, who is living in the castles. — *MS* VII.71

The castle, constructed after keeping certain strategy in mind, will surely be useful for the soldiers at the time of war.

> Even a single archer staying inside the castle may be able to face hundreds of warriers and an army-contingent consisting of just hundred soldiers may challenge ten thousand of strong soldiers. — *MS* VII.74

> The castle should always be well equipped with weapons,

money, food, transport, artisans, grass and water.

— *MS* VII.75

All these things should be in surplus for rainy days. The royal palace should be in the centre of the castle surrounded by a wide and deep water canal. — *MS* VII.76

Art of War

The whole detail depicts that at that time the art of war was well developed. Manu considers that a king should not be scared of the battle and should not lose his enthusiasm.

If once the king is challenged by his weak, strong or equally strong enemy, being a kṣatriya, he should not turn his back and should move on for the sake of his subjects.

— *MS* VII.87-88

The king is the guarantor of *dharma*, and so, in protecting the people, he is acting in accordance with his *dharma*.

The kings, who are fighting with vigour and not getting disheartened till the last moment, may acquire heaven.

— *MS* VII.89

Manu-Smṛti declares that the battle fought by the king is a *dharma-yuddha*. Therefore he is required to follow the code of war strictly, according to which:

No king is supposed to use the deceitful means or an arrow furnished with pointed knots or an arrow treated with poison or fire weapons. — *MS* VII.90

The main purpose for setting forth for the war was to protect the kingdom and to check the enemy king from entering inside the territory. The war should never be the demonstration of king's strength or wealth. A foe in a disadvantageous position shall not be struck.

A sleeping soldier, a soldier without armour and helmet, an unarmed one or fleeing one shall not be attacked. In the

> same manner a soldier engaged in fight with someone else shall not be attacked. A warrior who wants to surrender must be given security. — *MS* VII.92, 94

A war should be fought between two kings and it should not disturb the life of common people.

> The people standing nearby or watching the battle or doing their own jobs and innocent ones should not be harmed. — *MS* VII.92

It was the responsibility of the king to look after the general welfare of the common people during a war. The life of the subjects should not be disturbed by the war. The king has to take care of the wounded soldiers even if they are of the enemy's side.

> A soldier with a broken weapon, agonized with grief, wounded with sharp weapons and running away from the battlefield should never be attacked. It is the strict law of the war. — *MS* VII.93

Special care was taken of the soldiers, fighting for the sake of the country. They must get some incentive for their difficult job.

> A winner may take the captured wealth, horses, elephants, animals and gold. All these articles have to be given to the winner king. It is the duty of the king to distribute all conquered wealth among his soldiers. — *MS* VII.97

Manu-Smṛti has given much emphasis on this subjects and has warned the king not to violate it. The war brings destruction to the state and one side has to lose. Therefore, a king must try to avoid the war. It should not be fought until or unless it is a must. The war should be taken as the last expedient.

> A king should try to influence the enemy through conciliation or negotiation, bribery or by showing dissensions. Punishment should be the last effort for subduing the enemy. — *MS* VII.199

The four expedients (*sāma, dāma, daṇḍa* and *bheda*) have to be used in a very wise manner. A king must know the correct time, correct method and correct situation for using these expedients. The foreign policies specified in *Manu-Smṛti* are just riddles to the people of ordinary intelligence due to their secret and diplomatic nature. *Manu-Smṛti* has given more emphasis on the use of *sāma* and *daṇḍa* in comparison to *dāma* and *bheda*, as the first two are more effective. The learned people have praised the use of *sāma* among the four expedients, as it will prosper the kingdom. Bribery and dissension should be given second preference, but if a man does not stand firm by first three means, a king must bring him into the subjection by gradual force.

> A king should be like a farmer, who takes away the weeds and protects the crop. — *MS* VII.110

> He should also be totally absorbed in protecting the kingdom and warding off the enemies. — *MS* VII.107

He cannot follow the same tactics to conquer every enemy. He must keep on changing the nature of the war every time. It does not mean that a king should be benevolent to the enemy and should be reluctant from his side.

> A king must keep his army well equipped and ready to fight. There should be a regular practice of fighting with the enemy. He must try to know the weaknesses and loopholes of the opposite force and maintain the secrecy of his own plans. — *MS* VII.102-05

A king, who is possessing a strong and big army, which may be drawn in the battle-array at any time, may create terror among the enemies.

> A king should try to capture the wealth of his enemy just like a crane, should demonstrate his valour like a lion,

> should wait for the opportunity to kill his enemy like a jackal and should disappear like a rabbit. — *MS* VII.106

Manu-Smṛti brings out the very planned and systematic method of art of war.

> In the case of war the king has to take care of the movement of the mediator and the efforts made by the king desirous of victory, the psychology of the neutral kings and the position of the enemy. These are the four *prakṛtis* (sovereigns) that should be considered at the time of the war.
> — *MS* VII.155-56

Apart from these four components, there are another eight elements, making it altogether twelve.

> Each component may be divided into five based on *amātya, rāṣṭra, durga, artha* and *senā*, besides the king, thus making it in brief seventy-two. — *MS* VII.157

> The king must be careful about his friends helping the enemy in a hidden manner, and a dissatisfied servant who had left and has come back, as they may turn to be painful enemies.
> — *MS* VII.186

Diplomacy and Protection of Boundaries

Manu's picture of diplomacy is noteworthy. According to him:

> The king should consider his neighbouring states and their alliance similar to enemies. The states located beyond that may be taken as friends. The states other than these two are to be treated as neutral countries. — *MS* VII.158

The protection of the boundaries should be the first step before declaring war against any country. The enemies may try to exploit the states situated on the boundaries. The international relationship plays a vital role during the war. A king is bound to develop alliance with resourceful countries. In order to promote relationship with other countries a king has to use diplomatic vision. A king may take recourse to an alliance to other king only when he thinks that he is going to gain something at present and in future from him.

> A king may control other kings through *sāma, dāma, daṇḍa* and *bheda*. He too has to consider the six types of diplomacy. The expedients used by the king in foreign policies are alliance (*sandhi*), war (*vigraha*), march or expedition (*yāna*), halt (*sthāna* or *āsana*), seeking shelter (*saṁśraya*) and duplicity (*dvaidhibhāva*). — *MS* VII.159-60

Having considered what is to be done, a king should employ encampment, marching, alliance, war, stratagem and take recourse to protection. He has to show much of his presence of mind, foresightedness and analytical ability for making the best use of all these. *Manu-Smṛti* describes in detail the nature, method, impact and consequences of all these six expedients.

> A king should attack his enemy only when he is fully confident of his resources and army, and he knows that enemy's army and vehicles are in a bad condition.
>
> — *MS* VII.171

> In the same way, whenever a king thinks that elements like ministers, treasury, kingdom, fortress and army are very exalted and he himself is very mighty, then only he should go for war. — *MS* VII.170

Marching against the enemy should be done when a king is having a prosperous army and his enemies are in a feeble state. He may also wait for enemy's unfavourable state. It is easy to win an enemy who is financially weak.

> During the course of marching whenever the king feels that his army, including elephants, horses, chariots, etc. are not in good condition, then and there he should think of encamping. — *MS* VII.172

When a king realizes that it is impossible to conquer the enemy, he may seek the alliance of an equally powerful king.

> A king who knows political policies should make use of all the expedients to see that allies, neutral kings and enemies do not become superior to him. — *MS* VII.177

A king must try to check the number of enemy's friends and neutral kings.

> The excess number of friends may increase the strength of the enemy and the enemy may influence the neutral kings. — *MS* VII.178

The king has to think deeply about the past, present and future; he should not take any hasty decisions.

The war cannot be fought only with a big army. Before planning any attack, a king has to know the facts pertaining to enemy's financial condition, his relations with his subjects, the state of the army and his alliances. This type of information can only be collected through a strong spy system. *Manu-Smṛti* provides details of the espionage system.

> A king must send a spy to the enemy's country in disguise to know the whereabouts of the foe.
>
> A king may penetrate in any country through his spy; the spies are just like wind and, therefore, they may move everywhere. — *MS* VII.122; IX.256, 261, 268, 306

It becomes necessary to follow certain strategy during the war. The person who is leading the army must have a definite planning and direction of the whole operation. The proper position of the different sections of the army in the battlefield has also to be pre-planned.

> The king should make the arrangements at his base for the march, secure his position, establish his spies properly, clear and secure three kinds of roads and his own sixfold armies and gradually advance against the enemy's fortress in the martial manner. — *MS* VII.184-85

The three kinds of roads go through open country, marshes and forest, or through villages, forest and hills. The six parts of the army include elephants, horses, chariots and infantry. The last may be workmen and the weapon bearers. The leader should know the best method of utilizing the available resources. *Manu-Smṛti* provides a unique system of combating the enemy force with a small army.

> A king should ask his subordinates to arrange the army in the battle array by forming different types of *vyūha* (military array). While moving on the road leading to battleground *daṇḍa-vyūha, śakaṭa-vyūha, vārāha-vyūha, makara-vyūha, śūcī-vyūha* and *garuḍa-vyūha* may be formed.
>
> The king should protect himself first at dangerous places. He may keep himself inside *padma-vyūha,* which may cover him from all sides. — *MS* VII.187-88

The formation in the shape of a rod is in straight columns or in oblong; a cart is a wedge, broad in front and narrow in the back; the boar is a rhombus, pointed in the front and back and wide in the middle; the crocodile is narrow in the middle and broad in the front and back; the needle is a long line and eagle is rhombus like boar but with wide wings. The lotus formation is a circle that spreads out on all sides, with the king in the middle. All these *vyūha*s were complicated way of arranging the army for trapping the enemy and protecting the king. The presence of the king shall provide a great moral support to the army staff and will keep on boosting their performance.

> The chief of the army staff and the generals should be placed in all directions. The army should face the enemy side.
>
> — *MS* VII.189

The position of the army chief should be such that he may keep an eye on the enemy army, may assess the strength of the enemy and may induce terror among them by demonstrating his own power.

> The capable, firm, skilled and experienced officers should be placed around the *vyūha*. —*MS* VII.190

Manu-Smṛti provides details and useful hints for a successful battle.

> The soldiers should use code language, which cannot be understood by the enemy side. The language used by the army should not be palatable to the foes. In the army the recruitment of coward, timid and ungrateful should not be done.
>
> If the number of the soldiers is less, they should come closer, but if the number is more the soldiers may form *śūcī-vyūha* or *vajra-vyūha* by extending themselves. —*MS* VII.191

The formation of the *vajra-vyūha* (thunderbolt) is created by making a threefold division of the troops. These arrangements were prescribed mainly for protecting the king and to create hurdles for the enemy. The references found in *Manu-Smṛti* indicate that those days the kings used to have armies containing charioteers, horse riders, archers, foot soldiers and special types of boats used by navy force. Weapons like swords, discs and arrows were used for ground battle. The preference was given to the soldiers coming from the countries like Kuru, Matsya, Pañcāla and Mathurā. The soldiers dwelling in these countries were of strong built and were great warriors. The soldiers should be cheered up before the commencement of the war. They should be in good spirit and full of enthusiasm.

> A king should remain alert and should keep on monitoring the performance of his army even during war. There must be a desirable communication among the king, chief of the army and the warriors. —*MS* VII.194

Some efforts should also be made to shatter the confidence of the opposite camp.

> A king must take some action to disturb the food and fuel supply to the enemy country. The water resources of the enemy should also be destroyed totally. — *MS* VII.195-96

Manu recommends even to attack the enemy during night time, when they are fast asleep. This code does not go well with the ideology of righteousness expressed by Manu. It seems that perhaps Manu wanted to convey that small things might be surrendered for achieving a greater goal.

The external sovereignty is incomplete without well-established internal public administration. During the period of Manu the position and function of a king appear to have attained a much greater volume in comparison to the earlier periods. The most important development was the rise of the political organizations. The king could not manage the load of the enormous responsibilities fallen on his shoulders. There was a need of bureaucracy, the officials of the central government. These officials were supposed to share the king's duties.

> The public work should not suffer at any cost. The officials have to be appointed by the king to deputize for him during his absence. — *MS* VII.226

Appointment of Ministers and other Officials

The Indian monarchy was a unique one. Though the king used to be the head of the state, he was not free to take the decisions pertaining to different departments on his own. There used to be a group of officials for giving him advice from time to time. *Manu-Smṛti* presents many references, where the king is asked to appoint various categories of officials to help him on various matters.

> A king must appoint seven or eight ministers, nobly born, brought in the service of the king for generations, learned,

> mighty, well skilled in bureaucracy and trustworthy.
> — *MS* VII.59-60

It is impossible for the king to discharge the endless duties related to kingship without assistance from others. The highest ranks in the official hierarchy were occupied by king's family chaplain (*purohita*), the military commander and the ministers. The views prescribed by Manu are of a practical nature.

> Even the simple and easy work may not be performed by a person alone. How the king alone can manage to govern the big state with ample of responsibilities? —*MS* VII.55

It was the duty of the king to decide the number of ministers.

> Depending on the situation a king may engage more in number, the well-qualified, born in high family, high-minded, honest and well-tested ministers. — *MS* VII.62

Manu-Smṛti lays more importance on the qualification and capability of ministers, as they are going to help in the administration of the state. These preferences have also been extended even for the appointment of the army chief, helpers, bodyguards, warriors, ambassadors and spies. An officer, coming from a noble family, will certainly inherit good qualities, and with those personal qualities he will be more dutiful, wise and loyal. Advisors having all these qualities may render the needed advice to the king. The ministers belonging to the different departments are the indispensable part of the state constitution. In order to have perfect governance, a king may devolve his duties on his ministers. Manu states:

> The cabinet may consist of as many ministers as the needs of a kingdom call for, and the ministers should be competent to look after their affairs in the best manner. — *MS* VII.61

If the department allotted to a particular minister is not to his taste, he may not pay due attention needed for the business transaction.

> The people of mild and quiet nature should be given the charge of harem. — *MS* VII.62

Manu-Smṛti gives much emphasis on the appointment of ambassadors.

> An ambassador should be the master of all sciences. He must be capable of studying the gestures shown by different people. — *MS* VII.63

> A king should engage an envoy, born in high family, skilled, prudent, honest, fearless, affectionate, good in public relations, having charming expressions and possessing a pleasant personality. — *MS* VII.64

The international relationship depends totally on the efficiency of the envoy. An ambassador may bring two countries together and even may separate them. The job of the envoy is to represent the state in other countries and to take care of international relations. He is the mediator between two countries.

> He should try to know the relation between the kings of other countries and their subordinates. He should also judge the attitude of the opponent. — *MS* VII.68

Therefore, the king has to keep an eye on him in a very secret manner.

> The king may depute a spy to keep an eye on a suspicious envoy, posted in any other country. — *MS* VII.153

Brāhmaṇas enjoyed an important part in the royal assemblies. It was a must for a king to appoint a *purohita* and to seek his advice on every matter.

> A king must obey the order given by the brāhmaṇas. A king should receive the lesson of modesty and polity from him. A king must employ a *purohita* with the purpose of performing rituals and sacrifices. — *MS* VII.78

Brāhmaṇas are the real asset of the king. The service rendered by them may prove to be the greatest boon for the king.

> A king should enter in the court of justice along with brāhmaṇas. —*MS* VIII.1

It depicts the interdependence of both the king and brāhmaṇa on each other. Brāhmaṇas would seem to have been considered as the pillar of strength for the king because they were regarded the necessary adjunct and were characterized as the protector of the realm.

> The assembly, consisting of three brāhmaṇas sitting there as the representatives of the king, should be known as *brahma-sabhā*. —*MS* VIII.11

> In case the king is not in a position to attend the court, he may appoint a prudent brāhmaṇa as his representative. —*MS* VIII.9

> Two or three brāhmaṇas may stand in the court and may take care of the administration. —*MS* VIII.10

It may be reasonably inferred that there were two types of brāhmaṇas posted in the royal court: one section was of priestly class, taking care of the domestic rituals, and the other section was of the knowledgeable and highly competent brāhmaṇas involved in the administrative jobs. The brāhmaṇas were also appointed as judges in the court and were given the power of passing crucial judgements. In the judicial system presented by Manu, lawyers were largely of priestly class. They were regarded as the exponents of *dharma*. *Dharma* was above the sovereign and, therefore, it had to be obeyed by the executive.

The appointment of *koṣādhyakṣa* (the officer-in-charge of treasury), *koṣāgārādhyakṣa* (the supervisor of weaponry) and officers of the local government were also the integral part of king's administration. For these posts too, he has to follow the same criteria as were dictated for other appointments.

King used to be the overall in-charge of all departments.

> The judiciary and army should be under ministers, kingdom and treasury should be taken care by the king himself and envoy should look after the external affairs. — *MS* VII.65, 81

The most significant part of the monarchy, as discussed by Manu, was its democratic pattern of governance. In spite of his quasi-divinity, the king was supposed to depend on the advices rendered by the ministers, *purohita*s and other officials. *Manu-Smṛti* brings out the detailed procedure of *mantraṇā* (deliberations). A king should hold deliberations with his ministers for each and every affair.

> The king may discuss with his ministers the problems related to security, general development of the kingdom, seeking alliance with other kings, war, treasury and the investments of the earned capital. — *MS* VII.56

> The king may ascertain each minister's opinion separately as also their conjoint opinion, and then decide upon the course that may be the best. — *MS* VII.57

Ministers may give different opinions according to their skill and efficiency. The king has to analyse those views before taking the final decision. At the same time, he also has to consider whether the decision is going to be of greater help or not. The advice tendered by the ministers should enforce strict obedience to orders. Therefore, Manu is of opinion to appoint brāhmaṇa ministers, as they are well acquainted with the real nature of *dharma*.

> Brāhmaṇa is the most talented and prudent among other ministers, therefore the king should discuss with him the problems pertaining to six components of diplomacy. The brāhmaṇas, as ministers are the most trustworthy. A king may rely on them fully. — *MS* VII.58-59

Confidentiality of the consultations has to be maintained at every cost. Manu prefers to have a closed-door deliberation.

> The deliberations related to alliance and war should be conducted only among the ministers and army officers.
> — *MS* VII.146

> The venue of meeting should be well protected and safe. A king should ponder over different subjects with his counsellors in a hilly cave or in the inner part of the palace or at a remote part of the forest. A king by maintaining the secrecy of his deliberations may enjoy the prosperity of his kingdom.
> — *MS* VII.147

Statecraft

Manu's statecraft is based on the efficient system of vigilance. The officials belonging to the secret service should not leak out any document related to administration. Strict action must be taken against those, who try to pass the secret decisions to the enemy country.

> The dull-minded person, deaf, blind, and dumb people, a bird which can mimic human voice, women, person of low caste, a sick person and a handicapped one should be kept away from the place of deliberation. These people, because of their narrow-mindedness may feel humiliated at any time and may disclose the secrecy. — *MS* VII.149-50

While doing *mantraṇā* the king should expel inauspicious animals such as dogs and crows. The talking birds like parrots or mynahs should also be kept away because they might expose the counsel. A real concentration and much of patience are needed for a fruitful counselling. Any type of distraction may ruin the whole purpose.

> A king must hold counsel at midday or midnight along with his loyal ministers with a sound health and sound mind. — *MS* VII.151

> He may discuss the affairs related to the internal and external security, kingdom, treasury, and the administration of the surrounding districts. — *MS* VII.152-54

Holding a counsel should be the part of king's daily routine.

A king must know the ethics of the administration. He has to be tactful for extracting work from his officers. Administration needs a sharp diplomacy.

> Depending on situation, a king should be harsh or polite towards his officers. — *MS* VII.140

A king should try to develop a congenial relationship with his ministers and counsellors.

During Manu's period a great development of social and political life took place. The kingdom got extended and the load of administration also increased. It was not possible for a king alone to look after the whole kingdom in a smooth manner. This gave rise to the local self-government and guilds. The local self-government was taking care of the general administration, while the guilds were taking care of trade and commerce. In *Manu-Smṛti* one may find the references of the formation of *jāti*s, *kula*s and *śreṇī*s taking care of the different trades under the authority of the king. They were the group of people following common professions, such as tradesmen, artisans, moneylenders, coachmen and so forth. They used to frame rules for cooperative undertakings for controlling the market. These guilds had their own chief who worked under the directions of the king.

> The people belonging to different *grāma*, *deśa* or *saṅgha*, who were not fulfilling their duties, were liable to be punished by the king. — *MS* VIII.219-20

Manu has advised to decentralize the power of king or central government by creating small units of provinces.

> The king should appoint an *adhipati* (village headman) for every village, and one chief each for the cluster of ten, twenty, hundred and thousand villages. The *adhipati* should report the problems of the village to the chief of ten villages (*grāmapati*) who should report the matter to the chief of twenty villages, and likewise, the problems will be reported to the chieves of hundred and thousand villages.
>
> — *MS* VII.115-17

The term *kula* has been used as a technical word. It may designate the amount of the land that a family can live off or the amount of land that one can plough.

> The master of ten families gets the amount of taxes that one family pays, and the master of twenty families will be getting the amount of taxes paid by five families, while the superintendent of hundred families gets the taxes from an entire village, and the overlord of thousand gets the taxes paid by the whole town. — *MS* VII.119

> The salary of these officers will be paid with the grains, food and other things given to the king by the villagers.
>
> — *MS* VII.118

The local government has to bear the burden of the salary payable to its officials. It will save the central government's expenditures.

> A king should appoint a skilled, bright and forward-looking officer of high level. The officer shall manage the multifarious development of the town. It is the responsibility of the *nagarādhikārī* to manage the welfare of all surrounding villages. He may appoint spies to have vigilance on his subordinates. The junior officers should never be allowed to take extra advantages from the people. — *MS* VII.121-22

> The *nagarādhikārī* may have the power to send in exile the corrupt officer after confiscating his whole property.
>
> — *MS* VII.123-24

> The salary structure of the different officers has to be decided by the king. The king should decide the salary of the officers based on their efficiency. — *MS* VII.125

The above-mentioned references indicate that the kingdom was divided into few sub-divisions and zones. The king and king's officers governed these sub-divisions in descending order. Manu allows the king's officers to investigate disputes in the descending order of their enumerations. The guilds, like *śreṇī, kula, saṅgha* and *jāti* were also working under these zonal officers. The king used to be the overall in-charge of all these bodies. The guilds were something like cooperative societies working together for a common purpose. These sub-bodies were paying tax to the king through their chiefs. It was the duty of the chief to regulate his members. Their position was one of the high social standings and they had to bear the great responsibility with sincerity. The king was to set the chief on the proper path and to banish him in the event of his recalcitrance.

A king must possess a rich treasury and sufficient resources to maintain all departments of the state and to provide a progressive life to his citizens. Manu advises the king to keep the finance department under his supervision. It is the duty of the king to take proper care of *koṣa*.

> He should know the correct method of earning money. He should also be aware of how to keep on increasing the earned capital and how to invest the surplus wealth.
> — *MS* VII.99

The king has to appoint an efficient, honest and skilled treasury officer for handling the matters related to *koṣa.*

> A king may procure much of wealth by invading other prosperous countries and for that he must have strong and well-equipped army. — *MS* VII.96

> The conquered wealth has to be well protected and preserved. The king may increase that capital by investing that in trade and commerce. He has to look for some long-term measurements to keep the earned profit in circulation through trade. — *MS* VII.101

In Manu's time the whole affair related to finance was taken care by a very efficient treasury officer known as *koṣādhyakṣa,* who used to work with the help of a few other subordinates. Even then it was the responsibility of the king to supervise the performance of finance department regularly. The king decided the salary of different officers working in the various sections of the administration of the kingdom. The king should fix the salary of the males and females employed in government, based on the nature of the jobs. The king took care of the collection of the revenue and taxes. The king also decided the rates of taxation for different categories of the people. The king also had the power to give relaxation or exemption from the taxes to a particular section of the society. The officers-in-charge for the collection of taxes were kept under strict vigilance and were not given chance to cheat or to exploit the common people. According to the references found in *Manu-Smṛti* it is clear that trade and commerce was flourishing well under the care of vaiśyas. The vaiśyas were well trained in business and marketing. The king took care to provide them the needed infrastructure and facilities to improve and promote their trade. The market was fully regulated by the king. He had to fix the fares for different modes of transport and make suitable arrangements for the security of goods. The king must examine, from time to time, the weight and measurements used in trading and the traders should not be allowed to cheat the customers at any cost.

> The king who is taking due care of the income and expenditure of the state, managing the treasury and mines,

> and is capable of maintaining the infrastructure, goes to heaven. —*MS* VIII.318

It is rather impossible to find a trouble-free society. The people who, because of their selfish intentions, deviate from the proclaimed path of *dharma* and create trouble and disturb the normal life of the common people deserve to be punished. The king, being the guardian of his citizens, has to dissolve disputes and to induce law and order.

> The king must watch the behaviour of his subjects, they may otherwise be inflicted with the vices and may ruin the harmony of the society. —*MS* VII.13, 19

Manu says that the king must undertake the responsibility of maintaining security of people's life and property. Therefore, the basic duty of the king is to punish the criminals and to give justice to those who are victimized. The justice has to be proclaimed on the basis of law common to everyone. The law is in no way other than *dharma* or truth. The ruler needs to implement law in a fair manner for the welfare of the state. The citizens of a state must appreciate the law.

Manu has empowered the king to take care of his people by deciding the disputes through his judgement.

> The king has to pronounce his judgements for the disputes related to borrowing or lending money, debts, deposits, pledge, mortgages, labourers, fulfilment of the contract, partnership, revocation of sale and purchase, property and land, inheritance, partition of the ancestral property, marriage, remarriage, dowry and divorce and violence, slander, assault, theft, gambling. —*MS* VIII.4-8

The judgements have to be pronounced only after the king having consultations with the members of the law counsel. The codes were based on the divine inspirations.

In a court where the members are not in a position of

> separating divinity or *dharma* from injustice, they themselves are going to be ruined by injustice. — *MS* VIII.14

Manu introduces the concept of eternal or perpetual law, which never loses its relevance. The kings occupied the highest post in the court of justice and were the pillars of judiciary. Even then the law was above the sovereign. The laws were not made by any person or any counsel or group of people. These were the products of highly mature, sophisticated and sensitive brains of ancient sages and were passed down through generations. The perpetual laws were regarded as over and above all the human authority.

> The king has to follow the line of perpetual laws, while dealing with the disputes or pronouncing the judgement. — *MS* VIII.16

The doctrine of the perpetual law also extended to social laws, as laws were the tools to regulate the social problems. Manu provides a free hand to judicial system and advised to keep it separated from the executive. The king had no power to enter in the court of justice alone. Few members, well-versed in law should accompany the king. These members must express their views fearlessly and should support the truth.

> A member, who does not speak or tries to contradict the facts, is a sinner. — *MS* VIII.43

The king used to invite the opinion of learned members on the disputed points to facilitate the justice. The members should not have any leaning towards the litigants present in the court of justice. The king is bound to protect *dharma* (law) in every way.

> The protected *dharma* protects everyone, the unprotected *dharma* may destroy everyone. — *MS* VIII.15

It is the most important duty of the king to preserve *dharma*. All the members of the court of justice are equally responsible to dispose justice. The impact of the sin caused by injustice has to be shared as follows:

> The one-fourth part of the impact of the injustice falls on the person who has done it, another one-fourth part of the impact goes to the witness for his false statement, the next one-fourth part of the sin caused by injustice sticks to the members and the king has to share the last one-fourth part of the sin. — *MS* VIII.18

The juries were supposed to examine the dispute. The judge, mainly a brāhmaṇa, used to be the president and king has to inflict the punishment.

The power of proclaiming the judgement should only be given to the deserving persons. *Manu-Smṛti* has given much emphasis on the validity of the judgement delivered by the court.

> A king should examine and analyse each judgement carefully before announcing the punishment. He should sit in the court well-dressed and after saluting *lokapāla*s, he should ponder over the matter with full concentration.
>
> — *MS* VIII.1-2, 23

> He should go through the details of the disputes and should come to the conclusion only after considering the pros and cons of the decision. — *MS* VIII.24

> A king must not depend totally on the statements given by the person who has filed the case or the persons against whom it has been filed. Very often they may be wrong.
>
> — *MS* VIII.25

> A king should try to infer the facts related to both parties by judging the pitch of their tones, the expressions coming on their faces, the gestures or movements of the different limbs of the body and the movements of their eyes. — *MS* VIII.26

The court is a place where everyone has to speak truth

otherwise imparting justice will be impossible. The biggest culprit is the one who tries to twist the facts. Manu has warned the kings to take severe action against these people. Every case has to be taken up in an honest manner and verdict also has to be given without any delay.

> A king or any of his representatives has no right to extend the case beyond limit. The members of the court cannot nullify any proceedings or lawsuit in between, out of greed and unwanted pressure. —*MS* VIII.43

> As the hunter reaches to the deer by seeing the blood drops, in the same manner the king must reach to the truth through occular proof or through inferences. —*MS* VIII.44

It is not an easy job to dissolve the disputes. Most of the criminal or civil cases are usually very complicated and extracting the facts is also not an easy task.

> A king, while dealing with any case, must consider the validity of the truth, his own conscience, evidences presented from both sides and the place, nature and the situation of the dispute. —*MS* VIII.45

Manu-Smṛti presents a very graphic picture of the king, the court and the procedure. A king has to move according to the framed rules. He has to listen the whole proceeding carefully. The system of judiciary as presented in *Manu-Smṛti* is in no way different from the procedure of the modern court. The king was advised for every case by the chief justice, minister of justice and juries. All the members of the court had to examine and scrutinize the proof. Although the law propounded by Manu is considered to be a very traditional law and it does not leave much of scope for change or alternation, there was a provision to alter certain laws by the rules of interpretation. It was the powerful instrument in the hands of the king for studying and deciding the individual case. The judicial system introduced by

Manu encouraged to interpret the laws and to extend them to meet the changing situations. The evidences played a very important role for interpreting the individual case and for extracting the truth. A king had to supervise the whole judicial procedure personally. A king should start the civil action only after receiving the complaint from a plaintiff. A vexatious litigation has to be avoided. In the case of criminals, a king must take notice of a crime without a formal plaint. The criminal cases need speedy action. The procedure for filing the case and collecting the evidences may provide sufficient time to the dangerous criminals to manipulate the facts. The statement given by the plaintiff has to be noted down. The king and the court members are entitled to ask several questions to the plaintiff to clarify the complaint.

> The case should not be discussed if the plaintiff is hesitating to answer or avoiding the questions or keeping mute or trying to converse with the witnesses or is not in a position to produce the evidences. — *MS* VIII.73

The plaint was required to be precise, comprehensive, direct, unequivocal, consistent, concise and yet not deficient in meaning.

> The members of the court have to go into the details of the case and the plaintiff has to explain the case in detail to make his allegation specific and definite. — *MS* VIII.45

Manu-Smṛti has recorded few rules showing who should lose the case:

1. A person who is not giving the correct answer to the questions asked by the members,
2. a person who is being called upon to answer and remains silent,
3. a person who is putting hindrance to the progress of the procedure, and

4. a person who is not present in the court.

Manu-Smṛti gives more stress on the law of evidences. It is a must for a king to collect all types of evidences before deciding the case. The evidences may be in the form of documents, witness and the conduct of the witnesses. A plaintiff has to produce at least three witnesses in the court. Manu has enumerated many qualifications for the witness.

> He should be religious minded, generous, of a respectable family, devoted to truth, a lover of virtues, candid, impartial, healthy and possessed of offspring. — *MS* VIII.63-67

Truthfulness was the most desirable qualification for the witness.

> A witness, who speaks truth, gets name and fame, a witness giving wrong information suffers for several births. The witness should be compelled to speak the truth.
>
> — *MS* VIII.81-82

The king must not accept the criminal, helper, enemy or the friend of the plaintiff, cruel, old man, child, handicapped, distressed, drunk, grieved, furious, tired, love stricken and a robber as a witness. "The cases related to women should be supported by female witnesses" (*MS* VIII.68). "In the case of different castes, the witness should be of the same caste". The conduct of the witness also has to be noticed for reaching to the facts. The king has to be very alert to study the conduct of the witness.

> The contrary statement given by a witness should not be considered. The statements given fearlessly and in natural way should be accepted. — *MS* VIII.73, 78

In order to clarify the statements given by the witness, a king has to study his psychology.

The court should be the neutral place and everyone has to be treated without any discrimination.

> The king should summon both plaintiff and defender in the court. He should address the witness in a polite manner and should listen to him carefully. —*MS* VIII.80

A witness is supposed to know the detail of the conflict, which has taken place between the two parties.

> He should say exactly, whatever he has seen or heard.
> —*MS* VIII.81

> He should be warned and threatened not to speak untruth.
> —*MS* VIII.82, 90-92

While giving his deposition, the witness should be placed closer to both the plaintiff and defendant. In case of the unavailability of the witness, the king may invite any other person, who has seen the conflict with his own eyes.

> Even the headmen of four villages may be called for giving the witness. If the headmen are not available, other persons familiar to the case may be called in the witness box.
> —*MS* VIII.258-60

Manu-Smṛti has emphasized the necessity of putting plaint, defendant and witnesses under the oath.

> In order to know the truth, the king should put the plaintiff and defendant under oath. According to Manu, if there is any doubt about their statements, they should be asked to take oath which is a traditional rule. Even the great sage like Vasiṣṭha had taken the oath before *Paijavana* for proving his innocence. The oath must be taken in an honest and truthful manner. —*MS* VIII.109-10

> A person, taking false oath, goes to hell. —*MS* VIII.111

Touching the fire, water and the forehead of son or wife were the different modes of oath taking. *Manu-Smṛti* prescribes punishments for presenting false witness or taking a wrong oath.

> If the king is not satisfied with the procedure of the court or feels that the case has been presented in a wrong way, the case may be reconsidered. —*MS* VIII.117

> The witness given out of greed, fear, friendship, lust, anger, ignorance, innocence and compassion should never be accepted. —*MS* VIII.118

The king should not allow any trial to be held behind closed doors. Every trial was given much of publicity to teach a lesson to others, not to get involved in any type of crime. In the case of a severe crime, mostly the criminal was taken throughout the city. Manu advises the king to construct the jails on the main road of the town, so that the citizens may watch the criminals suffering because of their being punished. The main aim of the theory of judgement was to curb the crime through harsh punishment and to create a terror among the others not to indulge in similar or any other type of crime.

No account of the duties of the king can be even reasonably complete without some reference to the theory of the procedure of criminal law, which a king has to evolve and adopt. It was the law of equality and justice. Even a king could not avoid the punishment. Manu says:

> No one who has transgressed the law is exempted from the punishment, be he the king, or a brother, a son, an object of worship, a father, a teacher, a priest, a father-in-law or a maternal uncle. —*MS* VIII.335-36

The people have authorized the ruler to take care of their welfare by giving them the needed justice. They will surely lose their faith and trust, if the king is partial or unjust. Manu has carried the doctrine of the equality of the law to its highest point. Manu declares:

> Where an ordinary man is punished with a fine of one *kārṣāpaṇa*, the king himself committing the offence should

> be punished a thousand times the amount. — *MS* VIII.337

The responsibility increases with higher position and authority. Therefore, the king is supposed to show higher standard of behaviour. Manu prescribes punishment to the king even for the violation of the justice. A king, being the father of his subjects has to set an ideal example before his citizens. The punishment should be inflicted only after examining well the intention and the frequency of the criminal for committing the crime, the place and the time of the crime, the physical and the financial status of the offender and the gravity of the crime. Punishing the innocent persons and leaving free the criminals may defame the king.

> The subject rushes towards a restrained king just like a river rushing towards the ocean. — *MS* VIII.175

> A king, who is inclined to the selfless service of his people, is worshipped by everyone. — *MS* VIII.306

The king has to protect the life, wealth and the conduct of his subjects.

> The king has to bear the sin of the theft, if he is not in a position to control the thieves. — *MS* VIII.316

> A king who forgives the criminals will be destroyed and people will hate him. — *MS* IX.253-54

In Manu's penal code, no brāhmaṇa could be tortured for any criminal offence, nor could he be awarded death penalty.

> In the case of an offending brāhmaṇa, a king may banish him from the country after branding him with a mark on his forehead. — *MS* IX.241

Kaṇṭaka-śodhana (removal of the thorns or anti-social elements) is also a part of the numerous duties assigned to the king. It relates to the protection of the public rights against deceitful and fraudulent elements in the society; fraud in respect of the weights and measures, seizure of the criminals on suspicion, protection of the public from the oppression of the government servants, outrage of modesty of girls and punishment for the transgression of social obligations.

> A king dedicated to the service of his people should try to eliminate *kaṇṭaka*s (evil-minded people) from the society. The country may revolt against the king, who is charging the tax from the people and not providing them full protection. — *MS* IX.253-54

> The kingdom, which is well protected under the strong arms of the king and is free of the atrocity caused by the wicked elements, grows and flourishes like a well watered plant. — *MS* IX.255

The king is the head of the state, and state is a region where everyone should be in a position to lead a peaceful and trouble-free life. The dissatisfaction of the people, caused by anarchy prevailing in the state, may generate serious consequences and may destroy both the king and the kingdom.

> There are two types of thieves engaged in grabbing other's property; the visible thieves, who cheat the people by selling them spurious commodities and others are those who prefer to seize other's wealth in disguise. The king has to catch hold of both of these with the help of spies. — *MS* IX.256-57

> The people who are taking or offering bribe, fraudulent people, the fake monks, fore-tellers and doctors, painters and prostitutes are also like thieves and the king has to remove those thorns. — *MS* IX.258-59

> These elements are the real threat to the society and they need to be punished publicly. Manu asked the kings to form an ideal and peaceful society by controlling the undesirable elements. The cheaters prefer to stay in a lonely place; the spies appointed by the king must visit those places and

> should try to bring them to the king by hook or by crook.
> — *MS* IX.264-66

Manu-Smṛti shows the unique method of tackling the bad elements in the society and how the king has to implement those means. In case the spy is not able to catch hold of the thieves, the king should put the friends and relatives of the criminal in the prison. The thieves must be caught and killed by the king. The responsibility of the security of the village or town should be with the local people. In the event of any mishap, the local people have to take care of it.

> If the local people fail in their duties, the king is entitled to banish them from the country. — *MS* IX.271-74

> The security officer, found guilty of helping thieves should also be punished. — *MS* IX.273

There is no rest for the king. He has to toil day and night.

> In spite of being tired, he has to keep on working and has to accomplish all the works started by him for the sake of the country. — *MS* IX.300

The prosperity of the kingdom depends on the conduct and efficiency of the king. The king alone may induce progress, peace, harmony and development in the state. He may change the whole scene of a particular period by his planning and action.

> It is Kaliyuga when the king is asleep, it is Dvāpara when king is awakened, Tretā approaches when the king is ready to endeavour, and Satyayuga appears itself when the king is in action. — *MS* IX.301-02

> A king should always devote himself towards his duties and also should motivate his subordinates to work for the welfare of public. — *MS* IX.324

The actions performed by the king might change the face of the country. It will happen only when the king is aware of his duties in a genuine manner and considers his subjects just like his own kith and kin. *Manu-Smṛti* has made no difference between a *yogī* and a king. The rules designed for the king are of ethical and spiritual nature. His character must be higher than the common people. The king has to perform these duties with the spirit of *niṣkāma-karma.*

The above-mentioned points are the gist of *rāja-dharma* propounded by Mauu. These are those concepts which were evolved and practised at various periods of the Indian history. *Manu-Smṛti* points out the continued tradition of a successful monarchy, working in a real democratic pattern. *Manu-Smṛti* associates kingship to high dignity, prosperity and authority. The quasi-divinity of the king made him the lord of the earth. The king, the head of a strong central government, exercised his authority consulting highly efficient counsellors in a harmonious manner. The most conspicuous feature of the kingship was its promise of bringing up a society free of vices and corruption. The king was portrayed as the embodiment of all virtues and was made responsible for inculcating the same virtues among his subjects. The king was not supposed to leave any stone unturned for bringing the society on the right track, i.e. on the track of *dharma* and righteousness, which the king and his people have to follow. *Manu-Smṛti* expounds the ethical conception of law. King is the maker of the age and the promulgator of the principles of virtues and vices. The king was empowered with the tool of *daṇḍa*. The *daṇḍa* itself was regarded as a powerful god coming to earth, just for curbing the vices. The statecraft and society-craft were dependent on each other. The king has to take care of both. In short, the whole concept of kingship as presented by Manu is based on the practice of *dharma* in day-to-day life of each and every person.

Manu's idea of kingship is an ideal one and it does not leave any scope for alterations. It may be considered the most rigid one and difficult to be practised. That is why, the later Smṛtis and *Arthaśāstra* dealt with this subject in a different manner making it somewhat easier for the king to discharge his duties. They introduced many relaxations to suit the changing society and to make the duties pertaining to the king more practical. At this point, it may be said that the rigidity or relaxation of the rules must be governed by the maturity and the standard of the society. There may be objections to the stiffness of the law, as it controls actions and reduces the individual freedom of choice. But at the same time, it cannot be denied that Manu's scheme of *rāja-dharma* does allow choices within a limit. The freedom of choice can be given only to the highly-disciplined society, which will not misuse the freedom. The proclamation of rights alone cannot build the strong foundation of any country. The constitution of the country should emphasize on the duties to be followed by each and every citizen. Duty is *dharma*, and *dharma* alone can generate prosperity. The duties of a king as designed by Manu have the potential of elevating all people to the highest ideal of life. The casual approach towards implementing the laws may sometimes prove fatal to the society, and in order to avoid that situation a tough and effective administration needs to be put in place. Nevertheless, the idealism should not be ignored at any point of time. That is precisely the reason why Manu's *rāja-dharma* proved to be the proper model.

5

Manu's Codes Pertaining to Punishment

Concept of Welfare State

GOVERNANCE is needed to look after the demands of the people living in a given state and to take care of their day-to-day necessities. A state is a geographical area consisting of groups of people living together under single governance. It becomes mandatory for the government to keep the people satisfied in every manner. Food, clothing, shelter and security are the basic needs of the people of the state and it is the responsibility of the government to provide all these to them. In return, people of the state have to observe certain rules and regulations for proper growth and steady development of the state. Every state has to form certain laws and has to see that those laws are properly implemented. As such, human beings are governed by their own impulses and instincts and it is rather impossible to expect perfect behaviour from everyone. In many cases, people governed by their selfish motives, try to break the laws and create problems for other citizens. This situation may also have the negative effect on the working of the government. A state can only be considered ideal where people are conscious of their duties towards the state and towards other members to the society. The governance depends very much on the general conduct of the people of the state and those involved in the governance. In a welfare state both people and government need to work jointly to bring about progress and development to the state. The special feature of the welfare state is that people living in that state are not required to worry about their needs, as the government bears the burden of their requirements. The public money is used in a just manner and the transparency of the expenditure is well maintained. People feel secure both internally and externally. It is the ideal situation and is not very easy to achieve. Our ancient lawgivers, particularly Manu, have tried their best to introduce the concept of a welfare state. Manu thinks that the concept of a welfare state can become a reality only when the fear of punishment is created among the people. He has discussed the whole matter in the light of *matsya-nyāya.*

Theory of Matsya-Nyāya: Its Nature and Repercussions

The word *matsya* means "fish" and the word *nyāya* means "law or justice". It is a common maxim used for special purposes. *Matsya-nyāya* is a condition wherein the duties meant for the citizens of a state come to an end and the state submerges into anarchy. The anarchy can be described as social and political disorder or the lack of governance. This situation may lead a state to the stage of non-state, where law and order situation has completely collapsed and everyone is set against everyone else. It may be called as "jungle rule", where there is no one to govern and everyone behaves on his own without thinking about others. It surely will be the state of confusion and commotion and will initiate unruly conflict. In the absence of a proper government there will be no one to control the situation. The continuity of the conflict may destroy the very existence of that society. History of the civilization has witnessed similar situations many a time. In order to protect the state, the government is very much needed which may impose certain restrictions and may control the existing conflicts. The strict administration imposed on the unruly people is the only way to bring back normal life. The political philosophy introduced by Manu has brought in many solutions for achieving the desired level of governance and for addressing the lawlessness in the society. Manu's political philosophy has its base in spirituality, morality, truthfulness, justice and righteousness. The politics having all these elements will be an ideal one and sustainable. It will provide a fair deal to every citizen without any discrimination. The fair dealing of the administration will not have the element of favouritism and everyone will be able to get his due share. It will not allow anyone to design the right of might. The right of might leaves a group of people unattended, frustrated and deserted.

This situation may lead to several types of crimes and even revolt. Manu knew that certain groups of people are always prone to interfere with the rights of others and do not hesitate to violate the path of righteousness. It is the starting point of the induction of corruption, injustice and lawlessness and if this condition continues, it would be rather impossible to have a just society. Manu says:

durlabho hi śucirnaraḥ

It is difficult to come across a man who is perfectly pure.

— *MS* VII.22

Thus every person cannot be just and fair. Most of the people want to keep hold of the power in their own favour and use it for their own purposes. No one likes to share the power with anyone else. This situation surely will not be favourable for a healthy society and needs to be curbed. Impurity and vices of human beings can only be checked by punishment. Manu, being the advocate of *dharma,* wanted to have a pure and honest society. His main concern was to create a society where everyone may lead a dignified, safe and honourable life. No one should be deprived of his due share of the enjoyment of worldly life. Manu wanted to maintain the high standard of morality as it was the best way to dissuade people from committing crime. In normal case no one should deviate from the path of allotted duties, but in case someone has forgotten the duties, he has to be reminded through punishment.

How to Prevent Matsya-Nyāya?

According to *matsya-nyāya,* the weaker group has no right to survive or they have to face many challenges from the mighty side. The weaker side loses its very right of survival because of its feebleness. It is a matter of fact. In the society, there are many powerful men, well-equipped with physical power, money power and manpower, who often become fierce and unruly, and exploit the weaker people. Apart from these, there is political power, which surpasses all other powers. The weak person has no place to stand. This situation may cause lawlessness and chaos in the society. Manu says:

> If a king is not able to restrain the prevailing vices carefully by inflicting *daṇḍa* (punishment), mighty people may get the upper hand and may annihilate the weak just like the fish which has been put on an iron spit for roasting.
>
> — *MS* VII.20

Fish is a little and tiny creature and can be captured easily and even may be roasted without much effort. The fish is exploited always because of its feebleness. The powerful man demonstrates his power by catching and roasting a weak creature like fish. This situation should never occur in the society. Unfortunately, this tendency is rising day-by-day. It is the most common phenomenon that people who are superior by wealth, might or knowledge tend to show their supremacy and exploit the weaker group of people. People, by nature are very possessive and do not like others to have anything which they are having. A person wants to dominate over others in every sphere of life. It is a selfish motive and may lead to various crimes. The exploitation of weak people will result in the division of the society and the desired harmony of the state will be disturbed. It has to be checked at all costs for the welfare of the society. It is the king, the ruler, having powers, who has to look after the welfare of his subjects. There is no place for injustice in a lawful society. The weaker has to be protected and should be given security and confidence to lead a peaceful life. The protection of the weaker group of people can only be done by checking the crimes perpetrated against them. Manu suggests that *daṇḍa* is the only way to check the exploitation of the weaker group. It will create the sense of fear among criminals.

Nature of Daṇḍa

Manu has kept *daṇḍa* parallel to *dharma*. *Dharma* is the manifestation of *Brahman* Himself. He is the Supreme Power, controlling all other powers, and no one can challenge His commands. Through *dharma* even the weak becomes strong and defeats the strong one. To *dharma,* weak and strong are equal.

> *Daṇḍa* is the glory of Brahmā and the creation of *Īśvara* himself. For the king's sake the lord in ancient times emitted the rod of punishment, his own son, the incarnation of justice (*dharma*), to be the protector of all living beings, made of the brilliant energy of ultimate reality. — *MS* VII.14

> *Daṇḍa,* as the creator of the universe, may regulate everyone without any discrimination. — *MS* VII.15

The other name for Yama (the king of death) is Dharmarāja. He carries a rod of punishment (*daṇḍa*) in his hand. The king also holds a rod of justice in his hand and is regarded as the incarnation of justice. The verbal meaning of the word *daṇḍa* is rod. In the case of a king the rod symbolizes power of inflicting punishment for controlling the subjects.

> That rod is king, he is the inflictor, he is the chastiser, traditionally regarded as guarantor for the duties of the four stages of human life. — *MS* VII.17

> The rod (*daṇḍa*) chastises everyone, the rod protects the subjects, the rod stays awake while others are sleeping, wise men know that justice is rod. — *MS* VII.19

The power of *daṇḍa* remains vigilant always and keeps on watching the actions of different people. Through fear of *daṇḍa*, all living beings, stationary or moving, allow themselves to be used and not to swerve from their duty. *Daṇḍa* brings everything in order and nothing is possible without maintaining the proper order. Each and every component involved in the creation and existence of the universe moves in an order. The proper function of the society also needs an order and in the absence of that, there may be chaos. Criminals are those who are confused, misguided and have forgotten the high morals and their duties and are indulging in unlawful activities. Any action that harms the society in any manner and disturbs its peace has to be considered a crime. The criminals, by doing wrong deeds, spoil their own lives and even the society. Thus they are committing a double crime. The crimes taking place in the society have to be checked by all means. People as such are peace loving and wish to lead a quiet and comfortable life. No one relishes the mental agony caused by violence or any other aggressive type of vices. The negative activities may kill the creativity of human beings and may destroy their talents.

Why Do We Need Daṇḍa

The main reason for the growth of the crime is the lack of punishment. The vicious people take the advantage of this situation and keep on harming others for their own selfish motives. They do not bother about the problems of others as they know that there is no one to challenge them. Even the innocent people get tempted and are encouraged to follow the line of crime. Thus the criminals also initiate other people to get involved in the crime. This condition should not continue for a longer period as it may cause uproar among genuine peace-loving people. Inducing a sharp sense of fear is the most effective method for curbing the crime. The fear of the punishment may play the double role. First, it will provide a secured life to common people so that they can live without any fear. Otherwise there are chances that the mighty people may take away their possessions by force. Second, the fear of punishment will not allow people to move away from law. The restraint thus imposed by the state on the people is called law. But the existence of law alone cannot solve the problem of crime. It has to be supported by its implementation and the infliction of punishment.

Manu was well aware of the human psychology. He knew that most of the people prefer to preach others about their duties and may criticize them for not following the duties. But when it comes to them, they forget everything and violate the laws. Many people may not like to continue within the limit of prescribed duties and by hook or by crook will try to find out some way to cross the limit. These people are always busy in planning as to how the law can be broken for their own advantage. But what will happen to the society if everyone starts behaving in accordance with his own will? It will be the rule of beasts and no one will be able to lead a normal life. The oppressive happenings will take place and life will become miserable:

> The crow will eat the sacrificial cake and the dogs would lick the offerings; there will be no lordship; all will be upside–down. —*MS* VII.21

Creation of a Trouble-free Society

Any person engaged in any type of work expects a definite result. But it will bring a real frustration to him if he does not get the fruit of his work because of the mischief played by someone else. It is the common tendency of the ill-minded people that neither they work themselves nor they allow others to work. Such people are of destructive nature and they enjoy spoiling others' good deeds. Therefore it is a must for a state to have a government for controlling the undesirable elements in the society. In a state everyone has to be treated equally without considering one's position, wealth or rank. The government has to be equipped with laws which may be uniformly applied to every member of the society. Law is a tool which helps the ruler for inflicting punishment and maintain justice. Law cannot be changed and is based on truth. The truth always prevails, so no one is having the right to challenge the law.

> A king should never alter the law, he never should move away from law. — *MS* VII.13

Role of Punishment in Maintaining Peace and Order

The political theory of Manu treats law as *dharma* (truth or even justice or duty). As such the law is a guideline to the people to know of their duties and at the same time, the law has to be observed by everyone. Law and *daṇḍa* move together and work jointly for the welfare of the community. Law is associated with men's duties and *daṇḍa* keeps on reminding those persons not following the law that they have to face the consequences. The absence of these two vital elements may convert even an ideal society into a real hell. *Daṇḍa* brings surety to law and both of these together provide confidence and security to the common people. Manu thinks:

> The gods, titans, centaurs, ogress, birds and snakes work in order only by being pressurized by the fear of punishment. — *MS* VII.23

The same reference we find in *Kaṭha* and *Taittirīya Upaniṣad*- where it has been said:

> Through fear of Him the fire heats, and through fear the sun heats; and through fear Indra, wind and the god of death run. — *KaṭhUp* 2.3.3

> Through fear of Him the wind blows, and the sun rises; through fear of Him the fire runs. — *TaitUp* 2.8

Fear is needed even for the proper working of the different elements of creation, what to say of men? But one thing is clear that fear of punishment is the main tool to make someone work diligently. It is also obvious that everyone, howsoever powerful and superior he may be, comes under the authority of *daṇḍa*. No one is allowed to disobey the law or duty.

The main concern of Manu was to bring up a society where everyone knows his duty and does it very seriously. In order to be serious towards the duty one also has to remember the morals and values prescribed for an ideal life. The person who follows the social codes may lead a fearless and free life, and may get the best of it on the earth. Manu wanted to provide a life to every individual free from any type of interference from any side. The violation of the duties may generate problems for the person involved in it and at the same time may disturb others' life. So, it is better to stick to one's duty. The concept of *daṇḍa* as given by Manu, on one hand, tries to create a terror in the minds of criminals and at the same time it tries to purify and civilize the wicked people.

Manu, with his strong spiritual background was aware that basically, all human beings are pure at birth. But because of certain reasons a man becomes wicked. The *daṇḍa* will offer a chance to a wicked man to realize his mistake and the fear of *daṇḍa* will alert him not to commit the same mistake again. A punished person will understand the importance of law and will learn to observe the law. Punishment is a form of justice. Ignoring the infliction of punishment to offenders can be treated as denial of the justice to the people who are engaged in their duties properly. Punishment only protects the people. It puts a psychological pressure on the mind of a person to think about the consequences of his actions and he gets a chance to perceive the reality of the right and wrong. The main purpose of the punishment is to improve a person externally as well as internally. The fear of the punishment may compel a person to identify the contrasting nature of *dharma* and *adharma*. Many a time, a person commits a crime because of ignorance or because of bad company. In such cases the punishment may be an eye-opener for a person and after that he may improve himself. Manu has portrayed a very fierce picture of *daṇḍa*.

> When the dark red-eyed *daṇḍa*, destroying sin, advances, then the people are not confounded. —*MS* VII.25

The furious form of punishment can only be successful to fight against dishonesty, corruption and crookedness. Punishment has to be severe, otherwise people may take it easy and will not be terrified. Punishment serves as security among people to lead a calm life. It plays an important role of providing a better service to humanity by persuading people to improve their moral character. The disregard to morality and human values promotes crime. Punishment, by checking crime, may revive morality. The revival of morality and values may improve the future of the society. The awakened people may surely understand the nature of sovereignty of law and justice in a better way. The main reason of corruption, leading to crime, is the disappearance of the code of conduct needed by a society. Punishment serves as a reminder to the people not to move away from the track of code of conduct. A society, always, is a mixture of the people of different ranks, statuses and classes. But this should not lead to exploitation of one section by the other. The division of the society is very much in the existence everywhere in the world. One should know that people belonging to different classes living in a society are very much dependent on each other for many purposes. The physical or economic dependence in a society is a common phenomenon. But it should never be exploited. In this context it may be mentioned that though Manu has created class or order in the society and has given more power to the upper classes, in no way the upper classes were given the right of subduing the weaker classes. Everyone must have equal opportunity to avail the right of protection and security, without the discrimination of class or status.

Punishment has direct link with the security and welfare of the society. The society must possess a certain level of dignity and refinement of behaviour. The refinement of behaviour can only be achieved by the training of morality received through tradition. A desired behaviour of the people living in a particular community uplifts the status of the society. The growth of undesirable elements spoils the very spirit of the society. In order to have an ideal society the anti-social activities have to be curbed. The verbal instruction or gentle advice may not have any effect on the negative personalities of the offenders, as they are not in position to understand the seriousness of their deeds. The offences will keep on taking place repeatedly. Punishment is the only solution to solve this dangerous development.

Who May Have the Power of Inflicting Punishment?

The concept of punishment as propounded by Manu is based on the doctrine of spirituality. Honesty, equality and fairness are the very basis of Manu's idea of punishment. Every person cannot be given the responsibility of inflicting punishment. In order to establish the credibility of the punishment, the power of punishing someone has to be given to a worthy and deserving person; otherwise the power can be misused. The misuse of power itself is a crime. The most important thing is to decide that who should get the power of inflicting the punishment? It is a big question as the person having the power of punishing the offender must possess enormous qualities. His own conduct, seriousness towards the allotted work, and mode of working needs to be verified. Apart from these, the person must have a detailed knowledge of existing laws and a sharp presence of mind for the application of laws. That is why Manu gave the power of inflicting punishment only to the kings who were well-equipped with all desirable conditions needed for a person selected for the job of inflicting punishment.

> The Lord has created the king for the protection of the world. Taking lasting elements from Indra, Vāyu (wind), Yama, Sūrya (sun), Agni (fire), Varuṇa, Soma (moon) and Kubera (the lord of wealth), God created the king. —*MS* VII.4

All these gods are the basic components of the creation of the universe. A king must have vigour like Indra, swiftness like Wind, truthfulness like Yama, brightness like sun, energy like fire, fairness like Varuṇa, coolness like moon and the capacity of accumulating wealth like Kubera. The king has to look after many departments attached to governance. Therefore, he has to be qualified enough to look after all departments with equal efficiency. But even these are not sufficient for possessing the power of inflicting the punishment. The king responsible for punishing the offenders must maintain high standards of moralities, virtues and conduct.

> Day and night the king should make great efforts to conquer his sensory powers, for the man who has conquered his sensory powers may control his subjects. —*MS* VII.44

It is the unbriddled sensory powers which deviate people from the path of truth. The main function of sensory power is to first create the endless series of desires and then to submerge the person in the deep pool of desires. Injustice, corruption and all types of crimes are the outgrowth of desires. The person with the power of inflicting punishment has to be free of all vices. He has to present himself as an ideal person in the real sense.

> The king is the proper inflictor of punishment as he is free of six enemies (passion, anger, greed, attachment, false pride and jealousy) of human being and has restrained his senses.
>
> — *MS* VII.53

> The king who inflicts punishment correctly thrives on the triple path (virtue, pleasure and wealth), but if he is lustful, partial and mean, he is destroyed by that punishment.
>
> — *MS* VII.27

> Punishment has a brilliant energy, and for those who are indisciplined it is hard to maintain; if a king swerves from justice, it strikes him down along with his relatives.
>
> — *MS* VII.28

Points to Be Taken Care of at the Time of Punishing Someone

One who possesses power needs to have lots of qualities and sensibility, otherwise power becomes a real curse for the owner. Pronouncing the punishment is an extraordinary job even for the inflictor. Even the simple mistake done by the inflictor may cause serious problem for him. The injustice done at any step of pronouncing the punishment may lead to disaster.

> Punishment can oppress the king's fort, his territory, the living and non-living objects of the world, and even the hermits and gods who have gone to the other world.
>
> — *MS* VII.29

In such a situation, the inflictor of punishment has to keep certain things in his mind. He has to follow a prescribed process. A king has to make his realm happy by the proper use of *daṇḍa*. Though the king was responsible for granting punishment, he too was not totally free to give the final verdict. Manu has accorded supremacy to the judiciary where even a king is not free to pass any judgement without conducting proper investigation and without seeking the advice of the prudent members of the court. The ruler first has to decide that whether the act committed by a person is really a crime or not. Many a time the affluent people can manipulate the situation in their favour and make someone else as the scapegoat for the crimes committed by themselves or by their kith and kin. This needs to be checked at all costs. The maladministration of *daṇḍa* may cause the fall of the king. A king is required to follow certain norms needed for the proper delivery of justice.

> Justice, properly wielded, with due consideration, makes all the subjects happy; but inflicted without due consideration, it destroys everything. — *MS* VII.19

A person having the power of inflicting *daṇḍa* must have analytical power to make the analysis of the whole case at once. He should also have patience to hear the case and to note the important points related to the case. A king needs to examine the place, time, gravity and the effect of crime. He also has to follow his *dharma*. In no way, he should misuse his privileges.

> Upon men who persist in behaving unjustly, king should inflict the punishment they deserve, having truly considered the place, time, power and knowledge, of the evil-doer.
>
> — *MS* VII.16

It is a must to know the time and place of crime as it may give many clues for further investigation and for cross-questioning the offender. A powerful offender may try to change the nature of the crime by using his power. He should not be allowed to do such things. The knowledge possessed by the evil-doer also needs to be taken into consideration while punishing him. Many a time, a person commits a crime unknowingly or he gets implicated by or is involved because of someone else in a false manner. These things need to be considered before punishing someone. The punishment should always be in accordance with the type of crime and its magnitude. The king cannot betray the law. He must have a sharp insight to go through the whole case and to find out the truth. Even a small negligence while examining the case may create serious error in proclaiming justice. He should not trust anyone in studying the case. He is supposed to examine the details of the case himself intelligently.

> Just as a hunter traces the track of the wild animal by tracking the drops of blood, the king should trace justice by inference. — *MS* VIII.44

The person having the responsibility of pronouncing the judgement must know the gravity of his work. The judgement delivered is going to have a permanent impact on the whole society. His words at the time of delivering the judgement are not ordinary words. They carry much value for the welfare of the society. The name, fame, credibility and status of a king depend on how is he tackling the crime and how is he inflicting punishment for justice. His personality is going to be an example for his people. A dishonest ruler cannot expect honesty from his subjects. A corrupt ruler corrupts the entire community and makes everyone's life full of difficulties. He never can be admired just because of his kingship. There is no place for comfort or lust or passion in a king's life. His virtues earn wealth and prosperity for him. The right application of law gives correct direction to justice and justice proclaims the principle of equality. Punishment is a sure means to enforce law for bringing about an order among the unruly people.

> If justice is violated, it perishes the state, if preserved, it

> maintains the state. Therefore, justice must not be destroyed, as the destroyed justice may kill us. —*MS* VIII.15

The person destroying justice should be considered as sinner and should not get any status in the society. The survival of a state depends on the observance of *dharma* and justice is *dharma* itself. No one should be exempted from the purview of punishment. Manu wanted that not a single member of the society should cross the limit of law. Law has to be the same for everyone.

> Neither a father, nor a teacher, nor a mother, nor a wife, nor a son, nor a domestic priest should be left unpunished; if they do not keep within their duties. —*MS* VIII.335

There is no place for emotion or sentiment in the course of judgement. It does not matter how close is the person who has committed wrong, he has to be punished. Manu has laid much importance on the observance of *sva-dharma*, the duties allotted to different stages of life and allotted to different sections of the society. The observance of these duties will make a person disciplined, and a disciplined person will never cross the limits of code of conduct. Such a person will understand the significance of law and justice and will not be moved by momentary effect of emotion.

Code of Punishment

The theory of punishment given by Manu is fully based on the principle of social justice. Manu considers that justice is the impartial application of law. The inflictor has to be free of any type of favour. He has to rise up from the individual level. Favouring someone means falling on one side and this results in injustice. The injustice will be a disgrace to law, and punishment is an impartial implementation of law. As both justice and punishment are directly related to the society, it is a must to maintain their required standard. Punishment should always fall on those who deserve it. The human rights should never be violated. The wrongly inflicted punishment may have a negative effect on the common people and may spoil the reputation of the ruler.

> The unjust punishment injures the reputation and destroys the fame of a king, in this world, and debars him from heaven after death. —*MS* VIII.127

> A king, who punishes those who should not be punished and does not punish those who should be punished, gets a very bad reputation and then goes to hell. —*MS* VIII.128

The wrong infliction of punishment will breed dissatisfaction among the masses, and this situation may easily be exploited by enemies and even may produce extremists. It may also make people aggressive and there may be a revolt. Therefore, the ruler has to check his personal feelings and has to proceed in accordance with the law. In fact, the law is a real help to a ruler as it may save him from many controversies.

> Therefore a ruler should disregard his own likes and dislikes, just like Yama he should behave by conquering his anger and his sensory powers. He should keep aside his own pleasure and displeasure in every matter. —*MS* IX.307

> If any evil-hearted king conducts his affairs with injustice through want of discernment, his enemies will quickly get him in their power. —*MS* VIII.174

Importance of Law and Its Implementation

A non-discriminatory and just punishment can preserve the public order and may safeguard the public interest. Thus the social justice has to be taken care of in every respect.

In *Manu-Smṛti* the theory of punishment has been dealt along with the duties of a king. As a matter of fact, the necessity of applying forces arises only when persons decline to shape their actions voluntarily. The undesirable actions of people also have to be checked carefully and legally. There should be a definite, uniform and positive pattern of punishment. The whole arrangement of the punishment has to be systematic and reasonable.

> The king should take his place on the throne of justice with his body covered and his mind concentrated, bow low to the guardians of the world, and begin to hear the case.
>
> — *MS* VIII.23

One also has to study the nature of the crime and its impact on the society. The main purpose of the punishment is to make a person realize his fault and to make a promise of not to repeat the same action again. One also has to consider that how the punishment is going to have its impact on the rest of the society. Justice, truth and values also need to be maintained. Manu has considered all these points while prescribing the grades of the punishment. He has followed the old tactics of *sāma, dāma, bheda* and *daṇḍa*.

> Let the king inflict first punishment of voice, next that of reproof, third that of confiscation of property, then last that of corporal injury or capital punishment. — *MS* VIII.129

Manu perhaps thinks that man as such is pure, but many a time he commits crime being pursuaded by certain unavoidable circumstances. Everyone should be given a chance to improve himself.

> The ruler should discover the inner emotion of the men from the outward sign, by their voice, the colour of the face, involuntary movements and facial expressions, by their gaze and by their gestures. — *MS* VIII.23

The facial expressions of a person are very helpful to study the inner mind. Even in modern days the psychologists are appointed to study the behaviour of criminals. Face is the indicator of the inner mind and heart of a person. To begin with, the milder punishment should serve the purpose of giving a signal to the offender that he is on the wrong path. The punishment of voice given by a supreme authority in a mild and humble manner will be a warning to the evil-doer and the reproof will bring the criminal to shame. Seizing the property forcibly in front of the public may generate defame for the criminal and will cause financial problem to him. But many a time the criminal is habitual to the crime without any shame or does not feel guilty even after the loss of possessions. They do not regard their work as a crime and even they are not scared of punishment. The criminals of this category are the real danger to the society. The state must know the strong means of controlling them. These criminals can only be controlled through severe or deterrent punishments. They surely deserve corporal and capital punishments. There is no sense of showing mercy or softness to them, as they may exploit the gentle behaviour shown by the authorities. Manu puts forth his thought clearly:

> If even by corporal injury, criminals are not restrained, then the punisher may employ on them all these four kinds of punishments. —*MS* VIII.130

It is permissible to use all types of harsh punishments to hardcore criminals, but they never should be allowed to walk free and trouble the innocent people.

Imposing Fine for Certain Types of Crime

Manu's approach to crime and punishment was very rational, accurate and balanced. He moved forward with two missions: first, not giving any chance to criminals to take the upper hand in any condition; and second, ensuring the welfare state by providing a flawless, secured and satisfied life to the society. That is why, Manu was very careful in determining the degree or level of punishment, which depended on the nature of crime.

It is a must to maintain balance between crime and punishment. If the degree of punishment is more than the degree of crime, it may initiate the unruly reaction, but if the punishment is lesser in comparison to the gravity of crime, it will not check crime. If the crime is not of violent nature the imposition of a fine is considered as the right type of punishment. Wealth is the most precious and first acquisition for most of the people, and so, the punishment in the form of fine may really serve the purpose. An ordinary criminal may learn the lesson after being deprived of his money. In *Manu-Smr̥ti* imposing fine has been prescribed for the crimes like non-payment of the debt, sale without ownership, misusing the partnership, non-delivery of what has been given, non-payment of wages, breach of contract, non-payment of taxes, sale of damaged articles or adulterated goods and cruelty towards animals. The fine can be paid in the form of currency, gold and silver. There are three categories of fines known as *sahas* (level of fine).

> A fine of two hundred and fifty *paṇa*s is traditionally regarded as the lowest level, 500 *paṇa*s as the medium level and 1,000 *paṇa*s is the highest level. —*MS* VIII.138

The determination of the grade of the fine is rested on the status of the criminal, the impact of crime on the society and the intention of crime. The amount of the fine for a criminal who is well-educated and enjoys a higher position in the society will always be more. The crime becomes more serious if a person commits that crime after being fully aware that it is a crime and is going to have a wrong impact on others. In that case, imposing more fine is reasonable. Manu has followed the doctrine of justice even for determining the grade of the fine. If a person holding a higher position or a higher social status or a person working with administration commits a crime, he has to pay heavier fine than that of an ordinary citizen committing the same crime.

> In the case where a common man is required to pay 1 *kārṣāpaṇa* (the coin made of copper), the king has to pay 1,000 *kārṣāpaṇa*. It is the established rule. — *MS* VIII.336

As the king cannot take the fine himself, he can give it to a priest or may throw it in the water as an offering to Lord Varuṇa. But he cannot escape from the punishment. Even the well-educated and most respected brāhmaṇas were not free from the grip of punishment.

> The fine, imposed on a brāhmaṇa and kṣatriya for mutual insult, is small in the case of a brāhmaṇa and medium in the case of a kṣatriya. — *MS* VIII.276

Brāhmaṇas as such were not rich in comparison to the ruling class, that is why they were asked to pay less. But they have to face the punishment at every cost. The people of high caste and occupying high position were required to maintain the high standard of conduct strictly, as they were supposed to be knowledgeable and responsible citizens. They had to be the role model of good conduct to the rest of people.

The intention of the criminal was also a criterion for determining the amount of fine. Manu introduced a very strict court proceeding. The testimony given in the court was considered false if it had been given by error or because of greed, fear, friendship, love, anger, ignorance or foolishness.

> If one gives false testimony through greed, he should pay 1,000 *paṇas*, if by error, the fine will be of first grade (250 *paṇas*), if by fear the medium fine, if by friendship, the fine has to be four times more of the first grade, if through love, the fine will be ten times more of the first grade, if through anger the fine will be ten times more of the highest, if through ignorance, the fine will be 200 *paṇas*, but if through foolishness the fine will be 100 *paṇas* only.
>
> — *MS* VIII.120-21

Giving false testimony in the court out of anger, greed or

love indicates the immoral intention of the person who has come to the court for giving testimony. The emotions of anger, greed and love themselves are immoral acts. In that case the person is committing a double crime and, therefore, deserves higher fine. The wrong testimony given out of foolishness or ignorance invites lesser fine as the offender has done it without understanding the case or unknowingly.

It is the main duty of the king to give full security to the property and possession of the public, as they are the main source of sustenance for people. The loss of property may cause a mental tension for its owner. A creditor has the right to get back his money from a debtor. Failing to return the money, the debtor should be treated as an offender.

> A creditor is entitled to get back his money by law, by legal action, by a trick, by the usual customs and even by force. Even the creditor may recover his money himself.
>
> — *MS* VIII.49-50

> But if a man denies the debt that has been proven by the legal instruments, the king should make him pay the money to the creditor and a small amount of money as fine according to his ability to pay. — *MS* VIII.51

A person, taking the debt, will surely be in the need of money. His only crime is that he is hiding the truth. But in view of his financial difficulty, the amount of the fine has to be small and in accordance with his ability to pay. It is a real example of social justice.

> If debtor denies the debt, the plaintiff must call a witness who was present at the time when the debt was given, or adduce some other legal instrument. But even if the witness is having discrepancy in his statement, the case must be dissolved. — *MS* VIII.52-56

The disputes related to the boundaries between two lands

were handled with much care. No one had the right to grab even an inch of land belonging to someone else. The victim may approach the court along with authentic witnesses and may have justice.

> The witness about the boundary should be questioned about the sign (the stones, bones, husks, bricks and many similar things kept between as sign dividing the land belonging to two different persons) of boundary in the presence of the village families and two disputing parties. The records of the statements given by the witnesses have to be maintained. Their statements have to be true. The witnesses giving wrong information should be fined 200 *paṇa*s. — *MS* VIII.254-57

> If the neighbours lie concerning the boundary over which men are disputing, each of them should be imposed the medium fine. — *MS* VIII.263

The court proceedings were very systematic and rigid. No one had the right to play fun with the members of the court and only authentic cases were entertained. The person wasting the time of the court was also required to pay certain amount of fine. Fine was also recommended for the persons taking illegal occupation of others' property. The mighty persons, sometimes, try to procure the land, house and garden belonging to weaker sections of the society. This situation has to be checked instantly.

> A man who by frightening the owner takes possession of the house, pond, garden or field should be fined 500 *paṇa*s. — *MS* VIII.264

The illegal occupation of someone's property reflects the complete failure of the administrative machinery.

Causing verbal injury was also considered as crime and great care was taken to discourage the offender. The desired decency in behaviour is the essence of human personality and it has to be retained at every cost. People are identified because of their humility and humbleness, not because of their money, rank or because of their knowledge. Everyone living in a community should be treated in the same manner. No one should have the power of looking down, insulting or abusing others. Everyone should enjoy a life of dignity and reverence.

> If one of the twice-born abuses the man of the same caste, he should be fined 1,200 *paṇas*, but the fine should be twice of this amount for the words that ought not to be spoken.
> —*MS* VIII.269

Who Are Liable to Be Punished?

More serious punishments were recommended for using bad words to brāhmaṇas or to ruling class (*MS* VIII.271-74). Manu wanted to secure a free and fearless life to everyone. Even the handicapped and physically deformed people should also avail respect and honour and should be treated equally. No one should look them down because of their deformity. A person causing hate by making slanderous statement to any deformed person was considered a criminal and was subjected to punishment.

> If anyone insults a man with one eye or a lame man or any other person deformed in any manner, he should be fined at least 1 *kārṣāpaṇa*, even if he speaks the truth. —*MS* VIII.274

Manu taught universal brotherhood, love and respect for everyone. His theory is very conducive to the utmost welfare of human being. The non-payment of the salary was regarded as crime as it amounts to exploitation of the worker. This act was considered as theft and the person not giving the promised money had to pay fine (*MS* VIII.211-12). Contrary to this, a person who has given word to work and deviates from his promise is also punishable.

> If a hired man, although not ill, insolently fails to work, as agreed upon, he should be fined 8 *kṛṣṇala* (berries) and his wages should not be paid to him. —*MS* VIII.215

Economic development is very much needed for every country. It needs the equal support of every member of the community. The people of any state have to understand that the land belongs to them and they are responsible for its allround progress. It is the ideal state, but in case it does not happen, the ruler has to take some concrete steps for reminding people to work seriously. No one should be allowed to deviate from his allotted work. Manu considers that the violation of any agreement is an offence and needs to be tackled strictly.

> If a man enters into a sworn agreement with a group from a village or district and then breaks it out of greed, the king should banish him from the kingdom. —*MS* VIII.219

Government servants are also supposed to finish their work within the stipulated time.

> A king should arrest such a breaker of agreement and should fine him 4 gold coins, 6 *niṣka*s (coins), or 300 *rattī* of silver. —*MS* VIII.220

Fine was also a way of punishing the parents who did injustice to anyone by marrying him their daughter without telling her defects.

> If a man gives away a girl in marriage who is having some defects, without first making the defects known, the king himself should impose the fine of 96 *paṇa*s on him. —*MS* VIII.224

But this punishment was not one-sided. It was a must for a groom to follow the agreement made at the time of marriage. The sacrament of the marriage should be consciously accepted as it is the doorway of spiritual accomplishment. No one was allowed to spoil the sanctity of married life.

> When a man, because he dislikes his wife, asks her to go away, should be fined 500 *paṇa*s. — *MS* III.225

Manu also recommended fine on economic offenders and on those who destroy public properties. It was a must for everyone to earn money for the interest of the community and for the country. The householders were responsible for maintaining the patches of forests and wastelands. The people not discharging their duties for maintaining the greenery were liable to be punished (see *MS* IX.329, 332-33). The members of the village community were jointly liable for keeping their roads, water canals, tanks, rivers, reservoirs, mechanical agencies, granaries and temples in efficient repair as they were the sources of economic progress. Anyone damaging these structures had to be punished heavily.

> One should slay a person who destroys a pool, destroys granaries, or temples. He should be imposed the highest fine. A person destroying the pond should be physically punished by drowning or by simple killing.
>
> — *MS* IX.279-81

Acts Disturbing Public Life a Crime

It was the duty of the citizens to keep the roads of the town clean.

> If anyone without pressing need emits impurities upon the king's highway, he should pay the fine of 2 *kārṣāpaṇa*s and clear up the impurities at once. — *MS* IX.282

A fine was also imposed on a person who destroyed the stile, sign on the road or anywhere else, or a pole.

> Such a person was required to replace all that he has destroyed and should pay a fine of 500 *paṇa*s. — *MS* IX.285

> But one who destroys the city walls, one who fills up the mote or breaks the gate should be banished at once.
>
> — *MS* IX.289

As agriculture was the most vital sector of the economy, the conservation of land and tools related to cultivation became a must. Anyone destroying these articles was punishable.

> For destroying things used in ploughing, weapons or medicinal plants, one should be fined heavily. —*MS* IX.293

Manu has visualized the importance of capital, industries and other productive undertakings. The rate of the interest, taxation and the holdings of the people have to be well guarded. The supervision of financial resources needs to be done for the economic progress of the country. Traders, usurpers, herdsmen, artisans and craftsmen were not allowed to misuse the government property. Markets were kept under sharp vigilance. No one was allowed to sell damaged, adulterated or broken goods.

> One thing mixed with other should not be sold. Even no one should sell the spoiled, deficient or concealed goods.
> —*MS* VIII.203

Prices of different articles were decided by the king and he was responsible to ensure the quantity, measures, time and place of delivery.

> If the king sees that anything has been pledged or sold through artifice or anything has been given or accepted through artifice or whenever he sees any cheating, he should cause the whole transaction annulled. —*MS* VIII.165

The rules regarding loans, deposits and interest were also well guarded.

> He who does not return the deposits, and he who without having made a deposit falsely claims one, are both to be punished as thief or fined the sum equally involved.
> —*MS* VIII.190

In the matter of trade and money transaction, both the debtor and creditor must follow a fair dealing. Any type of fraud or breach of contract was not allowed.

> A debtor denying the debt has to be fined twice the amount of the debt. A minister or a judge performing any illegal business should be fined 1,000 *paṇas*. — *MS* IX.234

Manu realized well the importance of government treasury and considered revenue as the basic requirement of the state. Provision had also been made to keep some extra amount to be used during natural calamities. The richness of the royal treasury depends on the proper and fair collection of taxes. Manu mentioned several types of taxes and declared that it was the duty of each and every citizen to pay tax at the time of the demand. The king had all power to punish the one who had falsely declared his income or had not paid the tax in due time.

> A tradesman who slips from the place, where the tax has to be collected, or gives a false statement in regard to the amount due to be paid as tax has to be fined the eightfold of that amount he has evaded. — *MS* VIII.400

Everyone was required to remain present at the time of tax collection. The fine was determined by the value of the tax required to be paid by the person. The amount of the fine may be eightfold of the amount of the tax if someone denies paying the tax. The provisions were also made to take away the whole property of a man who was trading in an illegal manner, or smuggles the goods through avarice (*MS* VIII.399). Fines were also imposed for illegal import or export.

Protection of Ecosystem

The preservation of the environment occupies a special place in the ordinances of Manu. He had realized in true sense the interdependence of man and his environment. The strict rules were framed for preserving the greenery in every township, maintaining the pastures and fields and for taking care of the flora and fauna. Cruelty to domestic animals was regarded as serious crime. Even the wild animals were to be given due protection.

> A fine must be imposed for injuring trees in exact accordance with their usefulness. — *MS* VIII.285

The fine was to be imposed in direct proportion to the amount of pain caused when someone strikes animals to give them the pain (see *MS* VIII.386). A fine was imposed even on injuring the trees. Plants are vital for human life and injuring them is an act of violence.

> Someone destroying the flowers, roots and fruits of trees has to pay the fine of the amount five times more than the real value of those. — *MS* VIII.286

> The drivers of the cart and other vehicles driving on the road were cautioned to drive carefully and not to destroy the vegetation or to kill any animal. Failing in that the driver deserves fine. — *MS* VIII.295

All castes were reminded to take care of all types of animals and birds. A fine of 200 *paṇa*s was set for killing of small animals and birds like crow or parrots, and the fine should be of 50 *paṇa*s in the case of propitious animals and birds (*MS* VIII.297). It includes different types of antelopes, deer, flamingoes and other types of birds.

> The fine for killing donkeys, goats and sheep should amount to 5 *māsaka*, but 1 *māsaka* should be the fine for destroying a dog or a boar. — *MS* VIII.298

As agriculture was the main occupation, the rural economy was accorded much priority. Cattle breeding and dairy farming constituted one of the most important activities of the society. The people of all castes were allowed to go for these occupations. The animals like sheep and goat were economically more useful and their killing was considered a crime as it meant an economic loss.

Protection of Human Rights

Justice is the root of all happiness for the people of any country and injustice brings all sorts of troubles. The judicial system propounded by Manu is remarkably modern. No civil case was entertained in the court without the complaint of the plaintiff. Strict rules were framed for pleading. Evidences and witnesses were a must for every trial. There was a detailed description of the qualities and demeanour of a reliable witness. A witness had to be truthful and virtuous. A witness giving false statement was regarded as a sinner and was liable to be punished. A ruler had the power to banish such a person from the country. Punishments were oriented towards *dharma* and were used for the suppression of the wrong. Imposing fine was a mild way of suppressing the evil-doers and was used for controlling petty crimes. But it could not serve the purpose of controlling the crimes of serious nature. The seriousness of the crime was determined on the basis of the impact of that crime on the society. There were several crimes that might shake the whole society and cripple the very spirit of the common man. These crimes had to be tackled in a quick and an effective manner. Then obviously, there arises a need for rigorous punishment. Manu graded harsh punishments carefully depending on the nature of the crime. As the primary aim of punishment was to remove bad elements from the society and to provide full protection to the common people, proper consideration was given to determine the severity of the crime. Manu advocated corporal punishment for the crimes related to violence, theft, assault, crime against women, terrorism, non-payment of fine, robbery, slander, adultery, dicing, kidnapping and even for homosexuality. Corporal punishments included imprisonment, mutilation of organs, penal servitude, beating and even death punishment. The corporal punishment was also prescribed for the person repeating the same crime again and again. The observance of the law was to be maintained even at family level.

> Family members, on committing crime, should be beaten by bamboo cord or cane stick. — *MS* VIII.299

It seems that Manu wanted that the strict training of discipline had to be started right from the home. If a person does not follow the code of conduct at home, he may behave in the same manner even in the society. But the training of the discipline at home has to be a mild reminder and should not cause any serious type of injury, specially, on the vital parts of the body.

> Beating should be done only on the back of the body; never on noble parts of the body like the head, eyes and nose; if anyone does that, surely he has to be punished like a thief. — *MS* VIII.300

Types of Crime and Punishment

The ethics of the punishment had to be maintained at all costs. The common people are always careful and attached to their belongings, as they have earned those things through hard-work. Priority has to be given to the safety of their possessions. Manu considered theft and robbery as serious types of offences and instructed the king to check these crimes by inflicting harsh punishments on the perpetrators.

> In restraining thieves the king should exert the greatest possible effort, because the fame and the realm of the king are increased by restraining the thieves. — *MS* VIII.302

The denial of the protection of the common people is the denial of duties on part of the administrator. Any government receiving taxes from the public is bound to give full protection to its citizens.

> King who bestows security upon his subjects is ever to be honoured. — *MS* VIII.303

The sense of insecurity may trigger dissatisfaction among people and even may cause serious social and political problems. Thus the person who is posing danger to the security of common people has to face a befitting punishment. Manu prescribed corporal punishment for all types of thieves (see *MS* VIII.320). Inflicting punishments to the thieves was considered as the most important duty of the king.

> A king, not punishing a thief, himself receives the crime of the thief. — *MS* VIII.316

The punishment related to theft was based on the value of the amount/material stolen by the thief. If the amount stolen by a thief is not much or the article stolen is of not much value, fine can be imposed. But if the amount is high or the valuables are more, the thief deserves capital punishment.

> Death is the penalty if one steals more than 10 *kumbha* (jars) of grains; if the amount is less he may pay a fine eleven times more than the value of the grain. — *MS* VIII.320

> Death also has to be inflicted for stealing more than 100 finest garments or articles made of gold and silver. — *MS* VIII.321

> If the number of articles is less than 100 and more than 50, his hands can be chopped off. — *MS* VIII.322

Reasons for Inflicting Harsh Punishments

The harsh punishment is necessary for stealing valuable articles to check the loss to the state economy and hindrance to trade and commerce. Thieves, stealing valuable articles, may be professional ones and even may be the habitual ones. They may commit the same crime again and again. Therefore they need to be controlled by rigorous punishment. Capital punishment was also prescribed for kidnapping a man of high family or of high status (see *MS* VIII.323).

Manu asked the rulers to keep a vigilant eye on the robbers. Robbery involves the loss of property and is even a serious act of violence. It creates a sense of terror in the minds of the victims and may cause mental disorder.

> Any act of robbery done by force in the presence of the owner will be an act of violence. — *MS* VIII.332

It has to be treated similar to the crime of murder. It is an open assault on the guarded property and on the life of the owner of the property. Therefore, the robber has to be punished in such a manner that he may not even think of committing that crime again. Such a crime has to be dealt without any sense of mercy.

> With whatever limbs the robber executes his purpose, that limb has to be cut off, so that it may be an example for others.
> — *MS* VIII.334

A person, with chopped limb, will neither be able to work nor may lead a normal life. He even cannot face others.

> If a robber commits the theft in the night by making a hole in the wall, the king should cause both his hands to be cut off and the chopped hands should be fastened on a sharp stake.
> — *MS* IX.276

> If a thief takes away the gold or money tied in a cloth by opening the knot, at first instance, his fingers should be chopped off, if he commits the same crime again, his hands and feet should be chopped off, but if he does the same act for the third time, he deserves capital punishment. — *MS* IX.277

Committing the same crime again and again indicates that he cannot be improved and then he has no right to live in this world. The corporal punishment is also granted to the person for stealing the royal treasury (see *MS* IX.275). The supervision of internal and external security is also much needed from time to time. Many people from within or from other countries, with vested interests try to terrify the people and disturb their normal life. These criminals use all sorts of violent means and do not hesitate to kill anyone.

> Any person supplying food, shelter and weapons to the terrorists or concealing the crime should also be accorded capital punishment. — *MS* IX.278

Terrorism is the worst crisis for any country. It creates stress and fear psychosis among the people and arrests the development of the country. This act has to be checked instantly.

> A man who creates violence should be regarded as the worst of evil-doers, worse than the one who injures with voice, or than a thief or than one who smites with a stick.
> — *MS* VIII.345

A ruler, tolerating the act of violence, is digging a pit for himself, as the violence will cause his destruction. A perpetrator of violence ought to be punished according to the enormity of his crime, with death or mutilation. A terrorist, regardless of his position or status, should not be given any privilege.

> Let a king without any hesitation kill anyone attacking with a weapon in his hand. — *MS* VIII.350

A person, holding a weapon in his hand for killing others, should be known as *ātatāyī*, regardless of the fact whether he is a brāhmaṇa or of a low caste.

> No sin comes at anytime upon the slayer for causing, openly or secretly, the death of one who attacks him with a weapon, for thus anger meets anger. — *MS* VIII.351

Violence gives birth to violence and may transform a noble man to a wicked man. Keeping in mind the seriousness and complicated nature of the crimes related to violence and terrorism, Manu suggested:

> While handling such cases, no evidences are required and the criminal can be punished on the prima facie basis.
>
> — *MS* VIII.72

These criminals deserve capital punishment. The punishment can also be given in the form of mutilation of the privy parts, belly, tongue, two hands, feet, eyes, nose, ears and even the whole body. Usually, the part of the body used for committing the crime has to be mutilated.

The progress of the country depends on the efficient working of the people involved in the administration.

> If a minister or a judge performs business in a wrong manner, a king himself should attend to the matter and should punish him without any consideration of his status.
>
> — *MS* IX.234

People involved in different jobs had to work diligently.

> All physicians treating a patient incorrectly or carelessly were also punishable. — *MS* IX.284

Manu wanted to inculcate in the human mind a strong sense of duty, acceptance of the allotted work and voluntary submission to discipline. Anyone violating the ordained duties had to be punished for the sake of the country.

Gambling and drinking of liquor were strictly prohibited. These addictions give birth to many vices and ruin the person and even his family life. A person loses his senses and may indulge in several types of crimes, which may disturb the harmony of the community. Even betting in any form was considered illegal. The group of people, engaged in the business of gambling or promoting gambling in any form, are liable to be punished.

> People, indulging in gambling and prize-fighting, or causing them to be carried on, should be punished corporally. — *MS* IX.221-22, 225, 228

Manu regards gambling as open robbery and the people involved in gambling are the internal enemies of the country distressing the common people in disguise and a ruler must make a constant effort to tackle them. They should be physically punished. These vices are like epidemics and grow very fast. Therefore, the gamblers and drunkards need to be banished from the country then and there.

Taking or giving bribe was considered a major crime. People sometimes offer bribe to the concerned officials in order to get their work done in an unfair manner or for getting undue favour. It is the starting point of corruption and leads to many other unfair means. It spoils the very functioning of the administration and initiates unlawfulness. Giving or taking bribe, both are equally harmful for the proper growth of the society as both of them are moving away from the path of truth. The person, receiving the bribe accumulates lots of black money in a wrong manner and thereby the economy of the country suffers. These people are the real enemies of the country and are liable to be punished severely.

> Those who are being commissioned for looking after certain business and are reversing the whole affair because they are cooked by the heat of the money, the king must deprive them of their property. — *MS* IX.231

Capital punishment was also prescribed for a government official giving false statement or making a statement that gave rise to a strife or gave any type of favour to enemies (*MS* IX.232). Manu considered home and family as the bedrock of any society. The stability and sanctity of the family depend on women. Punishments were also prescribed for the women who moved away from the path of their duties.

> If a lady, being proud of her parental property or beauty,

> insults her husband and moves to another man, the king should devour her in some much frequented place.
>
> — *MS* VIII.371

Even a man doing any such crime should not be left unpunished. There were strict punishments for the crimes like adultery, insult, rape and for doing any type of evil act against women.

A unique type of punishment has been introduced in *Manu-Smṛti* for homosexuality.

> If a girl injures another girl with the finger, she should be made to pay 200 *paṇa*s and should give double of the marriage money to the injured girl and should receive ten whips (lashes). — *MS* VIII.369

> But if a married woman injures a girl, her head should be shaved or two fingers should be cut off or she should be made to ride upon a donkey and should be taken on the main road of the town. — *MS* VIII.370

Homosexuality has become a hot topic now-a-days. Manu considers it a crime and the punishment has been prescribed for this crime. Homosexuality is a deviation from the normal prescribed life of a married couple. It cannot be taken as a normal human behaviour and is not approved ethically. An unnatural act done by anyone may invite many complications. It may cause medical problems or may cause frigidity or impotency in a woman.

Manu interpreted punishment as the best method to control the crime. His main emphasis was to create an awakening and fear among people to behave in a desired manner and to follow the path of law. He advised the king to construct the prison house on the highway, so that most of the people while passing through might watch the sufferings of the criminals and the pain experienced by the mutilated evil-doers (see *MS* IX.288). Thus the punishment was a sure method to keep everyone in the limit of the order and discipline. Only the disciplined people had the right to stay in the community. Even the king was not exempted from the laws of punishment. The judge and jury had the full powers to punish the unjust king. Manu denied fully the eventual absolutism of the punisher.

A truly magnificent administration of justice and synchronization of the highest principle of the laws of punishment is the key to an ideal governance. This concept will never lose its relevance. Manu's theory of punishment consists of all those elements that are needed for desired governance and also provides much scope for bringing in change based on the need of time and place. The law of punishment in Manu's jurisprudence was above the sovereign and was free from any type of political or social interference. A criminal, regardless of his status, was regarded nothing more than a criminal. The imposition of the punishment was not just based on the number of witnesses alone but on the detailed investigation of the causes leading to the crime. Politicians did not play an important role in judicial procedures and the judiciary was kept separate from the executive. Only the exponents of *dharma* were appointed as judges. They too were subjected to harsh punishment in case they did not perform their duties. The job of the proclamation of the punishment was done in the presence of a group of people known as *sabhā*. The *sabhā* must act in a fair manner without interfering in the proceedings of the court and should participate actively. They should not remain silent under the influence of any kind of pressure. Manu declares that silence on the part of *sabhā* is culpable.

Manu accorded top priority to the welfare of the common man. Therefore, it was a must to prescribe harsh punishments for the permanent elimination of crime. Manu's concept of punishment is based on the principle of "an eye for an eye".

This method was adopted to get the strong impact of punishment on the criminal. Even during recent times, many countries have been able to bring about desirable changes by introducing rigorous punishments. Manu could remarkably interlink the degrees of the punishment and crimes. Prescribing capital punishment to the criminals like terrorists, kidnappers, hijackers, or to the offenders committing heinous crimes against women is really justified. No civilized country should allow these crimes to occur again and again. A person swindling crores of public money, if fined only few thousands, will surely be a relaxed person and will be encouraged to repeat the crime. There is no sense in putting a murderer in the prison for a long time. He should be given the same treatment as he has done to someone. The false witnesses should not get any chance to manipulate the case in any way. The human rights need to be guarded, but not at the cost of lives of thousands of people. The life of people living in a community is very precious and it has to be saved. The violation of the human rights has to be condemned strongly, but it never should be misused. The nature of crime keeps on changing with time and circumstances. Therefore, the laws of punishment need certain modifications, but the universal value system has to be maintained. Any government collecting tax from its citizens is bound to give them protection by punishing the undesirable persons. However, the innocent people should not be punished.

Relevance of Manu's Penal Codes in Present-day Social Challenges

The modern world has been progressing by leaps and bounds as a result of scientific and technological advances; however, there is also much to cause anxiety. The worldwide increase in crime has shaken the entire humanity. Selfishness has engulfed all human values giving way to unethical actions and practices. The common man has been forced to live under various types of constraints and pressures. The human values have been eroded giving way to violence and terrorism. In this context a judicious implementation of law of punishment becomes absolutely essential, so that the crime is effectively restrained. Human instincts and impulses have to be restrained for the welfare of the society as a whole. Moral laws and institutions were created for the coercion of the wicked people. Punishment is the only way to control the elements that ruin the society. The majesty of the law pertaining to punishment was never so eloquently described by anyone before Manu. His rules of punishment rested upon the double foundation of divine regulation and prudent human ordinances.

It is true that these days we have comprehensive law treatises and very systematic procedures for punishing those who indulge in various types of crimes. There is also a huge force in place to control the undesirable elements. All the arrangements related to administration are theoretically superb. Many types of state-of-the-art scientific methods are used to investigate and prove crimes. Several agencies are engaged in understanding the sociological and psychological reasons behind the increasing crime rate and they are trying their best to reach to the bottom of the problem. Nevertheless, the story of the common people continues to remain pathetic due to increasing incidences of crimes. They are gradually losing faith in governance. The well trusted judicial administration is also losing its credibility. There has been a tremendous rise in the socio-political crimes in recent years and the politically influential criminals consider themselves above the law. It is a global phenomenon, but it has assumed alarming proportion in the developing countries. The dreaded terrorism is simmering for a long time in many parts of the world and it has seriously slowed down the pace of economic growth.

The younger generation is totally misguided and is moving far away from the path of justice and truthfulness. The total personality of human beings has changed and they are living a life full of frustration and depression. The creativity of human being is diminishing day-by-day. There is under-utilization of the precious human resources and god-gifted talents. This situation is particularly distressing for a country like India where we boast of possessing the richest literature, telling volumes of words related to morality and human values. We are also having the most intelligent brains and a large number of awakened people. In spite of that, there is a sharp fall in moral values and moralities, causing serious crimes in different sectors of the society. Everyone wants to take the law in his own hand. The law has lost its very significance. The definition of criminals has also changed. There is much of disparity in designating someone a criminal. Powerful people are walking free even after committing serious crimes. They know how to manipulate law in their favour. No one can dare say a single word against them. Common people are terrified to oppose them. They have the power to destroy anyone. Even in prison they are getting special treatment and do not experience the pain of punishment. Thus the punishment becomes nothing more than a ritual for them. The misuse of power by these people has victimized many innocent people, whilst the real criminals move freely and are able to maintain the high profile. In most of the cases, either the justice has been delayed or denied altogether. The people sitting at the helm of affairs are themselves corrupt and they are trying to promote corruption. All this is happening because of the slackness in the proper implementation of laws of punishment. On the whole, the situation is worsening and there is no sign of any improvement in sight. But this situation should not prolong beyond limit. The country may become a "non-state", and there will be an anarchy. This situation needs to be avoided and there is a strong need to curb the existing trend immediately. It may be possible only through the strict adherence to the *nyāya-dharma* of Manu, which is based on the doctrine of equality, spirituality, ethics and truthfulness. *Manu-Smṛti* has solutions for the prevailing social and political evils. The social codes and the concept of crime and punishment as enunciated by Manu, if understood properly and followed in the right earnest, will certainly go a long way in meeting the contemporary social and political challenges.

6

Concept of Śūdras in Manu-Smṛti

Class and Caste in Vedas and Dharmaśāstras

MANU-SMṚTI comprises the codes of ideal life for an individual. Manu is of the opinion that an individual, leading an ideal life, may be the real asset of the community. The progress of the community depends on the proper management of human resources. The allotment of definite duties for different groups of the society, the correct observance of duties by the people of that group and the sincerity with which the allotted duties are performed are the prerequisites for the optimum utilization of manpower. The four divisions of the society proclaimed by Vedas and, later on, by Manu should be treated as the best technique for utilizing the talents possessed by the different groups of the people. While propounding the doctrine of *caturvarṇa*, Manu takes the help of the ninetieth hymn of the tenth *maṇḍala* of *Ṛgveda* (*ṚV* X.90.12). This *maṇḍala* belongs to the later Vedic period. It relates to the theory of origin of the universe.

Puruṣa-Sūkta and Other References

Puruṣa-Sūkta of *Ṛgveda* describes the origin of the four classes of the society as such:

> Brāhmaṇa was the mouth of the cosmic *Puruṣa*, *rājanyas* were created by his arms, vaiśyas were made of his thighs and śūdras sprang up from his feet. — *ṚV* X.90.12

The different classes were formed from the different limbs of *Puruṣa*, which makes it very clear that the whole community formed one unit. The same theory of the origin of four classes was accepted by *Kāṭhaka Saṁhitā* XXXI.2, *Maitrāyaṇīya Saṁhitā* III.1.1.10, *Āpastamba-Dharmasūtra* 1.3.40-41 and *Śatapatha Brāhmaṇa* 14.4.2.23-25. Manu, being the great supporter of Vedas, expresses similar views as mentioned in the Vedic literature. The only one point that Manu adds is that this division of the society was done for the sake of the welfare and prosperity of the world. It seems that the creation of four groups of the society was an amendment to the system of dividing the society into three classes during the early Vedic period. In Indian system, the social codes kept on changing, depending on the need of the society. The early Vedic text does not mention the concept of *caturvarṇa*. *Śatapatha Brāhmaṇa* II.1.4.11 and *Taittirīya Brāhmaṇa* III.12.9.2 speak of the existence of the three classes only. They do not mention śūdras as a separate group. *Atharvaveda* IV.6.1 and XV.8.1 also mention only three classes. Till that time the word *varṇa* was not in use for denoting the sense of class or caste. Even in the early Vedic period śūdras have not been mentioned as a separate class.

Śūdras in Early and Later Vedic Period

The word śūdra has been used more frequently in the later Vedic period. There is a probability that the concept of śūdras originated sometime in the later Vedic period. There is a question mark as to how the fourth class known as śūdras was included in the scheme of division of the society. Why Manu has moved one step ahead and declared that the reason for the inclusion of śūdras was "for the prosperity of the world"? In order to get an answer to this question one has to go deeper into the socio-economic and political situation of that period. In fact, Smṛtis have prescribed injunctions (*vidhi*s) and prohibitions (*niṣedha*s), keeping in mind a particular social surrounding. The mental, ethical and psychological statuses of the society kept on changing from time to time. New Smṛtis were complied with new concepts for catering to the changes taking place in the society. Many of the old concepts needed changes or modifications. The rate of the population growth was also a deciding factor for introducing changes in the social framework. There was also a change in what should be done and what should not be done. There were a number of people not fitting in the scheme of the three classes of the society. The old Vedic concept of three classes lost its relevance and it was thought necessary to introduce the fourth class of śūdras. Now the question arises as to what were the reasons for creating the new class called śūdra and who were śūdras? The critical study of the code of conduct prescribed in *Manu-Smṛti* for the four classes reveals that it was the duties ordained for the four classes that formed the basis for the division of the society into four distinct groups. The duties were based on the concept of *dharma* for leading a life of righteousness.

> *Dharma* slain verily slays, but *dharma* protected protects; therefore, *dharma* should not be injured. The injured *dharma* may slay us. — *MS* VIII.15

Evolution of Śūdra Concept: An Analysis

The introduction of a class system was an effort to develop a society free of vices by regulating its conduct. The conduct of an individual became very important for giving him the status. Manu has maintained a very clear dividing line between what to do and what should not be done. The actions, that are rational, are considered as virtues, and vices are opposite of virtues. The class system was not just a social structure, but it was meant to create a society in accordance with *dharma*. The duties allotted for different groups of the society were for uplifting the society and for providing an anxiety-free life to every citizen. It was an ethical order aiming at making every one a perfect one by sticking to own duties diligently. Therefore no one was allowed to meddle with the assigned *dharma*. The people of three upper classes were under severe vigilance and the rules were most stringent for them and if any of those three upper classes caused omission of the prescribed duties he was considered *adhārmika* (irreligious) one or *vṛṣala* (a person causing injury to *dharma*). Manu states,

> Lord Dharma is bull and anyone who puts an end to the bull is regarded by gods as an outcaste or *vṛṣala*.
>
> — *MS* VIII.16

The word *vṛṣala* is derived from the root *vṛṣ* with *alac* as suffix and meaning "śūdra".

Reasons for Including Śūdras in Class System

The people of three upper classes harming *dharma* were put under the category of śūdra. It was the denial of the duties, lacking faith in the spiritual life, misconduct and attachment to the sensual life, which brought the downfall of brāhmaṇas kṣatriyas and vaiśya to the fourth class of śūdras. A person is honoured because of his virtues and his dedication towards his duties, failing to that he will surely be considered of low moral.

Indian tradition has always given more value to the intellectual strength than the physical strength. It also has considered the worldly achievement useless without spiritual gain. The human life during Vedic period was treated as a blessing and it was supposed that everyone would justify his birth by doing good deeds. The control of the senses was very much needed for enjoying the life. Brāhmaṇas, were the most respected because of their great conduct and intelligence. They were expected to lead a life of high morality and spirituality. They were recognized for their unusual potentiality for performing every action with perfection. The moral action of a brāhmaṇa should be inspired by his inner conviction and not by outer compulsions. The outer behaviour of a person is always guided by his inner power and a person can improve his outer conduct only by controlling his impulses. One may expect perfect action only from a pure person. If a brāhmaṇa misuses his power and gets involved in earthly pleasures and comforts, surely he will lose his ability and potentiality and will not be able to follow the path of *dharma*. At this point he may not command the due respect and reverence and his downfall is inevitable. Manu has clarified the doubt about the position of *adhārmika* brāhmaṇa:

> A brāhmaṇa, who does not study Vedas, is quenched like grass in the fire. —*MS* III.168

At many points Manu has said that a brāhmaṇa, not fulfilling his qualifications, is not different from a śūdra. It is the śūdra alone who is excluded at god's feast where the *havya* (oblation) is offered. It is also mentioned in *Manu-Smṛti* that a brāhmaṇa, not performing his duties, should not be invited in the sacrifices.

> A brāhmaṇa who associates with the most superior persons and avoids inferiors, attains eminence, but by taking the opposite course he attains the status of śūdras. —*MS* IV.245

It can be proved with an example cited in *Manu-Smṛti*. Sukālina, who was the son of a great sage Vasiṣṭha, was a śūdra. He has been referred as the forefather of śūdras (see Govindarāja comm. on *MS* IV.185: *śūdrapitaraḥ sukalino vāsiṣṭhasya putraḥ* and Ramachandra comm. on *MS* IV.158: *sukalino vāsiṣṭhasutaḥ śūdranāmpūjyasmṛta*). Thus, it is very clear that the birth in the line of a brāhmaṇa was not sufficient to make someone a brāhmaṇa. Even the son of a sage may become a śūdra because of non-fulfilment of his prescribed duties.

The brāhmaṇas secured an unchallenged supremacy and

were held as the very guardians of the whole society and were considered as the human gods. Manu refers to *paurvikīṁ*, the remembrance of the previous birth, and gives details of how one attains the vision of his previous birth by the practice of Vedas, purity of life, penance and compassion to the human being. By remembering the previous birth he gets into the knowledge of *Brahman* and attains the infinite happiness (see, *MS* IV.147-48). By this process a brāhmaṇa may continue to gain the status of brāhmaṇa from one birth to another. But, in case the son of a brāhmaṇa does not carry on the rules and regulations ordained for a brāhmaṇa and indulges in undesirable actions, surely he deserves the status of a śūdra. The vices of anger, malice, passion, retaliation, intolerance and narrow-mindedness may convert anyone to a śūdra. Manu has also advised to have the company of good people. A person of a high class falling in the company of bad people may not be able to see the merits of good deeds and may deviate from the traditions of his family. A person learns many things in good company and loses many good habits in bad company. Manu says:

> One desirous to bring his family to eminence should ever form relation with the best and should avoid the low.
>
> — *MS* IV.244

The good conduct may enrich the life of a person and the bad conduct brings his downfall. A brāhmaṇa having a bad company will never be inspired to move on the path shown by his ancestors and it is natural for him to lose his status. A brāhmaṇa represents the highest of which human nature is capable. The lack of that high profile may not save his status and can make him a śūdra. The abilities of brāhmaṇas have to be properly utilized by the society. If a teacher does not teach the students in a correct manner, he cannot be considered a teacher and everyone will start disrespecting him. The job of a brāhmaṇa was to instruct the students selflessly and he has to make use of his eminence for imparting knowledge. The brāhmaṇa indulged in other jobs cannot make the best use of his knowledge.

> If a brāhmaṇa is looking after cowherds, is doing a trade, or who is a workman, actor, servant and moneylender, the king should treat him like a śūdra. —*MS* VIII.102

If a brāhmaṇa is doing other jobs, it proves that he is more concerned about earning money, leaving behind his noble job of teaching Vedas and has forgotten his rare ability and knowledge and thus he becomes a śūdra. The jobs other than teaching can be done by any other person but the teaching job involves extra talent and cannot be done successfully by others. Leaving the job of teaching Vedas was also a criterion for converting a brāhmaṇa to a śūdra.

Doing any type of business was totally forbidden for a brāhmaṇa. A businessman cannot avoid materialism. In order to earn money he will apply many types of tricks and will hide the truth. Manu has not given much value to the fame earned by enormous wealth. Knowledge is the prestigious source of gaining fame and that can be easily earned by a brāhmaṇa. Therefore, he should not go for any trade or business and should not abandon or waste his highly specialized knowledge.

> A brāhmaṇa falls at once if he sells meat, lac (resinous substance secreted as a protective covering by the lac insect) and salt; in the course of three days of him selling milk he becomes śūdra. —*MS* X.92

Thus it is amply clear that a brāhmaṇa, by not observing his prescribed duties, got placed under the category of śūdra.

Kṣatriyas, the ruling class, were placed second in the social order designed by Manu. They were holding the responsibility of protecting the country, preserving justice, and maintaining law and order. The guidelines given to the ruling class were also very similar to the code prescribed for brāhmaṇas. They were also advised to practise the austerity in every respect. The ruling class had to maintain the virtues of both a sage and an administrator. The job of administration requires certain qualities which a king must possess. The king is also responsible for curtailing the crime through the proper infliction of punishments. He is supposed to be honest and selfless.

> The king should protect everyone according to justice and should also receive the Vedic initiations. — *MS* VII.2

The transformative ritual (*saṁskāra*) is the initiation. It is a must for a king to be initiated formally for religious purposes. Thus a king should have the attributes of a good ruler and a religious person.

Kings are like the parents to the society and subjects are like their children. The king, therefore, has to care for their welfare. The king also has to maintain the justice and impartiality in all the affairs related to the welfare of the common people. He is in-charge of all types of resources needed for the survival of the society. He has to increase the resources for the betterment of the society. If he fails to do so, his downfall is inevitable.

> The fame of a king who does so, though he lives by gleaning corn or gathering single grains (it is a technical term for a modest kind of livelihood, see *MS* IV.5), is spread in the world like a drop of oil on the water, but if he does the contrary that may congeal in the world like a drop of *ghee* (clarified butter) in the water. — *MS* VII.33-34

The king has to maximize the utility of resources for the cause of common people. The misuse of resources will destroy his reputation and will make him unpopular. A defamed king loses his status. A sinful king has no right to be considered as kṣatriya and will be treated as śūdra.

> Gradually through the loss of sacred ceremonies and by violating the rules ordained by brāhmaṇa, a kṣatriya reaches the condition of a śūdra. —*MS* X.43

> The families of Pauṇḍrakas, Oḍras, Draviḍians, Kāmbojas, Yavanas, Śakas, Pāradas, Pahalavas, Cinā, Kirātas, Darads and Khaśas and many others were kṣatriyas, as age by age, they ascended by the virtues of their austerity to high positions, but descended by their sinful conduct to the condition of *vṛṣala* (the status of śūdras). —*MS* X.43-44

The Dravidians were the southerners, Yavanas were Greeks (Ionians), Pauṇḍrakas were the dwellers of southern Bihar and Bengal, Kirātas were the mountain dwellers and Khaśas were living in the mountain region of north India. According to Manu, they were considered as ruling class, but later on, because of their wrong conducts, they were treated as śūdras. These people were fitted into the degraded class. The degraded class was totally based on the non-performance of the prescribed duties of that particular class.

Kings Degraded as Śūdras

Kṣatriyas were given the status of gods and they had the authority over the people as long as they acted as the guardians of law. But if they started sucking the blood of their people their crownship was flung away. Manu has cited many references of different kings who were considered as śūdra kings. The brāhmaṇas were prohibited to dwell in the kingdom of a śūdra king.

> A brāhmaṇa must not dwell in the country ruled by a śūdra king or in the country which is full of unrighteous people.
> —*MS* IV.61

It indicates that the kings not practising righteousness were designated as śūdra kings and were not respected. The kingdom of a śūdra king was always in trouble because of the lack of morality and justice, and naturally, the life of the people living there was never safe. In *Manu-Smṛti* there are references of many well-known kings who were fallen from their status and were known as śūdras.

> King Veṇa was ruined by his bad conduct and also kings Nahuṣa, Sudās, Paijavana, Samukha and Nemi.
>
> —*MS* VII.41

These are the names of the kings who were relegated to the position of śūdras because of their unrighteousness. The story of the King Veṇa is also described in *Harivaṁśa Purāṇa*. Veṇa was king of Atri race and was the grandson of the lord of death (Kāla). He threw his duties to the wind as a king and started establishing an irreligious system of conduct. He also tried to change the ordinances of Vedas and was engaged in all types of lawlessness. The proud king was cursed by the *ṛṣi*s and became the founder of the race of Niṣādas and Dhīvaras, belonging to low caste (see *Mbh* 12.59.99-103). In *Manu-Smṛti* the name of Veṇa appeared as mixed caste (see *MS* X.10).

Another king who received the status of śūdra was Nahuṣa, the grandson of Pururavas. The story of Nahuṣa appeared twice in *Mahābhārata*, once in Vana-Parva and again in Udyoga-Parva. King Nahuṣa was leading a righteous life but after getting the position of Indra (the king of heaven and gods), he was badly addicted to amusement and sensual pleasures and even aspired for Indrāṇī, wife of Indra. The evil-minded king harnessed seven sages to his chariot in the place of horses. His understanding was enveloped in darkness resulting in his downfall.

The name of Sudās, the son of Paijavana, as a śūdra is mentioned in *Mahābhārata*, Śānti-Parva (chap. 60, verses 38-40). This name can also be seen in *Ṛgveda* VII.18, 23-25. Yāska in his *Nirukta* II.24 has also mentioned this name. *Viṣṇu Purāṇa* mentions this name as the descendant of famous King Sagar (*Viṣṇu Purāṇa*, chap. IV). Sudās was a king and his coronation ceremony was performed by Vasiṣṭha, a great sage. Later on, he became the enemy of Vasiṣṭha and killed his son Śakti. Viśvāmitra abandoned him and he was defeated (*ṚV* VII.18.7, 32; *Mbh* I.166-68). Sudās was a mighty king, but because of his unlawful conflict with Vasiṣṭha, a righteous man, he attained the position of a śūdra. The last episode recorded in *Manu-Smṛti* of the king who was thrown to the status of a śūdra is that of King Nemi. This story is described in *Viṣṇu Purāṇa*. Nemi undertook a great sacrifice and out of pride he did not wait for his family priest Vasiṣṭha; Vasiṣṭha cursed him to lose his body; when he died the priest churned his body to produce a son, Janaka of Videha (*Mbh* 13.91; *Devībhāgavata Purāṇa* 6). These are the examples of the kings who lost their position because of their bad conduct and because of them moving away from the path of assigned duties. They were mostly cursed by *ṛṣis* for their immoral behaviour. These kings were the descendants of high and well-known races, but because of their *adhārmika* deeds they were treated as śūdras. Curse was just an instant type of punishment inflicted on them. It is the history of conflict between morality and immorality. These stories help us to understand the fact as to how the kṣatriyas were degraded from second grade to the fourth grade of śūdras.

The degradation was not limited only to brāhmaṇas or to kṣatriyas. A man of any class, not observing the assigned duties, may fall from his class. Manu proclaims:

> One's own duty, even without having any good quality, is better than someone else's duty, which is well done; a man who makes his living by someone else's duty immediately falls from his own class. — *MS* X.97

The allotment of specific duties to different classes was done with the purpose of bringing a harmony and cooperation among the people of the society. Every class of the society depends on another class as the nature of their jobs is different. The harmony among different groups of the society is needed for maintaining the interdependence of the groups and crossing the boundaries of the jobs assigned to different groups may cause error in the management of the whole society. In fact, the classification of duties is aimed at bringing integration between different classes. Therefore, a person who deviates from his duties may harm the whole society and the expulsion of such person becomes inevitable. Manu says:

> He, who does not stand for morning and evening rituals, is to be expelled like a śūdra from every ceremony of the twice-born (*dvija*). — *MS* II.103

The word *dvija* has been used for three upper classes — brāhmaṇas, kṣatriyas and vaiśyas, who have to undergo through *upanayana saṁskāra*. Brāhmaṇas, being the guardians of the society, had the power of degrading other two classes of kṣatriyas and vaiśyas, but they too can be degraded by the society and the king. The degraded persons should not have any place in the community. Manu accepts this tradition when he tells:

> Ignobility, selfishness, savageness, laziness and negligence towards duties indicate that a man is born of a defiled womb.
>
> — *MS* X.58

A child shares the character of both father and mother and may behave just like his parents. The children of the degraded parents may not be righteous and their company may spoil other people living in the community.

> The realm where these caste-debasing mixtures are produced goes rightly and quickly to destruction.
>
> — *MS* X.61

Concept of Anārya

The people of impure origin were regarded as *anārya* or śūdra. The word *anārya* does not mean that they were of different tribe or different origin. Any person not following the law and behaving in an indecent manner was considered as *anārya* or śūdra.

> If a kṣatriya or vaiśya commits adultery with a woman of brāhmaṇa class who is guarded, he should be punished like a śūdra. —*MS* VIII.377

There is no difference between the two words *anārya* and śūdra. Both words are used for a person degraded from his status because of neglecting his duties and ignoring the value system prescribed by Vedas.

Apart from these codes prescribed for the three upper classes separately, there were several other codes of conduct which were essential for every class and failing to that the person of any class may be downgraded to lower class and may be regarded as śūdra. Manu says:

> A twice-born man who does not study Vedas but exerts himself doing something else quickly turns into a śūdra, even while he is alive and his descendants too are degraded. —*MS* II.168

The children of a person who is not observing the duties will surely follow the footsteps of their parents and thus, they will also become śūdras. Vedas were considered as the guideline for the most ideal life. A person not reading Vedas will not be aware of the prescribed value system needed for an ideal life and will not be fit for being included in the higher groups of the society. The purity of the progeny was also needed for maintaining the status of three upper classes. Manu had a firm faith in the hereditary factors involved in determining the personality of a person. That is why rules related to the marriage of three upper classes were rigid. A good marriage can only provide the desired line of descendants.

> A twice-born man marrying a casteless lady out of infatuation surly brings quickly his family and descendants to the status of śūdras. — *MS* III.15

A man can make certain sacrifices only with the assistance of a wife of a proper class. In the absence of a wife of a proper class the sacrifice cannot be performed and even the oblation cannot be offered, which is very much required for the people of higher classes. A person not performing the sacrifices in accordance with the Vedic rites has been considered as śūdra.

> A brāhmaṇa, having taken a śūdra wife to his bed goes to lower class, begotten on her a son is surely deprived of his brāhmaṇahood. — *MS* III.17

A person deprived of his brāhmaṇahood will be put in the category of śūdras. A blameless offspring may only arise from blameless marriage. The blamable child may possess many evils and may not follow the code of conduct designed for three upper classes. Thus, even the wrong marriage may convert anyone to the status of a śūdra. People belonging to the śūdra class cannot adhere to high morals and qualities required for the higher classes because of their sinful and impure nature.

Śūdras were the part of the mixed classes produced by the adultery done by the people of higher classes and by marrying those women who ought not to be married. These acts of upper classes were itself the violation of the code of conduct prescribed for them. Slowly and slowly the number of defaulters of the code of conduct kept on increasing. These people were refused *upanayana* (a ceremony needed for the twice-born men for entering in the *gurukula*), because of their blamable background. The *saṁskāra* of *upanayana* played an important role in the Vedic society. The purpose of this *saṁskāra* was to initiate a *brahmacārī* to the study of Vedas starting with Gāyatrī *mantra* by an *ācārya*. The validity of this *saṁskāra* continued throughout the life of the people of higher classes for all religious ceremonies. The people who could not understand the significance of this *saṁskāra*, because of their sinful nature, were deprived of it. The brāhmaṇas were prohibited to officiate in the *upanayana* ceremony of a śūdra.

> The brāhmaṇas are to be deemed unworthy to partake the oblation to the gods and manes who initiate the people of śūdra class. —*MS* III.156

The denial of *upanayana* to śūdras was on legal and religious grounds and perhaps the highly-intellectual tradition of the society needed that. Higher education or the teaching of Vedas was recommended only to those people who really deserved it and were worthy for that. There is no need of instructing knowledge to a person who does not follow that at all or who cannot make the good use of the earned knowledge. Manu is much concerned about the qualification of the people willing to acquire the higher knowledge.

> A good seed alone, when sown in a good land, is successfully raised, so a son who is born of a noble woman alone deserves complete initiation. —*MS* X.69

> The seed sown in a poor land is destroyed within that very land. —*MS* X.71

The success of the initiation depends on the mental ability of the pupil, which comes through noble birth. The effort of a teacher will be futile by teaching an unworthy student. *Upanayana* had a good deal of spiritual significance and śūdras had no faith in this type of spirituality. Therefore, the *upanayana* was not needed for them. The denial of *upanayana* became the major judging parameter between three upper classes and the śūdras. The disparity mentioned in *Manu-Smṛti* against śūdras should be treated as a punishment inflicted on them, with the purpose of encouraging them to improve themselves.

Status of Śūdras

It is true that because of their incapability, śūdras were subjected to innumerable ignominies, but at the same time they enjoyed a moderate social status. It was the duty of the householder and the king to protect their rights. While mentioning the duties of the householder, Manu says:

> If the vaiśya and śūdra both arrive together as guests, the householder must show mercy towards them and should feed them along with his own dependents. — *MS* III.112

The śūdras, approaching as a guest to the house of any person, were entitled to get the similar respect as a vaiśya guest was getting. The guest belonging to these two classes were treated in the same manner and both of them enjoyed the equal right of being welcomed. It was an earnest duty of the householder to offer food first to the guest even if he is of a low class. Manu advises:

> The husband and wife should eat their food only after serving food to brāhmaṇas and dependents. — *MS* III.116

Social Privileges of Śūdras

As far as the social rights are concerned, the privileges assigned to brāhmaṇas were many. But it does not mean that śūdras were kept without any pretension. The social law and justice provided in *Manu-Smṛti* do not discriminate between a brāhmaṇa and a śūdra. While mentioning the *prāyaścitta* (atonement) for killing a śūdra, Manu says:

> The slayer of the śūdra should practise exactly all those observances prescribed for other three classes for six months

> or he may give a priest ten white cows and a bull.
>
> — *MS* XI.130

Manu has suggested śūdras to serve brāhmaṇas with certain valid reasons:

> A śūdra desiring some means of subsistence may serve kṣatriya or he may support his life by serving some wealthy vaiśya, not for the duty sake but to gain property whereas by serving a brāhmaṇa he gets both. He should serve a brāhmaṇa for seeking heaven and even to be happy in this world. — *MS* X.121-24

This statement clears that śūdras had the right to earn money and property for their own sake. Serving a brāhmaṇa provided śūdras a good company to learn morality and spirituality. They might also get an opportunity to be in close touch with a person of good conduct and to learn the good behaviour directly. The Indian tradition also has given chance to sinful persons to improve themselves, and the improved one has always been considered a virtuous one. Manu states that even of a low class possessing virtues has the right to instruct others.

> A faithful man may receive pure knowledge even from a person of the lowest class, the knowledge of *mokṣa* can even be learnt from a *cāṇḍāla* (lowest class) and jewel of the women even from the impure family. Ambrosia may be extracted even from poison and good advice even from a child. The good advice may be acquired from anybody.
>
> — *MS* II.238-40

Means and Methods for Improving Status

Manu's treatment to śūdras was never one-sided. Manu followed the traditional theory of making everyone an ideal one for making an ideal society. The śūdras were ranked as the lowest and were less privileged. This ranking was never baseless as it was based on the bad conduct and immorality possessed by śūdras. But they were also given ample opportunities for improving their status. Manu says:

> He who is born of a noble man in an ignoble woman might by means of his good qualities become noble, while he who is born of an ignoble man in a noble woman remains ignoble.
> — *MS* X.66

It indicates that in spite of low birth one may improve his status by good deeds. A person of lower birth is also eligible to improve himself by following the path of truth and righteousness. The change of the status of a person of high class to low class and vice versa was quite possible.

> A śūdra may attain the status of a brāhmaṇa and the latter may be categorized as śūdra depending on their deeds. This may also happen with the children of kṣatriyas and vaiśyas.
> — *MS* X.65

Śūdras and Brāhmaṇahood

The real meaning of brāhmaṇahood was to possess the virtues of high standard and not just the birth in the line of a brāhmaṇa. In the same manner the śūdras may reach to the rank of a brāhmaṇa by acquiring the qualities needed for the brāhmaṇahood. Even the degraded kṣatriyas and vaiśyas may get back their respective positions by possessing desired qualifications.

> Those śūdras, who are desirous of performing meritorious acts (*dharma*), know the rules of right and follow the custom of good conduct earn the praise easily even without reciting Vedas.
> — *MS* X.127

The general behaviour of a person has to be noble. His wisdom does not matter much. The criteria for obtaining the higher status were to follow the ideals laid down by the virtuous persons. The practice of tenfold *dharma* has been recognized as the main basis for making anyone virtuous. The person of any class lacking these virtues may be degraded and the adherence of these virtues may upgrade anyone. But these virtues cannot be obtained by a śūdra in a single generation. Manu says:

> If someone born from a brāhmaṇa father and śūdra mother produces a child with someone of the higher class, the lower class reaches the status of higher class after the seventh generation. If a śūdra woman marries a brāhmaṇa and her daughter does the same and so on till the seventh generation, the last generation acquires the brāhmaṇaship.
>
> — see Medhātithi's comm. on *MS* X.65

The same method can be applied to other degraded classes for improving their rank. It was the method or process of transformation of the original character of śūdras towards good moral character. This reference had some valid scientific significance. The genes, responsible for determining a particular character of an individual, keep on changing from generation to generation. The good genes control the good character and bad genes are responsible for bad character. The bad genes can be modified to good genes by providing suitable environment. But it is an extremely slow process. The good marriages for seven generations may transform the bad genes to good genes. The gene–ecological changes are likely to occur after the lapse of a few generations under the influence of environmental conditions. The identity of a śūdra was fully based on his character and if in any case he is in position to change his character, he will no longer be considered a śūdra.

Rationality of Caste System

The classification of the society into different castes was an effort to envisage moral actions for different groups and was based on the requirement of the society. The determination of the class based on birth makes it easy to understand the exact nature of the duties related to that particular line. The social order presented by Manu is based on the concept of determining the exact position of that class in the society. Śūdras were assigned the jobs befitting to their capability. They were put in the separate group to enable them realize their shortcomings and were given chances to improve themselves.

The concept of śūdra as presented in *Manu-Smṛti* is fully based on the theory of the necessity of the adherence to the assigned duties. Manu appears to be very strict for efficient performance of the duties prescribed for different classes. The negligence of duties cannot be tolerated in any case. The people moving away from the path of their duties were dealt seriously and were degraded or amalgamated as śūdras. It became necessary to allot them the jobs to look after the upper classes as they were not able to do other jobs. Certain codes were also prescribed to make them realize the reasons for their degraded position in the society. Nevertheless, it needs to be emphasized in no uncertain terms that they too enjoyed many benefits given to the upper classes. They were not left unattended and the community was keen to look after them. They too were given all possible opportunities for their mental uplift and were given chances to transform themselves into ideal human beings by acquiring high levels of conduct. They were also given the chance to become a brāhmaṇa, which was considered the most honoured position in the society. It is abundantly clear that the class system recognized in the ancient Indian society was not as rigid as it is made out to be. It was the best possible combination of strict rules and certain amount of flexibility. The philosophy and doctrine of *karma-yoga* underlying the class system must not be lost sight of while analysing Manu's concept of śūdras in his monumental treatise.

7

Status of Women in Manu-Smṛti

Women in Vedic Period

THE philosophical, social, religious and political concepts depicted in *Manu-Smṛti* are fully based on the Vedic concepts. Manu, at the beginning of his work, has clearly mentioned that Vedas are the source of all types of knowledge and codes needed to have a desirable life on the earth. Vedas have declared both man and woman as integral part of the society.

> God parted his very body into two, from that came husband and wife. — *BṛUp* 1.4.3

Man and woman are the two divisions of the Cosmic Being and each is incomplete without the other like the two halves of a split pea. The two parts of a spilt pea are complementary to each other. The Vedic literature has maintained the dignity of man and woman equally. There is no element of difference of man and woman at the level of *ātman*. *Ātman* is beyond the gender distinction. Manu follows the same concept.

> The cosmic *Puruṣa* divided his own body into two and became a man with one half and a woman with the other half. In woman lord emitted *virāja*. — *MS* I.32

The whole world came out of *virāja*. The Vedic literature has taught us the lesson of happy inter-human relations, so that every person in the society gets his share of delight. As we come across the Vedic hymns, we find that women of the

Vedic India figure as the most civilized, cultured and enlightened beings. There are numerous references to various women composers of the Vedic hymns known as *ṛṣikā*s. Vāk (*ṚV* X.125), Śacī (*ṚV* X.159), Aditi (*ṚV* X.72), Dakṣiṇā (*ṚV* X.107), Indrāṇī (*ṚV* X.86, *AV* XX.126), Yamī (*ṚV* X.10.1) and Lopāmudrā (*ṚV* I.179) are the main *ṛṣikā*s referred in Vedas.

Women in Brāhmaṇa and Upaniṣadic Periods

Women were given appreciable status during the Brāhmaṇa and Upaniṣadic periods. The famous dialogue that took place between Yājñavalkya and his wife Maitreyī reflects the intellectual height of Maitreyī (see *BṛUp* 2.4.3). Gārgī, daughter of Vacaknu, who was the great lady philosopher and excellent speaker of Upaniṣad, had tremendous knowledge of the most difficult subjects like the nature of *Brahman*, the creation and space–time continuum. All these examples are the proof of the true status of the Vedic women. *Taittirīya Brāhmaṇa* states that a husband must be accompanied by his wife in all sacrifices (3.3.3.5). *Jaiminīya Brāhmaṇa* also expresses the same view (1.86). *Śatapatha Brāhmaṇa* comments that wife is the half part of any sacrifice (1.9.2.3 and 1.3.1.12).

Manu had before him the great tradition of glorified women and he has considered them the very spirit of the society. He was also aware of the potentiality preserved in the personality of a woman. He followed the footsteps of Vedas and has accorded equal importance to the creation of a woman. Manu examined carefully the role of a woman in the family and in society. Thus he tried to deal with the status of women from all possible angles. *Manu-Smṛti* contains a vivid account of the position of women in the family, her married life, her relation with husband, her public life, social rights, laws related to her and her right to property. One has to analyse all these points in a critical and fair manner for determining Manu's views on women. One should not stick to a single statement without thinking the reference and context and should not reach to any conclusion in a hurry. Many a time single word gets interpreted in a wrong way and changes the whole concept. It is not very easy to catch hold of author's intention for using a particular word. There should be an open-mindedness for interpreting any concept presented by any author. Manu had before him the ideal and grand picture of women presented by the Vedic literature. Being the faithful follower of Vedas, he had no intention of deviating from the path shown by Vedas. Manu has never discriminated between a daughter and a son.

> A son is just like ones self and a daughter is equal to a son.
> — *MS* IX.130

Pleasant Picture of Woman in Manu-Smṛti

In fact, Manu had a real pleasant, tender and beautiful picture of a woman. While dealing with the subject of four stages of human life, he makes it mandatory for every person to marry to a suitable girl and to enjoy the life in a righteous manner. The householder has to bear lots of responsibilities of his own family and also of the society. He needs to have a partner capable enough to walk side by side and ready to get herself associated with her husband's duties. Manu had given emphasis on marrying a beautiful girl:

> A man should marry a girl who does not lack any part of her body and who has a pleasant name, who walks like a goose or an elephant, and has slender hair locks, whose teeth are not big and who has delicate limbs. — *MS* III.10

Perhaps Manu was inspired by the female and divine beauty of Goddess Uṣas as portrayed in *Ṛgveda*. The picture painted of a woman in *Manu-Smṛti* is of an ideal nature. Manu was in favour of a wife who would devote her maximum time for household and other activities. She should always be by the side of her husband and should advise him in all of his deeds. It was necessary that husband and wife should stay together in taking care of the daily routine designed for a householder. That is why Manu did not like the idea of marrying a girl without having a brother as she might be an appointed daughter (see *MS* III.11). This reference also can be found in *Ṛgveda.* Women were regarded as the goddesses of the household. It was the time when women were required to take full care of the family members and the society. The population was scanty and men were in good demand for outdoor jobs. The outdoor life used to be tough and was not very comfortable for most of the women. Therefore the birth of a worthy son was regarded as the highest blessing for a household. The marriage became an important part of womanhood. Manu was more particular about the marriage codes to be followed among brāhmaṇas and kṣatriyas. These two higher castes were the main pillars of the society and were responsible for two important jobs — learning/teaching and governance, respectively. He did not give much attention towards the marriage codes of vaiśyas and śūdras. Manu had much faith in heredity as that might help in the protection of tradition and might maintain the level of the efficiency required for the jobs like learning and administration. Manu emphasized that Brāhmaṇas and Kṣatriyas must retain the quality of the progeny, and for this reason, the marriage with in the same caste became a must for them. It was a patriarchal society and the father had the power of taking decision on daughter's marriage. The maiden girls got loving care of their parents. Daughter's marriage used to be a celebration for the family. Manu insisted that a girl should be honoured in her father's house and even in her in-laws' house.

> Women are to be honoured and adorned by father, brother, husband and even by brothers-in-law. It is the way to achieve prosperity. — *MS* III.55

Father was responsible to choose a worthy husband for his daughter. The daughter should be given only to a suitable husband. Manu insists:

> Every man should give his daughter in marriage to an excellent youth of the same caste. —*MS* IX.88

The self-choice of the husband was allowed in certain conditions. In case there is no one to arrange for her marriage, the girl should not remain unmarried; she may marry on her own.

> A girl having reached the age of puberty may wait for the marriage for three years, but at the end she may marry on her own. —*MS* IX.90

A girl had the right to choose a husband on her own. If, because of any reason, the father was not in position to arrange a suitable husband for his daughter, the daughter had the freedom to choose a husband of her choice.

> If she herself selects a husband, when she has not been given one, she commits no error, nor does the man whom she selected. —*MS* IX.91

Institution of Marriage

The institution of marriage was considered the key to a happy and wealthy life and therefore much importance was given to marrying a girl to a worthy man. Manu says:

> It is better to keep a daughter at home till death than to give her to a suitor lacking in qualities. —*MS* IX.89

It is a clear indication that a girl was never a burden for her parents and for the family. Parents and family members always desired to provide a secured and happy future to the girls. Women were to be taken care and they deserved everyone's attention.

> Deities delight in a place where women are revered, but where the women are not revered all rites are fruitless.
>
> — *MS* III.56

Manu suggested eight types of marriages (see *MS* III.21). But he himself does not appreciate all types of marriages. Marriage is an institution where two families come together amicably and wish a prosperous future for the newly-wed couple. There is no room for any type of conflict or disagreement. It has to be mutual for the sake of the future of the married couple. The nature of the marriage is going to have an impact on the happenings in this birth and even in the next birth. It may have a direct impact on the progeny. Thus the type and process of marriage were important. In most types of marriages prescribed by Manu, women had the right to demand gifts from husbands. In *āsura* style of marriage a suitor can marry a maiden after having presented wealth voluntarily to girl's father or to the girl herself (see *MS* III.31). It seems that this type of marriage was prevailing at that time. But Manu himself did not give much importance to this type of marriage. He has forbidden brāhmaṇas to go for this type of marriage. For brāhmaṇas "the gift of maiden by pouring out water alone is the most approved marriage". As brāhmaṇas are entitled to lead the most pious life, they have to be careful from the very beginning of their married life.

Though the final decision of marrying a daughter to someone was taken by her father, it was a must to seek daughter's acceptance. The performance of the marriage took place only after getting daughter's consent. Manu has condemned the *rākṣasa* and *paiśāca* type of marriages where a crying and lamenting girl was taken away forcibly. "This type of marriage will give birth to a cruel and untruthful son" (*MS* III.41). A truthful son can only be begotten by a happy and satisfied mother.

> The son born of a *brāmha* marriage will be sanctified by spiritual pre-eminence and will be esteemed by learned men. He will be good looking, endowed with the quality of lucidity, rich and famous, religious and will enjoy the life for hundred years. — *MS* III.39-40

Blameworthy marriages bring forth blameworthy progeny, and with blameless marriage, where there is an agreement between bride and groom, comes a blameless progeny. This statement clearly supports the view that the desire of a girl for her marriage should be given priority by her father and relatives. The daughter should be sent to her husband's house in a graceful and humble manner.

> No learned father should take any price for his daughter, no matter how poor he is, for a man who, out of greed, extracts a bride price, would be selling his child like a pimp. — *MS* III.51

Relation between Man and Woman

The relation between man and woman is the very basis of a successful married life. In Indian tradition the institution of marriage is based on lawfulness, trust and spirituality. It is the most sacred relation based on the purity of understanding and fairness of thoughts. It is a divine relation where man and woman live together and enjoy the life in a religious manner. It is a mutual relation without any selfish motive. Manu was also in favour of a conjugal married life. He had few ideas for making the married life peaceful and free of jerks. No one likes to be over-burdened with too many responsibilities and works. Everyone is having a limited strength and capacity to toil. The prolonged or intensive work may surely irritate the person engaged in the work and may cause rift in the relation with the partner. In order to avoid this situation Manu wanted to introduce a division of labour between husband and wife. As a man has to go out for livelihood, it is a must for a woman to stay back at home for taking proper care of children and other household affairs. Manu has declared that the mother only can be the best teacher for sowing the seed of righteousness in a child. The long absence of mother from house may affect the future of the child. A child, up to certain age, needs full care and supervision. Thus, women were asked to stay back at home. But it should not be interpreted that women were illiterate. They were surely well-versed in rituals and rites as they accompanied their husbands for different sacrificial purposes. Even at home they were responsible to educate their children and look after the finances of the household. The main duty of a woman was to be faithful to her husband. But at the same time a woman was entitled to receive love and care from all quarters of the house. A wife was addressed as *gṛhasvāminī* (mistress of the house). It was a must for a husband to pay respect and honour to his wife. He should acknowledge his wife's contribution to the family and society and to his own career. The husband must be aware of the fact that all his goods will not bear any fruit, if his wife is unhappy.

> Homes that are cursed by a woman of the family who has not been treated with reverence, are completely destroyed, as if struck down by a witchcraft. —*MS* III.59

A sad and distressed wife can never look after the family affairs in a desired manner. Her mental agony may affect her physical health. What a person can expect from a sick wife? A dejected and disheartened woman can never do the allotted jobs faithfully. A woman should always be in a delightful state and should maintain a mental equilibrium. That is the secret of a happy family. In order to have a harmonious family, both husband and wife should take proper care of each other in an honest manner and have to be faithful to each other.

> In the family where husband is pleased with wife and so also the wife with husband, truly the prosperity is ever firm there. — *MS* III.60

A delighted wife will perform all her duties in a successful way and may take care of each and every member of the family.

> If a wife is pleased the whole family is pleased, if she is not pleased, all are not pleased. — *MS* III.62

Here at this point, one thing has to be noticed that Manu gave much emphasis on the mutual behaviour of man and woman. The married life is a phase in life where both husband and wife have to move together and must develop similar ideology. It is natural to have differences of opinion at certain points. But that situation can be resolved in a soft manner. Disloyalty and unfaithfulness must be discarded and should be replaced by mutual trust.

> The mutual absence of infidelity must continue till death. — *MS* IX.101

> A man and woman who have performed the Vedic ritual should always try not to become separated and unfaithful to one another. — *MS* IX.102

Life of Woman after Marriage

Married life generates a strong emotional attachment. It is not easy to break, and breaking it will bring in many types of emotional challenges. In order to avoid this situation the couple must have trust in each other. This will provide them a sense of forgiveness on petty issues and will ease the tension, if it arises.

> When a woman is joined with her husband in accordance with the rules, she takes on very same qualities that he has, just like a river flowing down in the ocean. — *MS* IX.22

The happiness of women is also necessary for the smooth sailing of religious rites. Extending the family was also considered as the main duty of the householder and for that also women have to be kept delightful and calm. The women have to be kept satisfied at all costs.

> A husband gets his wife as a gift from the gods, and not just by his own wish; by pleasing the wife, he is pleasing the gods. — *MS* IX.95

Women are usually fond of gifts and ornaments.

> The man who wishes to be prosperous should always revere the woman with ornaments, clothes and food at celebrations and festivals. — *MS* III.59

Controversial Remarks in Manu-Smṛti

The most controversial remark against Manu is that he was not in favour of giving independence to women. In the fifth chapter of *Manu-Smṛti* there is a statement given by Manu that women do not deserve independence. A woman is an object of being guarded at every stage of her life.

> Woman as young depends on her father, when married on her husband, and at old age on her son. — *MS* V.149

> A woman should not try to separate herself from her father, her husband or her sons, for her separation from them will make her own and her father's family contemptible.
> — *MS* V.150

This statement has often been wrongly interpreted. The word *svātantrya* is derived from the verbal root *tant*. This verbal root is having few meanings. This root also means "to support" or "to maintain". The word *svātantrya* also contains the meaning "self-dependent". Manu, whenever he talks about the dependence of women, has certain points in his mind. The dependence of women indicated by Manu does not mean that a woman should be kept in a prison house. Women are timid biologically and cannot perform every type of job. Second, they need support as they are staying back at home and looking after the household. Someone has to take care of her needs and has to give her financial support. The independence of women depends very much on the state of security provided by the society. Many a time, even in the present-day society, the girls needed to be escorted because of prevailing crimes. Everyday we come across many cases of crimes against women. Women cannot move freely everywhere. Manu has laid much emphasis on the protection of women. Protection was something similar to honour accorded to women especially of high castes. He blames father, mother or brother who cannot give protection to their daughters/sisters.

> The son who does not protect his mother after the death of his father is surely blamable. —*MS* IX.4

Here one more thing comes to light that sons were given the charge of looking after his widowed mother, and so, the widows were not helpless and were not forced to die. Widows had a comfortable life with their sons after the death of their husbands. In fact, it was the duty of a son to take care of his mother. The dependence of a woman does not mean that she was restrained from doing anything. Manu says:

> Women were not guarded by men howsoever cleverly they attempted it. Those women who guard themselves are alone well protected. —*MS* IX.12

> No man is able to guard women entirely by force.
> —*MS* IX.10

Here, guarding means the protection that women must get when they are in public places. As the duty of a woman was to keep herself occupied in saving and spending money, taking care of the servants and supporting staff, looking after children and other family members, she hardly had any time left for doing outdoor activities and she needed someone to help her for her outdoor needs. She was also supposed to perform all her duties with full concentration. Her movement outside the house may create trouble to all the people living under her care. Another reason for giving protection to a woman was to safeguard the progeny. Woman brings forth the progeny. By guarding women, progeny can be guarded well and the purity of the offspring can be maintained.

> Since the woman wishes to produce a son like her husband whose love she shares, a man should guard the woman with care so that he may obtain the purity of the race.
>
> — *MS* IX.9

Woman as Mother

The purity of progeny was necessary for the proper follow-up of the strict duties prescribed for different sections of the society. Worthy and able children were also needed for the continuity of tradition and for taking care of the family members and the society. Everything was associated with the birth of an able son. It was considered identical to true happiness. Motherhood was taken as a real boon for a woman and the birth of a son was regarded as the blessing of god. Thus the mother became the most precious one for the whole society and she needed all care and protection.

> When women are found blessed with offspring, worthy of honour, true lamp in the house, then there is not the slightest distinction between a woman and the goddess of prosperity.
>
> — *MS* IX.26

Women are auspicious and blessed as they bring delight to the house by giving birth to a child. The women were regarded precious as they have to train the child in his infancy. A child has to be trained for the future life right from the childhood.

> A son has to be well-trained as he only can take his ancestors to heaven. —*MS* IX.28

An able mother can save her progenitors from hell by giving a good training to her sons. For this reason Manu has advocated that a wife and husband must be faithful to each other. As the married life was taken as a divine one, the chastity was considered as the best virtue for a woman.

> Even a widow, firm in chastity, though childless, goes to heaven. —*MS* IX.160

> She, who has left her inferior husband and attaches herself to a superior man, is blamable and is called *parapūrvā*.
> —*MS* V.163

A husband also has to follow the same rule. The success of a married life depends on how both husband and wife are going to present themselves to each other. The superiority of any of the two can never be imposed. Both man and woman have to understand the very significance of married life and have to stick to virtues and morality. They have to put up their best for the sake of themselves, for their children and even for society. Their conduct is going to be reflected through their children and they are responsible for the success of their children. Any wrong step taken by any of the parents may have life-long impression on children. Thus they have to restrict themselves to morality needed for a married life. It is the gist of Manu's idea of a married life.

Modern India has become a country of paradoxes. We adore many goddesses and pay honour and regard to them. The Śakti cult is gaining considerable momentum and many new goddesses are emerging everyday. But we hold an entirely different view when it comes to the female child in the household. Even now the girls are not getting their due share of attention and care. The laws of the land have granted equal fundamental rights to females, and many provisions have been made to empower them but it is not very easy to avail the benefits of those provisions. As we turn the pages of *Manu-Smṛti*, we find that Manu was quite liberal in granting fundamental rights to women. In spite of being surrounded by many restrictions, women were permitted to enjoy many privileges given to them by the society. In many cases women get the equal share of rights. The marriage was considered as a sacred institution and it was desired for both man and wife to live together and to enjoy the life at their best. But in case, it is impossible for husband and wife to live together because of certain reasons, they can seek separation. Manu had permitted the separation of husband and wife in case of infidelity and impotency. The main purpose of marriage is to provide a happy and peaceful life to both husband and wife. But if they are not happy and the life has become miserable because of some reason, it is better to be separated. The dissolution of marital life, which may be called divorce, may have some advantages. It is not advisable to lead a suppressed and disgusted life and to suffer from mental disorder. One should not forget that life is a rare gift given to us by the Almighty and everyone is entitled to live in a befitting manner. The provision of divorce may be treated as an advancement of social values, which allows supercession of a wife. But the superceded did not lose any of her right as a wife. Manu has taken much care of handling this situation. The husband cannot abandon his wife just because he does not like her; the divorce has to be granted only on genuine grounds.

> A husband was allowed to set aside his wife only in the case when she is careless to her duties, drunkard or troubled by any disease, and that also only one year after the marriage has been performed. —*MS* IX.77

The wife had equal right of setting aside her husband in many cases.

> A woman can leave her husband if he is crazy, insane, impotent, or inflicted with an evil disease. — *MS* IX.79

The women were not allowed to go out and to work for their livelihood. Therefore, it was the earnest duty of a husband to take full care of their all needs. Women should not be deprived of their financial necessities because of their being non-earning members. Husbands were not supposed to go for a long trip without arranging the means of sustenance for their wives. The dependence of the wife on her husband had no evil motive as the husband had the whole and sole responsibility of taking full care of his wife.

> A man may go away on a journey or on business only after he has established a livelihood for his wife; for even a steady woman could be corrupted if she is starving for lack of livelihood. — *MS* IX.74

In case the husband is not in a position of providing livelihood, a woman may take up small jobs.

> If the husband goes away on a journey after providing a livelihood for his wife, she should subject herself to restraints in her life, but if he goes away on a journey without providing the means of sustenance for his wife, the wife is allowed to make her living on her own. — *MS* IX.75

Women were free to decide their future in the absence of their husbands. They had full right to take care of their needs. The husbands were not permitted to stay away from their houses without any genuine reason. The married life is meant for living together. A lonely wife may have to face countless problems. This situation should not be continued for a longer period. Manu gave liberty to women to choose their way if husbands leave them for a longer period without any substantial reason.

> A man should be waited by his wife for eight years if he has gone out for religious purposes, she should wait for six years if the husband moves away to attain wisdom and glory, but she is supposed to wait only for three years if the husband is out just for love sake. — *MS* IX.76

At this point it is clear that a woman was free to decide her future and was permitted to remarry for starting a new life. A husband cannot keep a wife waiting for a long period for superficial reasons. A woman too is entitled to think of her life and to take decisions needed for her future life. She also had the right to relish her requisitions just like her male partner. A husband should not disrespect his extremely sick wife.

> If a woman, who is kind and well-behaved becomes ill, she should be superceded by a man only after getting permission from her, but she should never be dishonoured. — *MS* IX.82

As the birth of a son was must for a family, even the sick wife will intend that her young husband should marry someone else. Only a wife who is in a position of receiving a selfless and natural love from her husband can take such a decision. It reflects the maturity of the relation that husband and wife have secured through their mutual conduct.

Widow Remarriage, Niyoga and Childless Women

As such, Manu was not in favour of a widow's remarriage. It will not be practically, psychologically or socially feasible for a widow to marry at a late age. She will also be busy with her children and grandchildren, and she herself will not think of remarriage. But Manu has allowed a young widow to remarry.

> If the intended husband of a maiden dies after troth (promise) has been plighted, her own brother-in-law should marry her. — *MS* IX.69

A widow has to depend on her son after the death of her husband. But she may have a difficult situation in the absence of a child, as no one will be there to look after her. Manu has taken a very bold step and has introduced a progressive provision for issueless widows known as *niyoga*. Under this provision a widow may approach her brother-in-law for getting a son.

> When the line of descendants dies out, a widow who has been properly appointed should get the desired children from a brother-in-law or a co-feeding relative. — *MS* IX.59

Manu does not mention the sex of the child. It even may be a girl. The provision of *niyoga* was given for widows so that they also may have someone to support them.

> But when the purpose of *niyoga* with the widow has been completed in accordance with the rules, the two of them should behave towards one another just like *guru* and daughter-in-law. There should not be a sense of lust in *niyoga*. — *MS* IX.63

Manu was able to imagine the plight of a childless woman, not in position to earn her livelihood and has no one to look after her in her late age. This practice was regarded a sacred one as it was performed in accordance with the rules. The society also gave sanction to it as it was a pure act. Widows also got support from the king. It was the duty of the king to look after the welfare of women and was to stand by their side whenever they needed it.

> The property of a barren woman, or the one who had no sons, or no family or is a widow, or is seriously sick, should be protected by the king. — *MS* VIII.28

Women have to be treated in a fair manner. No one has any right to relinquish women from their possessions.

> If any of the relative dares to grab the property of a woman, he is liable to be punished. —*MS* VIII.29

Apart from these provisions women were given many facilities and preferences. They enjoyed many social securities.

> A woman, more than two months advanced in her pregnancy, should not be made to pay toll at a ferry. —*MS* VIII.407

Women were also entitled to enter in the court of justice.

> Woman should be witnessed for a woman. —*MS* VIII.68

A woman knows better of a woman, while being appointed as a witness she may be more authentic and closer to the fact. Even for other court cases the credibility of a woman was much high.

> In the absence of qualified witness the evidence may be presented by a woman. —*MS* VIII.70

Women were entitled to get preference while moving outside the house by other people moving together (see *MS* II.138).

> The host, without any hesitation should feed newly-wed woman, small girls and pregnant ladies just after the guests. —*MS* III.114

Duties and rights should always move together. Only a person, who takes care of his duties earnestly, deserves the rights. Manu, who has constituted the social codes, was quite conscious of maintaining a balance between duties and rights. He had never ignored the rights of women. While allotting duties to women, he looks rigid. But it is not only in the case of women. In order to introduce a righteous society he wanted that every member of the society must observe the duties rigorously. There was a mutual dependence of all sections in the society. Any person falling from the path of his duties may cause hindrance in the proper functioning of the society. Woman, being the mistress of the house, had greater responsibility for the smooth functioning and progress of the family and the community.

Strī-dhana

Coming down to the provisions of inheritance by women, it may be said that Manu followed the rules formed by his predecessors and recommended that the property has to be divided between the sons. But it does not mean that he has removed the daughters totally from the list of inheritance. There is a very substantial provision of *strī-dhana* which only can be inherited by daughters. It was their personal possession and no one had any right to claim that. It was a customary duty of a father, mother, brother and husband to offer gifts consisting of money or ornaments to a woman from time to time. In fact, it was needed to keep her happy. It was also a practice to give some wealth or property to daughters at the time of marriage. This type of wealth was considered as *strī-dhana* and it was only meant for the daughter.

> The person who takes away women's property goes to hell.
> — *MS* III.52

> The wealth given at the time of marriage used to be merely honorific and mercy to the maiden. — *MS* III.54

As such also, every Vedic ritual was always supported by some gift meant for the deity. Further, Manu describes that women had six types of properties.

> That which is given over marriage fire, which is given at marriage procession or as a token of affection, given for an act of love, received from mother, father and brother is called the sixfold property of a woman. — *MS* IX.194

The gifts received from husband are also the part of *strī-dhana*. It is solely the daughter's share. This property cannot be shared by sons or by anyone else.

> Whatever separate property the mother has, is the share of her daughter. — *MS* IX.131

It seems that Manu was more liberal to daughters for granting *strī-dhana*. As the daughters were not getting any share from their father's wealth, at least they may have mother's wealth. In modern law mother's property has to be shared by both, sisters and brothers. Sisters alone cannot claim mother's property. In fact, *strī-dhana* was meant for the security of the woman, which she can use in her rainy days. Woman may be helpless if sons deny to look after their mothers after their father's death.

> The same security she can transfer to her daughters by offering them her personal wealth. If there is any common property of husband and wife, both brothers and unmarried sisters may have equal share. — *MS* IX.192

The daughters of a married woman were entitled to get something from their grandmother's share.

> Something should even be given to the daughter of a married daughters out of the estate of their maternal grandmother, through affection and according to their deserts.
> — *MS* IX.193

This practice exists even now in few tribal communities and in the villages in certain parts of India. The women had the freedom of having ornaments and any other valuables with themselves; it was their right. Even husband cannot take the valuables possessed by his wife. Children also cannot grab their mother's wealth as long as she is alive.

> The heir should not share the valuables or the jewellery worn by a woman during her husband's lifetime; if they share them, they will suffer. — *MS* IX.200

These provisions were made just to secure the life of women and to give them something for emergency. Married women need to wear ornaments as long as their husbands are alive; depriving them from ornaments will be inauspicious. This reference also proves that women used to possess plenty of ornaments and were wearing them even inside the house. In case a man is having more than one wife, the property of a brāhmaṇa wife in certain cases may go to her daughter.

> If a man gifts something to his brāhmaṇa wife and he is not having any child from other wives, the wealth will be inherited by the daughter of the brāhmaṇa wife.
> — *MS* IX.198

The brāhmaṇa wife is supposed to be more virtuous because of her righteous lineage. Therefore, she and her daughter have to be rewarded by her husband.

Old women also enjoyed certain rights pertaining to inheritance.

> The mother should receive the inheritance of a childless son, and if the mother is dead the father's mother should take the property. — *MS* IX.217

The significance of this provision was to help the old lady staying alone after the death of her husband and grandson and having no one to take care of. The childless widows also enjoyed some relaxations.

> The widow of a man who has died childless should adopt a son from the same lineage and should hand over to him her property. — *MS* IX.190

Many a time, it happens that after the death of a childless man the property is taken through fraud by someone else and the poor widow is left having nothing. This situation can be avoided if the widow adopts a son and gives him the property. In the old age she may even have to look after herself.

Provision of Putrikā

There is one more provision made by Manu which goes in favour of women. The birth of a son is considered important as he has to give offerings to the manes. But a person not having a son may transfer this right to the son of his daughter and may hand over his all wealth to his daughter and her son. This provision was termed as *putrikā*. It is an agreement between daughter and father when the daughter's son becomes his son. A man without a son is entitled to give his all property to his daughter assuming that daughter's son will give offerings to the manes. Manu says in firm words:

> A man with no son may make his female child *putrikā*, an appointed daughter by means of this formula: whatever children are born to her will offer the refreshment for the manes and the dead family members. — *MS* IX.127

A man has to say to his son-in-law:

> I am giving my married and auspicious brotherless daughter to you and the son born from her will take the place of my son.

It seems that Manu himself has recommended this idea as he has quoted many Vedic examples where many kings had taken up the advantage of *putrikā*.

> In ancient times Dakṣa (the lord of creatures) himself, created appointed daughters in order to increase his dynastic line. He gave ten daughters to Dharma, thirteen daughters to Kaśyapa and twenty-seven to King Soma, with honour and affectionate heart. Who else can take the property when a daughter just like father's own soul is standing here.
>
> — *MS* IX.127-28

(The story of Dakṣa's daughters (*Mbh.* Ādi Parva, 75.6-8) and the story of Manu and his sons (Vana Parva 221.4-15) are mentioned in *Mahābhārata*. The daughters that Dakṣa gave to moon are the constellations of lunar mansions.). The son born of daughter should have all the rights of a son:

> Daughter's son may inherit the entire property of his maternal grandfather and he must give two balls (*piṇḍa*) at the ceremony for the dead, one for his own father and another for his mother's father. —*MS* IX.132

When Manu says that daughters are just like one's own self, he means that there is similar blood relation with daughter as it is with son. In the absence of a son only daughter can take care of her father and mother and no one else.

> There is no distinction between son and daughter's son in worldly matters according to law, as the father of one and the mother of other were born from the same body.
>
> —*MS* IX.133

Yājñavalkya in *Mitākṣarā* has also supported the provision of *putrikā* (see 2.218). There is no apparent reason for discriminating between daughter and son as they are born from the same parents and heredity is also the same.

The laws of inheritance accorded to daughters as propounded by Manu are quite rational. Though apparently, she is not getting the lion's share in father's property, she is entitled to inherit many other things. Giving life-long security to women was the main aim of Manu and that he had accorded to women in so many other ways. Modern law has provided the equal right to property to both daughter and son. But it is just in law books. Daughters rarely go to claim that. The demand of the property by a sister may create a conflict with her brother(s) and this may spoil the pleasant relationship between them. These are very ticklish matters and the provision of law is not going to be of much use. The good training given by the parents to their children and children's own attitudes for other family members may be of more use.

Harmony among sisters and brothers is more important than anything else.

Punishment for Crime against Women

The biggest problem the society is facing at present is the increasing crime against women. No matter how influential, educated or financially independent the women are, they become the victim of some undesirable incidents. Law books contain many laws to avert crime against women, but in reality, the crime graph is moving up. The main reason is the weak implementation of laws and lack of infliction of harsh punishment on the perpetrators of crime against women. Manu suggested strong steps for checking crimes against women. Women, being the object of reverence, should be free of any type of fear from any side. In *Manu-Smṛti* we come across many laws framed for the safety of women. The abduction or kidnapping of women, adultery, harassment, murder, rape, stealing women's wealth were considered serious crimes and strict laws were put in place for punishing those who committed such crimes.

> Daughter is the supreme object of pity; therefore if someone is abused by her, one should always bear it without getting heated up by the fever of resentment. — *MS* IV.185

It shows that everyone has to be considerate towards women. Even her harshness should be taken lightly. A woman may face harassment even inside the house by her husband and by other family members.

> If a man, out of hatred, says of a virgin that "she is not a virgin" and cannot show her flaw, he should be fined by 100 *paṇa*s, even without having the details of girl's flaw.
> — *MS* VIII.225

Many a time in order to get rid of the wife with some motive, a husband blames her for adultery. Women and their family members, who wish to protect them, are usually shy of explaining personal things to everyone. Even they hesitate to move the court of law. No one should be allowed to exploit this situation. There was no place for adultery in Manu's code. No third person was allowed to enter in between the relation of wife and husband.

> If men persist in seeking intimate contact with other man's wife, the king should brand them with punishments that inspire terror and banish them. — *MS* VIII.352

Seeking intimate contact with other man's wife is a corrupt practice and may invite lots of repercussions. It is going to have a bad impact on a healthy relation needed between husband and wife and may create a problem even for the society. Many a time people think that it is their personal issue and there is no need for others to create fuss. But it is a wrong notion. Even the personal action of a man may have adverse effect on the society. The law has to keep an eye on these offences and must not allow the recurrence of these crimes.

> If a man who has been accused of such offences carries on the same offence, he should pay a fine. — *MS* VIII.355

Manu has not allowed any type of sexual misconduct.

> Speaking to someone's wife at a bathing place, in a wilderness or in a forest, or at the confluence of rivers, playing around with her, touching her ornaments or clothes, sitting on a couch with her are sexual misconducts.
> — *MS* VIII.357-58

Manu has dealt with rape cases very strictly. The rape causes mental and physical agony for the girl involved and even to her parents. It closes all avenues of progress for women. It is a shame for a cultured society. The men involved in rape cases deserve very harsh punishment.

> The man, who corrupts the unwilling virgin, should instantly suffer corporal or capital punishment.
>
> — *MS* VIII.364

There is no need of filing a case in the court or collecting evidence. It is the most heinous crime and needs to be smashed instantly. The action of rape is the outcome of man's blind passion, arrogance and madness. These vices may prove to be very harmful for the society. Such a person may commit many other crimes, as he is cruel and violent. He is in no way different than a demon.

> If a man in his arrogance overpowers a virgin and rapes her, two of his fingers should be immediately cut off and he should pay a fine of 600 *paṇa*s. — *MS* VIII.367

The punishment in the form of fine may not solve this type of crime. The affluent people pay the heavy amount of fine and walk away with dignity. It is a very dangerous state. That is why Manu has prescribed physical and capital punishment. Manu thinks that this type of behaviour is an addiction. A person, committing this type of crime gets addicted and does not know what exactly he is doing. The society has to ward off such an element by all means.

> Double punishment has to be given to a man who has already been convicted and does the same crime again within a year. The evil man can be burnt on a red-hot iron-bed and people should pile up wood on it and the evil-doer should be burnt up. — *MS* VIII.372

Manu advised that the culprit should be punished publicly. It will generate a sense of fear in others and they will come to know that the person involved in such a crime is going to be punished in a similar manner. Even a brāhmaṇa was not exculpated from punishment for rape.

> Shaving the head is ordained for a priest for raping a girl.
> — *MS* VIII.379

Manu condemned the kidnapping of women. It was considered as a major crime and rigorous punishment was recommended for it.

> The kidnapper of a woman deserves corporal or capital punishment. — *MS* VIII.23

The punishment for crimes against women needs to be very severe as it ruins the life of a woman and makes her totally miserable. Thus the ruler has to take special care for averting it fully. Murdering someone itself is a heinous crime and murdering a woman is the worst. It involves an extreme type of violence and anger. Women as such are not physically strong. Overpowering a woman is a sin.

> A king must punish a person severely who is involved in the murder of a woman, even the supporters helping him for the murder also have to be punished. — *MS* IX.232

The whole idea pertaining to the status of woman as presented in *Manu-Smṛti* is fully based on the teaching of Vedas. Manu framed strict ordinances for both men and women. He never considered women inferior to men in any respect. He formed a tradition of moral conduct for each and every person in the society.

> The moral conduct must have the predominance of *sattva*. It is free of desire and motivated by knowledge. — *MS* XII.89

> The man, who sacrifices the self, equally seeing the self in all living beings and all living beings in the self, becomes independent. — *MS* XII.91

It was the philosophy revealed by Manu in *Manu-Smṛti.* The rules and regulations declared for women had the same base. Virtues and moralities recommended for women were related to the effects of her acts on her future life. Manu wanted to take everyone to the level of supreme conduct which may enable them to reach to perfection. The perfection of a society depends on the perfection of an individual. Manu was a serious advocate of an established order having sharp scope of progress. Perfection is the very base of progress. Women, being the essential part of the community, were equally responsible for bringing all types of progress at individual level and even at social level. A woman should do what is agreeable to her conscience. There is a voice of God within us and one must have the power to listen to that. Any type of status can never be designated by someone else. It can only be acquired by possessing the needed spirit. It is women's force of thought and majesty of vision that may take them at the top of the world. After redeeming the lower nature, one's own impulse may provide the direction to move ahead. If a woman decides to move ahead on her own, no one can stop her.

Conclusion

These days, people have started talking about the status of women across the globe. Everyone talks about gender equality. But it has far-reaching consequences. We had a great tradition of advocating the importance of sex equality and everyone knows it. In order to hide our own mistakes, we start criticizing a particular tradition and try to put all blame to that. Why we cannot have our own tradition by improving the old ones? It is not the good old tradition that is causing obstacles for improving the status of women as they are based on truth. There is no sense of giving more power to anyone of the two sexes. Both of them complement each other and giving more power to one will make other to suffer. That will not be an ideal situation. We have to search out the real reason behind the non-implementation of laws for improving women's status.

Whether we look at the West or the East, the situation is almost the same. We say that we do not have faith in old sayings. But, in fact they are deep-rooted in our blood. Our life is more or less governed by the age-old myths. We are scared to violate those myths and do not bother to go to the underlying reasons. Myths have overpowered the whole subconscious of human being. We think that the violation of myths may have adverse effect. Though even women realize the necessity of improving the status of women, they themselves have not made any serious endeavour for achieving that. Even in the West, the situation is in no way better than any other country in the East. In many of the Western countries even today women are discriminated against in several spheres of life. Women draw less money for the same work in comparison to their male counterparts. The girls do not get the due share of the inheritance in the absence of a male child. The desire for a male child is also common among women. The concept of the difference between the jobs to be carried out by the males and females still dominates the scene. Women have taken it for granted that there are certain jobs meant only for them and they have to do that.

If you compare this situation of status of women in the West, perhaps, we are in a better position. Our scriptures have handled the whole issue in a reasonable manner. Our seers have given perfectly equal status to women. They have inspired us to create a society where the dignity of both men and women can be established at par with each other. It was the height of human evolution when our great sages had conceived that *ātman* is beyond gender distinction. If we really want to manifest this concept in our society, we have to change our attitude towards women. We have forgotten the tradition of women and their achievements and how they were in a position to stand side by side with males. It is apparent that modern Indian society has not granted the due status to women. The discrimination has paralysed the life of a women. They are talented and are capable of doing many things at par with men. But they are not getting proper opportunities which they should get.

We are living in the age of science and consider ourselves developed or progressive. But how can a society progress when half of the population is lagging behind. Even now we are governed by ignorance and superstitions. The whole situation can be transformed by introducing the messages passed to us by our ancient seers supported by modern scientific thoughts. Even women too have to come forward and justify their capability. No one can help them improve their existing status if they themselves do not take initiative. They themselves have to be convinced that they are equal to males and they have to move forward. Their limitations are also their own creations. There is a need for the application of old philosophy in a practical manner. The fulfilment of the life depends on a person's conduct and virtues. Women have to attain that stage of fulfilment through their deeds and training which they have acquired from the age-old tradition. Dependence is always bad as it lowers the self-confidence of individuals and crushes their reasoning power. A dependent person takes everything in a casual manner thinking that this thing can be done by someone else and his desired activities are ceased. An excess of dependence makes a man dull and lifeless. No one respects such a person and thus the person loses his dignity. The loss of dignity is the loss of existence. On the contrary, the independent person is free to use his mental faculties as well as physical activities freely. He can make the best use of his wisdom given by God. We should not forget that God has bestowed intelligence on everyone without the discrimination of gender. The women also possess the same level of intelligence. They have to make the proper use of that and should not be dependent on someone else?

Women, by not using their own brain, are disgracing the womanhood, a precious gift of God. They themselves may achieve the height of glory by their own virtuous deeds and may show the light to the rest of the world. Manu wanted to make every woman perfect and powerful and that was the reason why he accorded woman the status of Lakṣmī, the goddess of prosperity.

8

Manu's Concept of Prāyaścitta and its Significance in Maintaining Harmony and Peace

Meaning of "Peace" and "Harmony"

THE equivalent words for harmony and peace in Sanskrit are *sadbhāvanā* and *śānti*. The word *sadbhāvanā* means "amiableness to everyone" and word *śānti* denotes "cessation of hostility and passion". Every individual is an integral part of the society. Thus his every action may have its impact on the whole society. Being a member of the society one has to behave in such a manner that others may not be harmed. Hence, a person is supposed to take care of each and every member of the community. Any act which disturbs the tranquillity of the society has to be regarded as a criminal act. The global harmony and peace cannot be achieved unless we shun jealousy, hatred and harshness towards others. These are the root causes of the rising rate of many heinous crimes, which have now reached an alarming level and have disturbed the whole humanity. The misery of common people is beyond imagination. They are losing the sense of security and are living under tremendous pressure. The psycho-phobia generated by the repeated criminal acts has made the people deaf and dumb and has adversely affected their ability and efficiency. This will surely hamper the development of any community.

Every country is well equipped with courts of justice supported by laws of punishment. The crimes are handled employing certain prescribed procedures, which have their own limitations, and punishments are inflicted accordingly. But it is a bitter truth that the prescribed laws of punishments are not good enough to check the animal-like avenging spirit of the offenders. In many cases the offender commits the same crime again even after being punished harshly. Many a time, even the severest punishments fail to create the sense of fear among the offenders. The fear induced through the deterrent and preventive provisions of punishment is not good enough to create a permanent impact on the offender.

Harmony and peace cannot be expected in a society where people do not get speedy and proper justice. The laws of punishment and justice take their own time to pronounce the verdict. The verdict depends on the witnesses and the arguments presented in the court of law, which may or may not be correct. During the course of long court proceedings the criminal commits so many other crimes. Hence, the legal approach to curb crimes may not be a permanent solution, as it does not leave any scope for self-realization by a criminal that he has committed something wrong which may have serious impact on his own life as well as on the whole community. The deep-rooted evils provoking crimes cannot be uprooted permanently until and unless the criminal realizes his shortcomings himself. Keeping in view the temporary impact of regular laws of punishment, *Manu-Smṛti* and other Smṛti *grantha*s have brought in the concept of *prāyaścitta* (atonement) as an alternative and reformative method for averting crime. This concept is an outcome of the effort for correcting the limitations inherent in the legal system of delivering punishment as it strikes at the very root of the criminal attitude.

Definition of Prāyaścitta

Manu-Smṛti defines *prāyaścitta* as a "determined resolve undertaken by the offender to observe the penance for being free of his offensive attitude" (*MS* XI.46). It is a combination of severe austerity and strong determination for not committing the evil deed again (*MS* XI.48). Manu presents a systematic account of the contradiction of man's original purity of nature and the negative attitude of getting indulged in a crime. Every person is born with goodness but fails to continue those inborn virtues because of certain evil influences. The perpetual state of mental crisis is a common phenomenon. It is also true that crime is always a frenzied act. A person all of a sudden becomes overexcited and loses his mental balance. The lack of reasoning is the main cause of criminal acts. The crime is a conflation of various types of emotions developed in a person's mind. Emotions occur temporarily. Thus the criminal act is also an expression of momentary impulse. Many a time, a man, because of being addicted to sensory organs, commits a mistake unknowingly. Sensory temptations are powerful enough to deviate a person of weak will-power from the path of rectitude. *Prāyaścitta* is a means to reach to the very root of the criminal leanings.

First, it makes a person aware of the crime and then it generates in him the sense of repentance. The criminal broods over his act of crime and realizes his fault. This self-realization makes him decide not to repeat that act. But to control the passions is not an easy task. In the process of *prāyaścitta* the offender is required to torment himself voluntarily or sometimes with the command of the public (*MS* XI.45). The criminal acts have direct impact on the public and, hence, the public must have the power to pronounce punishment. The justice provided by the society will be more effective and quick. Atonement is a way to testify the inner approval of the ethical sense of the offender. Legal punishment is a forced one and it does not leave any scope for the criminal to analyse his guilt and to realize that he has really harmed the society through his deeds. On the other hand, the long process of atonement arouses the inner goodness in the person and helps him to restrain his senses. The criminal disapproves his guilt himself.

Modes of Prāyaścitta and Its Relation with the Theory of Karma

The mode of *prāyaścitta* depends on whether the crime has been committed intentionally or unintentionally.

> The crime committed unintentionally is cleansed by reciting Vedas, but the one committed intentionally, in confusion, is cleansed by different types of atonements. — *MS* XI.47

A person who commits a crime intentionally needs to be tackled more carefully as he may commit the same crime again and again. Such a person should be kept away from the company of the good people as he may influence them as well. In some cases, an offender realises his mistake and he, on his own opts for ex-communication, and this may prove an effective punishment for him.

The Indian tradition believes in the theory of *karma*. We reap what we sow. The criminals, who are not punished or have not observed *prāyaścitta,* may undergo a reverse transformation and may have deformity in their next birth because of evil deeds committed by them in the present life, and some criminals suffer because of evil deeds of their previous birth (*MS* XI.48). Because of the particular effect of their past actions, men are born idiotic, blind, mute, deaf and deformed. *Manu-Smṛti* describes types of physical deformity and disease caused by the evil deeds of a person's previous birth (see *MS* XI.49-53). Manu considers them the most undesirable and not fit for attending the religious functions (*MS* III.153). The evil-minded people may spoil even good people. Therefore, their company has to be avoided. The people born with distinguishing physical marks may be identified as criminals and should be kept away from the society. Atonement is the way to cleanse the dirt caused by the undesirable acts (*MS* XI.54). Most of the criminals fail to think about the fallout of the crime in their future life. They damage their own life and make the members of the society suffer due to their evil deeds. These notions were introduced for creating a sense of fear in the minds of those people who are prone to crime.

Prāyaścitta encompasses all those crimes, which may hamper the harmony of the community. The security of life and property, preservation of the ethical values, social justice, equal opportunity to enjoy the basic rights, freedom of expression and smooth atmosphere for religious practices are the prerequisites for attaining peace and harmony. Any act which infringes upon the rights of the common people and brings in disharmony in the society has to be checked at any cost.

Prāyaścittas for Different Crimes

The different types of atonements are based on the nature and seriousness of the crime. The crimes affecting the peaceful existence of the society are regarded as serious or major crimes.

> Killing a brāhmaṇa (*bramha-hatyā*), drinking liquor, stealing, violating the *guru*'s marriage bed, and associating with those who commit these acts are called the major crimes.
>
> — *MS* XI.56

Brāhmaṇas were regarded as highly accomplished people, and they were very much needed to guide the community. The violence against them might prove disastrous for the society. The society needed to give them full protection. Consuming liquor triggers many crimes, as after being intoxicated, a person loses his senses and gets involved in many anti-social activities. Women, especially those worthy to be respected, are to be taken special care of. A crime against them may make an uproar in the society. These crimes have been considered as major crimes, as they give birth to many other crimes. There are few other crimes, similar to these major crimes.

> Lying about one's superior birth, slandering someone to the king and obstinately displeasing one's *guru* are equal to the killing of a brāhmaṇa. — *MS* XI.55

> Discontinuing the study of Vedas, reviling Vedas, giving false evidence, killing a friend and eating a food that is despised or not to be taken are crimes equal to drinking of liquor. — *MS* XI.56

Stealing someone's property and crimes against women were also regarded as major crimes. All these crimes may have a direct impact on the personal and social life. A displeased person cannot contribute anything to the welfare of the society. Women are the backbone of any given society. They nurture its prosperity. Therefore, they deserve reverence.

Apart from these major crimes, *Manu-Smṛti* brings forth another list of crimes, which are regarded minor.

> Killing a cow and other animals, abandoning father, mother, son, relatives and *guru*, marrying a brother, usury, breaking a vow, selling wife, child, pool and pleasure garden, injuring medicinal plants, trees, flowers and roots, undertaking acts for one's own sake, failing to pay debts, and using magic spells are minor crimes. — *MS* XI.60-70

The theft of personal property and the property belonging to the community has to be condemned. Animals and plants provide life support to the society, and hence, they have to be taken care of. The Indian system has faith in the strong ties among the family members and the same closeness is recommended among the members of the society. Community has to be taken as an extended family. Everyone has to take care of his family members as well as the members of the society. The person not fulfilling this condition causes instability in the family and the society. Such a person must be declared a sinner.

The *prāyaścitta* recommended for major crimes is of a severe nature. A person committing a major crime has to undergo tedious physical torture.

> A brāhmaṇa-killer should build a hut in the forest and live there for twelve years to purify himself, eating food that he has begged for and should use the skull of the corpse as his flag. — *MS* XI.72
>
> Or he may, by his own wish, make himself the target of an armed man, who knows about the guilt, or throws himself three times into a blazing fire. — *MS* XI.73
>
> Another alternative for a person, committing a major crime is to walk thousand miles or to walk along the length of the River Sarasvatī against the current. — *MS* XI.72

The second option recommended as means of atonement for major crimes is to perform the sacrifices like:

> *Aśvamedha* (horse-sacrifice), *gosevā* (serving the cow), *svargajita* (heaven-conquering), *abhijita* (a part of the great sacrifice called *navāmayāna*) and *viśvajita* (a particular sacrifice) or even the triple performance of *agniṣṭoma* (fire-praise, a sacrificial rite extending over several days in spring). — *MS* XI.74-75

The third option of atonement for major crimes is to recite the entire collection of Vedic Saṁhitā three times or to donate one's whole property to a *veda-vijña* (a person well-versed in Vedas) (*MS* XI.76). All these prescribed means of *prāyaścitta* laid more emphasis on restraining the sense-organs. A person shows his deep gratitude to Almighty by performing different types of sacrifices. They develop trust in the Supreme power, which governs the whole universe. A god-fearing person will always hesitate to harm others and may feel the existence of the same God in every creature. Taking of religious vows invokes a sense of strong determination, and that will make a criminal rigid to his vow of not committing any misdeed again. The observance of *brahmacarya vrata* (a vow of chastity) may purify a person and may help him develop firm determination (see *MS* XI.81). The repeated recitation of Vedas may increase the will-power of the criminal and may enlighten him to lead an ideal life. The sense of detachment may subdue many vices and may widen the outlook as well. *Manu-Smṛti* prescribes highest level of detachment:

> One may, without hesitation, give up his life's breath for the sake of a brāhmaṇa or a cow, as anyone who serves a cow or a brāhmaṇa is freed from the sin of killing a brāhmaṇa.
> — *MS* XI.80

The life of a brāhmaṇa and of a cow has been given equal importance. All these methods of atonement cannot be observed unless and until a person keeps his vows constant and concentrates his mind on the purpose of the vow. In atonement the criminal's mind has to be fixed to his vows and he should constantly make efforts to get rid of the vices.

Digging out the deep-rooted evil-mindedness from a criminal's heart is not an easy task. It is a long process of purification. *Manu-Smṛti* says:

> A criminal, by keeping his vows intact, leading a chaste life and concentrating fully on his efforts, at the end of the twelfth year, dispels his crime. — *MS* XI.81

The confession of the crime by a criminal is itself a step towards reformation and an honest desire on his part to be free of guilt.

> But the confession of guilt has to be done in the presence of trustworthy and able persons. This confession has to take place before a brāhmaṇa or a king. — *MS* XI.82

> The brāhmaṇa is said to be the root of the law and the ruler is the tip, therefore a person is purified by announcing his guilt before these people. — *MS* XI.83

The brāhmaṇa and the king are considered the authority of pure knowledge, reasoning and justice. They have acquired these virtues through severe penance and are ready to impart these virtues to others. They are experienced and cannot be deluded by false confessions. The confession of the crime by the criminal before these people will serve few purposes. First, there will be a morale boosting to the criminal as he has approached a right person, and second, he may illumine himself by the proper guidance received from them. They are supposed to be the divine personage because of their accomplished and righteous personality. Hence the guidance provided by them will surely help the evil-minded people to choose the right path.

The higher class of the society enjoyed the highest glory and immense power. But in no way they were allowed to disturb the peace of the society. In fact, the rules for atonement for a criminal belonging to higher caste are more severe. Consumption of liquor was fully prohibited for a brāhmaṇa. Brāhmaṇas and kṣatriyas were the custodians of the society and were responsible for keeping the rest of the society on the right track. They were not allowed to break the norms meant for the welfare of the community. Failing to that, they had to suffer serious consequences.

> A twice-born man, who has consumed liquor, should drink boiling-hot liquor. Once his body is scaled by it, he may become free of his guilt. — *MS* XI.90

> He may drink boiling-hot cow's urine, water, milk, ghee (clarified butter), or liquid cow dung until he dies. — *MS* XI.91

The cow products have been considered as the means of

atonement. These may have some chemical property useful for pacifying the bad impulses. Cow urine and cow dung bear strong smell and are not pleasant to be consumed. The consumption of these things will help to restrain the senses. The crime of drinking liquor also can be dispelled by eating oilcake once in a day, wearing a hair-shirt, by having matted hair and by carrying the symbol of the crime. The different types of crime have their own marks or symbols. The criminals are required to carry that mark during the period of *prāyaścitta*. The purpose behind it is to identify a person as a criminal and to make the society aware of it.

The mental attitude of a person, up to some extent, depends on the type of diet he takes. The criminals, going through the process of atonement, are required to eat *sāttvika* food or the food which may keep the mind cool and calm and does not initiate the evil impulses.

> Wine (made by fermenting fruits such as grapes), meat, liquor (made by fermenting grains such as rice), and strong decoctions are the food of genies, ogress and ghouls. A brāhmaṇa should not eat that. —*MS* XI.96

The main occupation of a brāhmaṇa is to pursue higher knowledge and for that he needs the mental concentration and coherence. That is why brāhmaṇas are not allowed to consume liquor or to eat meat.

> A drunken brāhmaṇa, confused by drunkenness, might fall on some thing impure or even pronounce Vedic text wrongly or do something that should not be done. —*MS* XI.97

> A brāhmaṇa not engaged in studies is similar to a śūdra. Once the body of a brāhmaṇa is flooded with wine, his brāhmaṇatva disappears and he becomes śūdra.
> —*MS* XI.98

The atonement prescribed for a brāhmaṇa for violating his *guru*'s marriage bed is also of difficult nature:

> For this crime a brāhmaṇa has to sleep on a heated iron-bed or embrace a statue of a women made of heated iron or he should cut his sex-organs, hold them in his hands and should walk to south-west region, until he dies.
>
> —*MS* XI.104-05

Manu has taken a special care while prescribing rules of atonement for brāhmaṇas. He feels that this caste possesses many virtues and cannot be the habitual criminal. But if they disrupt the normal life of the society by their misdeeds, they too have to follow the difficult method of atonement. However, at the same time Manu opines that a brāhmaṇa can purify himself by his inner-heat (see *MS* XI.102). The inner-heat signifies his awakened consciousness, which others may not have. The crimes committed by an awakened person may be unintentional and it will not take much time for him to realize his guilt and to improve himself. That is why the brāhmaṇas have been asked to "restrain their sensory power and to carry out *cāndrāyana vrata* for three months. In this *vrata*, the daily quantity of the food, which consists of fifteen mouthfuls at the full moon, is diminished by one mouthful everyday during the dark fortnight till it is reduced to zero at the new moon, and is increased in the same manner during the bright fortnight. The food fit for an oblation or barley broth has to be taken during the *vrata*." (*MS* XI.107)

These *vratas* will surely revive their consciousness and they may command mastery over their senses.

The *prāyaścitta* recommended for major crimes, which are having a serious repercussion in the society, are designed in such a manner that after observing them once, the criminal may not dare commit the crime again. The main objective behind these rules is to root out the criminal tendency from a criminal's mind forever.

Apart from these major crimes and their atonement, *Manu-*

Smṛti brings forth another list of minor crimes. The methods of atonements prescribed for minor crimes are not as rigorous as for major crimes. Manu has given much importance to the lives of animals, especially of cow. The cow is the most useful animal in an agrarian society. Cow products are healthy and nutritious. That is why the cow is considered a holy animal and to worship her cow has become a part of the religion. Killing of a cow is regarded as a henious crime as the society depends on it for many things and a person committing this crime has to go through *prāyaścitta.*

> A person, killing a cow should drink barley broth for a month, he should have his head shaved and should live in the cow shelter, covering himself with the skin of the dead cow. — *MS* XI.109

Serving the cows diligently without caring for his own difficulties is another way of atonement for cow killing.

> By day, one should follow the cows and remain standing, inhaling their dust; by night, one should give them obedience and reverence and should sit in the yogic posture (squatting on one's thighs with the lower legs crossed over one another). — *MS* XI.111

The care of the cows involves freeing them from threatening dangers, making shelters for them in cold, hot and rainy seasons, feed them well without caring about his own food, loose them and allow them to move anywhere and to donate cows to the learned at the end of the *vrata* (see *MS* XI.113-16). These activities have to be continued for three months. All these methods of dispelling the crime of killing a cow are to remind the sinner the importance of cows for human life and to develop a congenial relation with them.

Social life has a direct connection with the personal life of each and every person. The crimes committed by any person even in his private life may create a wrong precedence and may corrupt the society. In order to avoid this situation one has to regulate each and every phase of his life. The life should not be chaotic; it has to be orderly. One is required to observe certain vows prescribed for the different phases of life. The members of the society have also to follow certain ethical norms for maintaining peace in the society. Passion and lust are the biggest enemies of human beings. Many crimes take place as people are not able to control these dangerous impulses. *Manu-Smṛti* condemns crimes motivated by lust and prescribes certain methods of atonement.

> A man who has shed his semen in violation of his vow should sacrifice one-eyed donkey to Nirṛti (the goddess of death and destruction) at the crossroads at night, according to the rules of *pāka-yajña* (a simple domestic sacrifice).
>
> — *MS* XI.119

But if the same crime has been committed by a *brahmacārī*,

> he has to put on the skin of the donkey and go begging to seven houses proclaiming his sin and should take only one meal in a day, for one year. — *MS* XI.123-24

When a person of high caste, who has undertaken certain vow and understands the law and expounds Vedas, does similar crime out of lust, his vows will be nullified. Since he is doing double error, he needs to go for deeper penance. *Manu-Smṛti* prescribes more difficult atonement for them (see *MS* XI.125-26). Sticking firm to the vows is a must for character building. It will also develop the sense of strong determination, which is needed for doing any good deed. These *vrata*s are meant for restraining the senses and also provide the strength for leading a disciplined life.

In an ideal society everyone should enjoy equal status. The crimes committed by persons of any section of the society should be handled in similar manner. The disparity may cause frustration among the discriminated section of the people.

> A man, who has killed a servant, should carry out the similar atonement as prescribed for killing other persons.
> — *MS* XI.131

Manu does not allow even the killing of small animals. These animals also contribute much towards making human life smooth and trouble-free. The protection of animals is also the responsibility of the society and killing them is considered a crime.

> If a man kills a cat or mongoose, a blue-necked jay, a frog, a dog, a lizard, an owl, or a crow, he should carry out the same vow as for killing a servant, or he may drink only milk for three nights or walk 10 miles or may have bath in a river or should recite the *mantras* such as *Āpohiṣṭa mantra* in which waters* are deity. — *MS* XI.132-33

> For killing a goose, a crane, a heron, a peacock, a monkey, a falcon and a vulture, one should give a cow to a brāhmaṇa.
> — *MS* XI.136-37

The killing of elephants, horses, bulls, goats, sheep and donkeys is also prohibited, as these animals are needed for the households.

Disturbing or destroying the natural habitat is a crime. Our life is fully governed by nature. The life on this planet depends on the coexistence of man and nature. A person destroying the natural resources has also to observe atonement.

> For cutting fruit trees, shrubs, vines, creepers or flowering plants, a thousand Vedic verses should be chanted as atonement. — *MS* XI.144

Atonement for pulling out medicinal plants is more difficult.

---

* In Vedas, water in always written in plural i.e. waters (*see*, *History of Sanskrit Literature* by A.B., Keith)

> For uprooting without any purpose, medicinal herbs grown by tillage or growing by themselves in the forest, a man should follow a cow for one day, living on nothing but milk.
> — *MS* XI.145

The nature renders a selfless service to everyone without any discrimination. Destroying nature is a crime. By protecting nature we are protecting ourselves. The recommended methods of atonement for destroying the natural vegetation signify the importance of plants in our life and command us not to go against them.

Type of Diet *vis-á-vis* Crime

The happiness of human being depends much on good health. In order to maintain a good health one has to be careful about the quality of food consumed by him. Having unhealthy food and drinks is also a crime. *Manu-Smṛti* prescribes atonements even for eating the food, which is not worth consuming.

> If a brāhmaṇa drinks *vāruṇi* (a spirituous drink) unknowingly, he may be cleansed by *saṁsāra* (the purificatory rites), but if a person drinks knowingly, he has to go through the process of atonement. A man, who drinks water kept in a liquor-jar, should take milk boiled with the flower of *śaṅkhapuṣpī* (conch shell flower or *Evolvulus alsinoides*, and *kuśa* grass) for five nights. — *MS* XI.147-48

> If a person has touched an intoxicating drink while performing any ritual or has taken water brought by the servant and kept for some time, he should drink water mixed with *kuśa* grass (a sacred grass). — *MS* XI.149-50

Both *śaṅkhapuṣpī* and *kuśa* grass have several medicinal properties and are in use for a long time. They must be having some elements, which may dilute the intoxication caused by consuming any type of decoction. *Kuśa* grass is an essential part of rituals and is used in religious ceremonies invariably for sprinkling the holy water.

The eatables have to be fresh, well preserved and clean. The vegetarian diet is the most suitable diet for human beings. *Manu-Smṛti* prescribes difficult atonements for eating prohibited food.

> For eating carnivorous animals, pigs, camels, cocks, crows and donkeys, the cleansing is done through *taptakṛccha* (hot painful) *vrata*. — *MS* XI.157

> Under this vow, one has to drink hot water, hot milk and hot *ghee* for three days. — *MS* XI.215

> Anyone who wishes to keep himself clean should not eat food that is not to be eaten, but if he has consumed, he should vomit it out. — *MS* XI.161

The left-overs of the animals, containing their hair, have to be discarded and should not be eaten at any cost.

Practical Approach to Prāyaścitta

A person needs the company of good people for developing good habits. It is very easy to learn bad things but it is difficult to accumulate virtues. The intrusion of a single undesirable person may spoil the whole society. Therefore, it is a must to avoid the company of evil-doers. According to Manu, the people who have committed four major crimes (killing, eating the wrong food, stealing and having sex with forbidden women) are the evil-doers and one should avoid their company.

> No one should sit with bad people and even they should not get the share of the father's property. — *MS* XI.185-86

> One should not live with the people who have killed children, women or the people who have come to them for refuge. — *MS* XI.191

A man who keeps company with these people should observe *taptakṛccha* or *cāndrāyana vrata*s (see *MS* XI.181-82). The social boycot may teach a good lesson to the evil-doers. The *vrata*s may make them realize their guilt and will purify them.

Stealing of others' property is also a crime as it causes mental agony to the concerned person. *Manu-Smṛti* prescribes *taptakṛccha vrata* for stealing other's grain, raw or cooked food, carriage, bed, or stealing the articles of less value from someone's house (*MS* XI.165-66).

> Keeping fast for three nights is the atonement for stealing grass, wood, dry food, tree, sugar, clothing and leather.
> — *MS* XI.167

> For lifting valuable articles like gems, pearls, coral, copper, silver, brass, iron and stone, one has to go without food for twelve days. — *MS* XI.168

> For stealing cotton, silk, wool, an animal with cloven hooves, a bird, perfume, medicinal herbs, or a rope, one should live only on milk for three days. — *MS* XI.169

The rules for *prāyaścitta* connected with different crimes aim to root out the crime from criminal's mind forever. These methods were based on the principle of self-control. The different prescribed *vrata*s provide the strength to restrain the senses. *Yoga* is a powerful method of controlling the impulses and inducing spirituality in a person. It may also increase the efficiency of a person for performing good deeds. The recitation of Vedic *mantra*s helps a criminal by generating in him the inner heat, which is needed for developing self-confidence. One may have the sacrificial attitude by donating personal belongings to someone else.

> An evil-doer is free from his guilt by declaring the act, by deep regret for wrong doing, by inner heat and by donating gifts to others. — *MS* XI.228

The suppression of evil passions may be possible by taking a particular type of diet and by transformative rituals. These methods may generate the inner heat in a person. The inner heat is the pure consciousness, which will show a person the right path.

> The intelligent men whose vision was based on Vedas have said that all the happiness of gods and humans has inner heat at its root; inner heat as its middle and inner heat as its end. — *MS* XI.235

The inner heat reminds a man about his own duties and keeps him away from sins. It broadens his outlook and he will be able to see the vastness of the creation of God. The self-acceptance of the crime reveals the inner goodness of a person.

> The more a man, on his own accord, declares the wrong that he has done, the more he is free from his guilt, like a snake from its skin. — *MS* XI.230

After being purified by atonement a person decides that he is not going to commit the same crime again and he stays firm on that. After that he will constantly engage himself in auspicious actions through his mind, body and speech.

In the present-day scenario where intolerance, selfishness and immorality have reached the climax, the concept of *prāyaścitta,* as enunciated by Manu, may prove effective in curtailing the crimes, thus bringing harmony and peace in the society.

9

Seeds of Modern Economics in Manu-Smṛti

According to Indian thinking, man is the supreme creature that God has ever created. A man possesses the light of the Self and has the power of illumining everything, whatever comes in his contact. He comes to this world with the responsibility of performing *karma* in the right order. Therefore, it is implicit that he has to discharge his duties in such a manner that it may reform his life in the present and next birth. There is a mandate for action, but the action has to be carried in such a way that it does not hinder the very purpose of taking birth. Being a part of the society, he too has to take care of social values. At the same time in order to lead a fruitful life he needs different means of sustenance and consequently, he requires money and other resources needed for his day-to-day life. Being a rational creature, he is also supposed to know the right way of earning and utilizing the available resources.

Place of Wealth in Indian Tradition

The ancient Indian seers were fully conscious of the importance of wealth in the scheme of life. That is why, *artha* got prominent place among four *puruṣārtha*s (four ends of human life), viz. *dharma, artha, kāma* and *mokṣa*. The ultimate goal of life is to attain *mokṣa*, but before that, one has to be free of the debt towards family and society. Though wealth never was considered as the only goal of life, even then the material aspirations for human being were considered as important as the spiritual gain. No one was allowed to move to asceticism without discharging the allotted duties towards family and society. The proper management of wealth was also needed for getting the utmost benefit from it. Economic ideas of ancient Indian thinkers have been reflected mainly in law books, epics and Purāṇas. The references pertaining to economics found in all these texts involve both the theoretical as well as practical sides.

> *Vārtā* (profession or occupation) got prominent place among four *vidyās*. — *MS* VII.43

Vārtā in Manu's Perspective

The word *vārtā* etymologically means *vṛtti* (livelihood). Later on, this word denoted the "occupation allotted to vaiśyas" (*MS* X.80). Smṛtis and *Arthaśāstra* brought out the detailed study on all topics related to wealth. Manu has considered *vārtā* (dealing with the study of economics) as a main branch of learning. According to Manu:

> *Vārtā* is a science, comprising the management of agriculture, cattle breeding, trade, moneylending, banking, industry, consumption and proper distribution of wealth and taxation. — *MS* IX.326-27

Thus, it covers roughly all the aspects of modern economic thoughts. The modern economics tells us how a person should satisfy his needs with limited means; in short economics teaches us to make the best use of our limited resources. It requires prudence, wisdom and proper planning. Economics is concerned with the material welfare of the people and economic development of the state. Manu realized that the proper care of all aspects of economics is needed for the desired growth of a country. Manu considered the science of economics as an essential and integral part of regal curriculum. It became the main duty of a king to look after the financial matters with optimum care. In *Manu-Smṛti* there are several references stressing the necessity of economic management for the stability of the country. "A king must preserve wealth against misfortunes" (*MS* VII.213). He also prescribes that the king should learn business from the people. It means that king should learn business, trade and commerce from the people who are well-versed and experienced in these fields. A king must have the theoretical as well as practical knowledge of trade and commerce in order to deal with the financial matters. In *Manu-Smṛti* one may find the reference of a particular word *vyavahāra*, which has been used mainly for trade and commerce. The requisite progress of the economy depends on the continuous growth and circulation of wealth. It may be possible only when the management of the wealth gets due priority. The mismanagement of wealth may slow down the development of the state. This can be avoided if all the components of economic growth are taken care of. The economic growth should never be static. There should always be a circular flow or movement of the resource for generating wealth. Manu says:

> A king should desire to gain what he has not gained, but at the same time he should guard the wealth which has already been gained. He should also increase the preserved wealth and should arrange the profitable investment of the increased wealth. — *MS* VII.99

The main idea behind this concept was to maintain the proper acquisition, consumption and suitable investment of the wealth. Prosperity is very vital for the multifarious development of the country. Manu has condemned poverty as it gives birth to too many vices, causing the downfall of the society. It is not enough for a country to increase its national income, it is also necessary to ensure that each and every member of the society is in a position to get his due share. Thus, Manu seems to advocate the socialistic pattern of society.

Components of Economic Growth

In order to have a proper understanding of economics it is necessary to consider the important components or sectors that have serious impact on economic growth of a country. The sectors that determine the economic status of a country include mainly the agriculture or rural economy, labour, capital, trade and industry, banking revenue and taxation. *Manu-Smṛti* contains minute details of all these sectors as described in the following pages.

Agriculture

It is quite apparent that even during Manu's time, India's economy was agrarian. Rural economics played a vital role as agriculture was the main occupation of common people. Life of each and every person depended mainly on agricultural products. Therefore, the focus ought to be on agriculture. The word agriculture means the "practice of cultivation of soil and rearing animals". In *Manu-Smṛti* agriculture includes farming, cattle breeding and dairy farming. The land was regarded as a source of wealth and was accorded high divinity. A good agriculture always needs a good land and its proper care will surely give the desired results. Manu considered agriculture as a technical job and advised that only skilled people should go for it. There was a division of labour and according to that, agriculture was prescribed mainly for vaiśyas and śūdras, but brāhmaṇas and kṣatriyas were also allowed to follow it under special circumstances.

> A king should make vaiśyas practise agriculture and cattle breeding with much care. — *MS* IX.326

Vaiśyas and śūdras did the job of farming for generations and became well-trained and more efficient in this work. At the same time the community also took the joint responsibility of taking care of agriculture. Manu has brought out a very scientific as well as methodical scheme of a successful agriculture. He has introduced the thorough knowledge and a fine scientific outlook on agriculture. He presents the process of farming in a detailed manner, and the steps prescribed by him are relevant even today. A progressive agriculture needs good management of land, the adjustment of crop to the soil, procurement of quality seed, rotation of crop, knowledge of the different modes of cultivation, effective agricultural tools, availability of good irrigation system, storage of the produce, transportation and congenial market. The precepts related to agricultural management as presented in *Manu-Smṛti* cover all these aspects. The state and community both were made equally responsible for the prosperity of agriculture. In order to have a trouble-free farming, it is a must to have a record of individual holding, and for that the proper demarcation of land is necessary. Manu has laid down many rules for conducting proper survey and demarcation of individual holdings.

> There should be a sturdy boundary with clear marks dividing the land owned by two persons. —*MS* VIII.245

> Ponds, springs and dams are to be made at the point of the union of these boundaries. —*MS* VIII.248

The construction of ponds, springs and dams on the boundaries may serve the dual purpose of ensuring the firm boundary as well as easy approach to water reservoir for irrigation. Boundaries were treated as legal restriction and through that common disputes related to land were checked.

Those who indulged in damaging or manipulating the boundary of crop fields were liable to be punished. These laws were made to check the exploitation of the weaker section by the rich. Those days there was no dearth of land as the population was less. There was a need to encourage farming. Many measures were taken to involve the common people in farming. Jobs like cutting the forest, improving the land and bringing the wastelands under cultivation were entrusted to the community. Manu created beneficial law in favour of the person who first cleared the forest.

> The land belongs to him who first clears the timber.
>
> — *MS* IX.44

Perhaps this law was introduced to encourage common people for providing free service to the state. It also indicates that the ratio between forest and human population was comfortable and cutting the forest was not causing any threat to the living beings. But at the same time, Manu was deeply conscious of environmental protection. He has mentioned about the necessity of maintaining green belt everywhere.

> Round about every village there should be a strip of land measuring one hundred bows, or even three casts of a staff in width; around the city it should be three times more.
>
> — *MS* VIII.237

The length of a bow is approximately 6 ft, and one cast of staff is approximately equal to 200 ft. This land was intended for the common use and was not to be tilled. These land patches could also be used as pasture and for community functions.

Manu-Smṛti brings out the minute details of different aspects of agriculture and its advancement for strengthening the state economy. The first step in cultivation is sowing of seeds. The richness of the yield depends on the quality of seeds. It was the job of the king to control the quality of seed. The people who were supplying seeds were supposed to know the process of treatment of seeds. Farmers had to use the wisdom of careful selection of seed grains. Manu insisted on using the good quality of seeds, as it was highly essential for a good crop. A farmer must have the knowledge of evaluating the quality of the seeds; he should also know what type of soil is needed for a particular seed grain (*MS* IX.330-32).

Not only that, Manu also advised to keep an eye on those who were supplying seeds. The persons supplying bad quality of seed were liable to be punished. It seems that during Manu's time strict laws were put in place against those who were not supplying quality seeds.

> He who sells bad seeds, or prepares worthless seeds, should receive corporal punishment, his limbs should be chopped off and body should be deformed. — *MS* IX.291

The tools used for ploughing the field should also be of good quality and should be made by skilled people. Stealing agricultural tools was taken as a crime.

> A person stealing plough, yoke, etc. should be punished by the king. — *MS* VIII.292-93

> A person found guilty of stealing or destroying rope, vessel or anything related to agriculture should be fined. Physical punishment should be given to the person stealing grain from the granary. — *MS* VIII.319

The next thing, which is very important for farming is to protect crops from thieves and animals. Farming involves lots of expenses and the loss of crop may cause serious financial problems. Thus, a farmer has to take care of his crop carefully and the owner has to secure the land from all sides.

> The owner of the field should make a hedge so high that a camel could not look over it, all the holes should be closed through which a dog could not thrust his muzzle, or a boar his snout. — *MS* VIII.239

> If the cattle damage the crop of an enclosed field, bordering on a road or lying on the outskirts of the village, the owner of the cattle has to pay a fine. — *MS* VIII.240

The fence or hedge should be made of thorns and boughs. It is the sincere duty of the cattle keepers to be vigilant on the movement of their cattle.

> If the cattle keeper fails in his duties, because of negligence and the crop has been damaged, he has to pay the value of the destroyed crop to the owner of the field. — *MS* VIII.241

The owner of the field is also equally responsible for the protection of his field.

> When the owner of the field is at fault and the crop has been damaged, the punishment should be ten times more than the value of the crop; the fine will be five times more than the value of the crop if the crop has been damaged because of the mistake done by the servant. — *MS* VIII.243-44

The state income depends on revenue collected from the farmers and it will be possible only if there is a good harvest. The negligence shown by an owner of the land will bring down the production and may deprive the state of its revenue, causing economic downfall.

Manu also realized the precepts of effective irrigation system. A farmer should never depend on rain, as at times there may be no rain or deficient rainfall, and the farmer will not get any produce. Every village was expected to have ponds, tanks, canals and water channels. Special incentives were given to those who constructed tanks (*MS* VIII.248). The community was responsible for the protection and maintenance of all these water resources. A person damaging water resources should be punished severely:

> A person should be fined heavily who steals water from the pool or breaks the dam, or diverts the course of the water (*MS* VIII.264).

If one takes or destroys the water of the whole pool or breaks the dam, he is causing a serious problem to irrigation and even to society. According to Manu, such a person has to suffer death penalty.

> The king should kill a person destroying the pond by drowning him in the water or by any other dreadful manner.*
>
> — *MS* IX.279

Ruining the water resource warrants punishment. In *Manu-Smṛti* agriculture and land management have been well supported by the principles pertaining to the knowledge of selecting seeds, selection of the crops according to the nature of soil, irrigation, eradication of the problems like flood and drought, and even warding off the pests. The storage of food grains has also been considered quite important. One cannot get good returns from the yield if the produce is not stored safe. Manu considered the construction and protection of the granary as the vital part of farming. According to *Manu-Smṛti* it was the duty of the king to facilitate the farmers with granary. Granary was treated just like a temple, and it used to be one of the most protected places in the village. Strict laws were formed against the person damaging the granary.

> One should also slay a person without hesitation who destroys a granary. — *MS* IX.289

The stock of sufficient food grains, well kept in the granaries may be of great help during flood or famine. Every effort was made to strengthen the rural economy. The persons engaged in agriculture must possess deep knowledge of the modes and methods of agriculture and the storage of produce.

Agriculture cannot be improved or promoted as long as cultivators do not get the good price for their produce. One should not forget that farming is the only means of livelihood to the farmers. The low price of the crop may discourage farmers from farming, causing serious challenge to state's economy. The state must formulate an honest and trustworthy body to regulate the price for agricultural products. A king himself should take care of this department.

---

* Other dreadful manner could include corporal or capital punishment.

> A king should establish the price of purchase and sale after considering the place of importation and exportation, the storage, the gain, and the loss of all goods bought and sold.
> —*MS* VIII.401

The price should include all the expenses incurred by the farmer in cultivating the crop and bringing it to the market. Any injustice done to the farmers may discourage them from farming. The farmers should not be oppressed at any cost.

> Every five days or at the expiration of every fortnight, the king should settle the price of the goods in the presence of the traders and experts. —*MS* VIII.302

The experts were those who possessed the thorough knowledge of all aspects of rural economics. This practice may serve the interest of common farmers, as they will know the correct selling price of the products and will not be cheated. The absence of the middleman may facilitate the farmers to get the best price for their hard-earned products. It will also help the state to know the correct position of the agricultural products for collecting the grain to meet the challenges caused by famines or floods. An approachable market is also needed where the farmers can sell their products without much difficulty. Agriculture was kept away from all types of social or political disturbances. Disturbing agriculture was considered a serious crime and any person harming the farming in any manner was considered a criminal. It is the duty of the king to make effective arrangement to safeguard agriculture even during internal or external unrest. Manu has given special importance to the cultivation of medicinal plants and other cash crops. He suggests the measures for conservation of medicinal plants and prescribes punishment for those who are engaged in stealing them (*MS* VIII.285). Thus it may be said that *Manu-Smṛti* has suggested various beneficial schemes for promoting the rural economy, which will ultimately contribute much to state's economic stability.

Labour

The term labour includes those who do mental or physical work and are paid wages for that. Any type of reward for human exertion whether paid by hour, day, month, or year, and paid cash or kind, or both, is called wages. The labour plays a vital role in achieving the desired turnover of any type of industry. The status of the production depends totally on the efficiency of the labourers. In order to increase and maintain the efficiency of the workers, certain steps have to be taken by the employers. First, there should be a division of labour. That means the workers should be divided into few groups, based on their qualification and skill. The right man should be at the right place. There must be a congenial relation between the employer and workers. An employer may maintain a cordial relation with his employees by giving them due wages and at the same time by keeping them under strict discipline. *Manu-Smṛti* lays down many labour regulations pertaining to the employment of labourers; the division of labour, the nature of their work, their qualifications, the payment of wages, and how to impose discipline on them. The workers were required to sign some agreement before joining their work. The remuneration of a labourer was fixed in accordance with his qualification and efficiency. The amount of wages had to be sufficient to meet the livelihood expenses of the worker and his whole family. Provision was also made to grant leave with pay to a sick worker. Manu says:

> If a hired man is sick and is not able to work according to agreement, he should get full wages in spite of his long absence from the work. —*MS* VIII.216

On the contrary to this:

> If a hired man, although not sick, insolently fails to work as

> agreed upon, he should be fined and his wages should not be paid. —*MS* VIII.215

The worker has to pay penalty for the breach of the contract. The negligence towards duty shown by workers on flimsy grounds will not only hamper the output of the production, but will also encourage other workers to do the same. It was a must for a worker to finish the work assigned to him.

> A labourer who does not finish his work because of his proud nature or due to his laziness is liable to be punished. —*MS* VIII.215

The diligence and dedication along with skill should be considered as basic qualification for workers. In order to safeguard the interest of the workers, Manu has made few special provisions.

> A sick labourer may get his work done by any other worker. In that case he is entitled to get full wages. —*MS* VIII.216

If a person is frequently out of work for some reason or the other, it will surely bring down the production. The main purpose behind all these rules and regulations was to create a healthy work culture and to ensure the growth of economy. Low productivity may cause serious problems. In order to avert that situation, the balance between production and wages was to be maintained. Competent supervision is also necessary for getting a work done in a perfect manner. The remuneration of a labourer has to be proportionate to his productivity and qualification. A skilled worker is entitled to get more wages, but a worker showing negligence in his work needs to be dealt strictly.

> If a worker does not finish his work as agreed upon, whether he is ill or well, the promised wages should not be given, even if only a small part of the work is left unfinished. —*MS* VIII.217

In no way workers were allowed to show any type of slackness towards their duties. They were required to make full use of their skill. Manu gave much importance to the agreement signed by the worker. The breaker of the agreement was considered as criminal and banishment from the realm was the recommended punishment for him. The disputes may occur, and it is, therefore, necessary to have some mechanism to settle the disputes with perfect justice. Thus, the codes presented in *Manu-Smṛti* for appointing skilled labourer, their training and conditions for the job, wages and punishment to the defaulters, prove to be of great value even today. The punishments were of harsh nature, but it is also a fact that strictness was needed for proper output. Result-based wage system encouraged workers to use their capability to the best of their ability. At the same time it boosted the output. There was a balance between incentives and punishments inflicted on the workers.

If one starts thinking in terms of the economic growth of the country, it becomes inevitable to take care of labour management. Manu seems to have very well visualized this aspect of economy in a proper perspective.

Capital

Capital has been defined as the part of a person's wealth other than land which yields an income or which aids in production of further wealth. Thus, capital is an instrument of production. The growth of productive undertakings depends totally on capital. The economic progress of any country depends on how much capital the country can generate. Capital is a man-made instrument of production. Therefore, it is possible to increase its supply when the situation demands. That is why the capital management has become the most vital part of the state economy. In fact, production would almost come to a standstill without adequate supply of capital. *Manu-Smṛti* deals with capital management bringing out all of its aspects in detail. The king being the head of the state was responsible to look after all types of money matters, and he had to accelerate the process of capital formation. It could be done through the development of agriculture, trade, industry and good banking.

> It is the duty of the king to earn money even by invading other kingdoms. He may increase the capital even through trade and commerce. — *MS* VII.65, 97

The money should always be in circulation. The stagnation of the capital may hamper the economy. The lack of capital usually results due to individual hoarding or extravagance by the state. There should be a proper distribution of wealth in the country. A king has to take care of all these issues (see *MS* VII.99). Manu has advised that the king should maintain a budget with heavy recurring surpluses to increase the state coffer, and he should formulate definite policies in this regard. The accumulation of too much of wealth by the private bodies may cause serious problem to the state. "The belongings of each and every individual have to be examined strictly and according to rules. There should be a record of the assets of each and every person residing in the state. A king must form certain viable policies for restricting the personal property for enriching the state coffer.

> A king may keep the property of which the owner is unknown. The owner may claim it within the period of three years, failing to that the property will go to the king.
> — *MS* VIII.30

It is essential for a king to generate recurring income for the welfare of the state. The inequality in income among the people may lead to serious economic and social consequences. Manu mentioned many ways for making money for the state treasury. He brought out the concept of ceiling on agricultural as well as urban property. Apart from this, he also introduced measures like the procurement of unclaimed property and stolen wealth, having the monopoly of few industries and charging high tax on luxuries.

> The property that has been lost and has been found again should be placed under king's guards. — *MS* VIII.37

> The king may take sixth part or the tenth part or even twelfth part of that property depending on the financial condition of the real owner. — *MS* VIII.33

In the same way:

> If a king discovers any ancient treasure hidden in the ground, after giving half of that wealth to brāhmaṇas, he should store the other half in the royal treasury. The treasure which is unearthed from the ground belongs to the royal treasury, but if the land is owned by some individual, the king may claim half of that wealth. — *MS* VIII.39

The main aim for introducing these policies was to check the private property and to boost the state treasury.

BANKING

Banking plays an important role in enhancing the state economy. It seems that during those days banking was under public control. It was a profession of vaiśyas to lend money and earn profit from the interest. There was a practice of taking loan from moneylenders by putting some security deposit. In order to regulate the moneylending business, Manu framed strict rules for both moneylenders and debtors. The moneylenders were allowed to charge interest on debts for increasing their capital. When money is lent, there is some risk of it not being returned. The borrower may be a cheater or he may not be in a position to return the money. The moneylender, therefore, expects a reward in proportion to the degree of the risk involved. At the same time, he also wants to make some profit. With this reason the lenders ask some security. It used to be in the form of land, jewellery, house or even cows and bulls. According to Manu, whole of this affair has to be monitored by the king. Moneylenders were not given power to decide the rate of interest or to do injustice to the borrowers. Both Manu and Vasiṣṭha have acknowledged that the normal rate of interest should be eightieth part of 100 a month (see *MS* VIII.140). This rate is equal to 15 per cent per annum. This rate of interest seems to be high. It may be because of the lesser availability of liquid money in comparison to demand. There may be other reasons as well. The high rate of interest will increase the gross capital, and this would help the lenders to pay some amount of their profit to the king as tax. The high rate of interest will also discourage the debtors to go for debt. The rate of the interest differed from caste to caste.

> Brāhmaṇas were to pay 2 *paṇa*s, kṣatriyas were to pay 3 *paṇa*s and the vaiśyas were to pay 4 *paṇa*s as interest on 100 *paṇa*s every month. — *MS* VIII.142

> The moneylender may take only 2 *paṇa*s as interest from noble people. By doing this, the moneylender is not committing any offence. — *MS* VIII.141

The learned people will not borrow money without any genuine reason. Even the moneylenders have to show respect to them by charging less interest. The rate of interest differed depending on the caste of the borrowers and their financial status. Special privileges were given to the farmers.

> A farmer, who has given his land to the lender as security, need not pay any interest. The crop earned from his land should be treated as interest. — *MS* VIII.143

MONEYLENDING

Manu-Smṛti also prescribes many laws for moneylenders so that they may not exploit the borrowers in any case. The moneylender has to do his business in a fair manner.

> A moneylender has no right to use or to sell the security kept by the borrower. If he is using the ornaments kept as security by the borrower, he is not entitled to charge interest. The objects of security always belong to the owner and the lender cannot use that. If the security is damaged or destroyed, the moneylender has to pay the total cost of the object to the owner. The security should be returned to its owner, even if he comes back after a long time. The security in the form of animals like cows, camels and horses or tools like yoke always belongs to the owner, it does not matter even if it has been used by lender. — *MS* VIII.144-48

> A pledge, a village boundary, the property of a child, deposit, something loaned for good cause, the possession of a king and the possession of a brāhmaṇa who knows Vedas by heart, are not lost even if used by someone else and belong to the owner. — *MS* VIII.149

> If a lender uses the security kept by the borrower without his permission, he must give up half of the interest as redemption for its use. — *MS* VIII.150

On the contrary to it:

> If a lender is keeping the security for more than ten years and the owner does not come back to take it back, the lender has all right to enjoy the ownership of that object. — *MS* VIII.147

As per the references found in *Manu-Smṛti* it is evident that the interest rates were fixed on humanitarian grounds.

> If the principal money and the interest are to be paid together, the amount should not exceed double of the principal amount. — *MS* VIII.151

> The interest has to be calculated annually and it has to be

> informed to the borrower and no one is allowed to charge excessive interest. — *MS* VIII.152

There was no provision of compound interest.

> The lender cannot charge the interest that extends for more than a year or what is not recognized by the king, nor compound interest, periodical interest, forced interest or interest in the form of corporal. — *MS* VIII.143

A lender cannot take the interest in the form of physical work. Manu has prohibited *cakravṛddhi* or compound interest, periodical interest, stipulated interest and corporal interest.

> If a lender has imposed the compound interest on the debtor and has stipulated the time and place of the payment, he should not reap the fruit of it. — *MS* VIII.156

In case someone is not in a position to return the debt, he can pay the interest at the end of the year and may get some grace.

> If a man is unable to pay the debt and wishes to make a new contract, he may pay the interest that is due and may sign a new agreement. — *MS* VIII.154

> If a father has taken debt for gambling or drinking liquor or for some undesirable purposes, the son is not responsible to pay his debt. The son has to pay his father's debt if the case is in the court of the king and is supported by any witness. — *MS* VIII.159

> In the same manner lender's son also has the right to procure his father's money after the death of his father by producing some witness. — *MS* VIII.160

> If the guarantor has received the money from the borrower and dies before paying the debt, his son should pay the money out of his own money. — *MS* VIII.162

> If the debtor dies and the borrowed money was spent for the immediate relatives of the debtor, the family members have to pay the debt from their own property, even if they have moved away. —*MS* VIII.166

> The lender has to give back the deposit in a friendly and amicable manner. —*MS* VIII.187

The lender also has to be a responsible and well-recognized person. Manu does not allow everyone to enter into this profession.

> A person who is seriously sick or intoxicated or fickle-minded or immature has no right to enter into the profession of moneylending. —*MS* VIII.163

The moneylender has no right to get anything done with force.

> What is given by force, enjoyed by force, and also what is written by force, should be declared undone. —*MS* VIII.168

> An intelligent man should make a deposit with a man of good family and good conduct, who understands the law and speaks the truth and has a large following and is wealthy. —*MS* VIII.179

Thus, the theories on interest prescribed in *Manu-Smṛti* denote that though the businessmen did the job of moneylending, they were not free to determine the rates of interest as these were regulated by the king.

Trade and Industry

Apart from agricultural products, a person needs many other things manufactured by other sources for day-to-day life. In fact, with the advancement of civilization, the needs of common people also increase, and this encourages many new industries to come up. Economy also rises with the growth of trade and industry as it generates employment and keeps the money in flow. Division of labour as prescribed in *Manu-Smṛti* provided ample scope for the desired progress of trade and industry. *Manu-Smṛti* carries many references dealing with different aspects of trade and industry. It seems that during Manu's time trade and industry was flourishing vigorously under the care of trading community and administrative staff. The charge of trade and industry was given to the vaiśyas. They were supposed to know the minute details of trading. That means special training was needed for entering in the business of trading.

> A vaiśya cannot go for any other profession. After marrying, he has to look after agriculture and trade. — *MS* IX.326

> He must possess the knowledge of the qualities of different articles, the cost of various goods, the means of increasing and promoting trade, the position of demand and supply and how to safeguard the produced material. He also should know the art of engaging the workers and the payment of their salaries. A trader should also know several languages.
> — *MS* IX.327-29

Manu wanted to maintain the sense of spirituality even in the field of trade.

> A vaiśya should do his trade with righteousness.
> — *MS* IX.333

A trade done in a fair manner will increase the credibility of the market and will be able to develop the trust among the buyers. It is natural for a businessman to get corrupt because of infatuation for money. In such a case, the proper monitoring is needed to regulate the whole affair. Manu advocated that trade and industry should be controlled by the state.

> The king has to take care of the sold articles; how much of the profit has been gained, to whom the things have been sold, how much of money has been spent on food and lodging of the traders and the expenses towards security of the goods. — *MS* VII.127

The references found in *Manu-Smṛti* depict that though there was a lack of heavy industries, even then the industries producing timber, perfumes, medicines, earthen pots, stone objects, clothes, furniture and ornaments progressed well. Apart from these, the leather industry, woodcarving, bamboo industry, bee-keeping and dairy farming were also there (see *MS* VIII.326-27 and IX.328-30). The traders were required to obtain licence and foreign traders were desired to procure special permission from the king. It is amazing to note that Manu had a very clear vision of the market. He was aware of all fundamentals related to price fixing. He also knew that the value of any product was governed by its demand and supply.

> Proper market survey is necessary for fixing the prices of different articles. —*MS* VIII.401

> After considering the place of exportation and importation, the storage, the gain and loss of all goods bought and sold, the king should fix the price of purchase and sale.
> —*MS* VIII.402

The satisfaction of the customers was given the highest priority. The traders in no way were allowed to deceive the customers in any manner (*MS* VIII.403). In order to ensure the fair dealing of the market, it was mandatory for the king to examine each and every balance as well as weights and measures carefully and to examine the same after every six months (*MS* VIII.404).

As the price of each and every article was recorded in the state office, no one was allowed to charge extra. The traders were supposed to give the details of the quantity, quality and the price of every article. The exorbitant prices of different goods may create dissatisfaction among common people and may bring defame to the ruler. A king has to avoid this situation and for that he should keep a strict vigil on the market. Manu advocates punishing the traders involved in taking undue advantage of the buyers.

> A trader selling adulterated goods, making the pure things impure, damaging the precious stones or breaking any gem with the purpose of decreasing the weight is liable to be punished. — *MS* IX.286

A trader has to sell all the commodities without discriminating against any buyer.

> It is a crime to sell the same article to one person on a cheaper rate and to give to someone else on a higher price. Similarly, selling the goods of better quality to one person and of inferior quality to the other person is also punishable. — *MS* IX.287

Market is said to be perfect when all the potential buyers and sellers are promptly aware of the price at which transactions take place and the consumers get a fair dealing. Market is a place where trader and buyer meet each other face-to-face. They are in direct touch as the buyers come there with the intention of purchasing the things they want and traders want to gain some profit by selling those commodities. The growth of the market depends on the goodwill of both, the sellers and buyers. The consumer's satisfaction is the key to trader's gain. Therefore, the consumers must have some right as they are paying the price of the goods bought. The consumers must have faith in the market. According to *Manu-Smṛti,* the traders should not be allowed to cheat their customers. There should be a proper weighing of each and every article.

> A customer was allowed to give back or to take back anything purchased by him within a period of ten days, in the case of dissatisfaction, but after the expiry of ten days the seller is not obliged to take back the sold article. — *MS* VIII.222-23

A good infrastructure is needed for the proper growth of the industry and trade. At the same time the traders must get some incentive and some relaxations for trading from the state. A good transportation is needed for transporting the goods to the market. Transport plays the role of eliminating the challenges of distance between the producer and the consumer. A speedy and cheap transport is a must, specially for perishable goods. Adequate transport facilities promote the movement of raw material to the industries or consumer goods to shops. Developed transportation means cheaper movement of materials. Cheaper transport will lower the cost of production and this will bring down the price of goods. *Manu-Smṛti* considers all these points in a very vivid manner. The king was responsible to provide a good transport system to the traders.

> A king must look after regularly the management of income, expenditure, treasury and transport. — *MS* VIII.419

During those days boats and carts were the main means of transportation. The tariff and transportation charges depended on the weight of goods. The king decided the rates for transporting goods.

> The transport charges should be within the reach of the traders. The traders were supposed to pay less for empty containers. — *MS* VIII.404-05

> For the long journey, the boat toll should be in proportion to the time of journey and the distance of destination.
> — *MS* VIII.406

The transport charges were charged according to the financial status of traders.

> The charge for a boat going to the direction of the wind used to be less. — *MS* VIII.409

Proper security is the most important factor for the growth of trade and industry. The traders must have a confidence that their products are safe. It was the responsibility of the boatman to transport the goods safely.

> If any damage occurs to the goods while transporting because of the negligence of the boatman, he has to pay the compensation to the owner. — *MS* VIII.408

As the state is getting much of the revenue, it becomes obligatory for the king to provide full protection to the traders. Manu was in favour of giving security to the traders against theft and other types of threats. He recommended harsh punishment for the theft of different goods.

> The persons found stealing gold, silver, expensive clothes and other valuable articles have to get capital punishment. — *MS* VIII.321-22

A thief has to give double the price of the stolen article. In fact, Manu was opposed to theft of any kind and it was mandatory for the king to check it by any means. Law and order was needed for the development of trade and industry. Punishments like fine, imprisonment or even mutilation were recommended, according to the gravity of the offences. Apart from this, elaborate rules were suggested to look after the establishment and management of the market.

> It is the whole and sole responsibility of the king to take care of the market. He should look after diligently the income, expenditure, balance, the amount received through taxation and the transports used for trade and commerce. — *MS* VIII.401

Manu advocated the state monopoly of several industries on the basis of the rarity or the cost of the articles. In monopoly a single producer or seller controls the market. There are no close substitutes for the product. In this case the state becomes the monopolist and the industries are completely under its control. The state took care of the mining of gold, silver, copper, diamonds, gems, precious stones and iron. It was also the state's concern to take care of the ocean mining of the pearl, conch and coral (*MS* VIII.399).

Manu has extended the royal monopolies even for the trade of elephants, silk, woollen materials, saffron and sandal.

> Any person smuggling these goods to another country is liable to be punished. The king should confiscate the entire property of a man who, due to greed for gain, exports the goods of which the king had a monopoly or which are forbidden to be sold. —*MS* VIII.399

It was an advance vision of controlling the state economy.

> Capital punishment should be given to a person found stealing horses, elephants. —*MS* VIII.324

Elephants were the most useful animal to the kings and were needed for different purposes. In the same manner the production of saffron was done only in Kashmir. Horses were brought from the north-west. Therefore the state had to control the sale of all these things.

> A king must appoint few trained and skilled officers to take care of all these affairs. —*MS* VII.81

During Manu's period the bulk of transaction was handled through barter system, but the currency in the form of coins was also in much use especially in urban areas. The coins, as the medium of transaction, were originated and developed in India at a very early time, or much prior to the arrival of foreign invaders. There are ample evidences proving the existence of gold, silver and copper coins even in 600 BCE. *Manu-Smṛti* also mentions the use of coins based on the weight system. The coins were made of copper, silver and gold. The smallest unit was *raktikā*.

> The fine particle of the dust which is seen in a beam of the light as it enters a lattice window is taken as first standard and was called an atom. Eight atoms in respect of weight are equal to one louse egg, three of these are equal to one grain of black mustard (*sarṣapa*) and three grains of black

> mustard are equal to one grain of white mustard. Six grains of white mustard are equal to one medium-sized barley-corn; three barley-corns are equal to one berry; five berries constitute in weight a bean (*māsā*); sixteen *māsā*s are equal to a gold piece (*suvarṇa*). Four *suvarṇa*s are equal to a *pala;* ten *pala*s to a *dharaṇa*. Two berries of the same weight should be regarded as a silver *māṣaka;* sixteen of silver *māṣaka*s constitute one silver *pūraṇa*. A copper *paṇa* of the same weight is known as *kārṣāpaṇa*. — *MS* VIII.132-36

> Ten silver *dharaṇa*s make one silver *śatamāna;* the weight of four *suvarṇa*s is called *niṣka*. — *MS* VIII.137

During Manu's period rulers, merchants and traders used the coins with their own seal, certifying the correct weight of the coin and the genuineness of the metal. No one was allowed to tamper with the coins. In royal courts coins were used to impose fines for different types of crimes. Taxes were also collected in the form of coins. The coins were also used for paying the fares for different modes of transports and the salaries for different jobs.

Revenue and Taxation

State's control and intervention in the economic sphere are essential for promoting the general welfare of a nation. The state must step in to make economic activity orderly and fruitful. The state has to look after security threat from external aggression and maintenance of the law and order within the country. Besides these, the state is also responsible to take care of administrative, social, economic and commercial activities. To carry out these functions, the state needs fund. The common people also have to contribute to the state revenue. Taxes are the most important source to generate funds to be used for the welfare of people. Tax is the compulsory contribution from the wealth of an individual or a body of persons for the service of the state. Taxes are mostly levied with the object of raising revenues. Revenue expenditure is an ordinary, routine type of expenditure incurred in running the administration. The purpose of tax collection is also to remove inequalities in the distribution of wealth in a society. A part of the tax is rolled out for the welfare of the common masses.

Manu could visualize the importance of revenue and taxation for the welfare of the state. According to him, *koṣa* (treasury) is one of the seven constituent elements of the state (*MS* IX.294-95). It was mandatory for the king to enrich the royal treasury by different means to tackle the external as well as internal problems. According to Manu, these seven elements are complementary to each other. The power of collecting tax was given to local self-government (*MS* VII.114-19). The greater portion of revenue was collected in kind and its deterioration was regarded as a serious calamity. The wealth collected through revenue was treated as the reserve fund, touched only at the time of calamity (*MS* VII.110). It was the policy of foresightedness, which a king ought to observe. The richness of the treasury depended fully on the surplus of the collected revenue over the expenses of the state.

Manu provided elaborate rules for procuring revenue and taxes. A king had the power to collect revenue through different types of fees, tolls, rentals and royalties.

> A king may charge the fiftieth part of the income from goldsmith, sixth part, or eighth part or twelfth part from farmers, depending on their earning. — *MS* VII.127, 130

> He may charge the sixth part of the income earned through the trade of timber, meat, honey, *ghṛta* (clarified butter), perfume, medicine, flowers, fruits, vegetables, grass, leather, goods made of bamboo and the articles made of clay or stone. — *MS* VII.131-32

> A king should not impose any tax on artisans, mechanics and labourers; instead of that they may be asked to work for one day without any payment every month: he should also not charge any tax from the businessmen of low income group. — *MS* VII.138

> A king must ask the traders in his kingdom who live on trade to pay a small amount as tax each year. — *MS* VII.137

Manu gave special treatment to the brāhmaṇas, teachers and to those who were well-versed in sacred learning.

> A king should not impose any tax on learned people even at the time of drought or any other calamity. It is the earnest duty of the king to look after the welfare of the learned people. The kingdom, where the learned people are made to starve, may lose all its glory. — *MS* VII.133-34

The guidelines for taxation as presented in *Manu-Smṛti* show that there was a mutual understanding between the ruler and the subjects. The system of taxation on the whole should be reasonable. Its burden should fall on broadest shoulders and not on the weak shoulder. It should not hamper the development of trade and industry. There should not be any rigidity. Diversity is needed for any type of tax system and special care has to be taken of the persons rendering rare and critical services to the society. The major consideration is to prevent the tax system from becoming too much of a disincentive. There should not be any loopholes, and defects should be removed. Defaulters should not go scot-free. *Manu-Smṛti* has touched all these points of a good tax system.

> A king should not charge too much of tax. He, in any case, should not put increasingly higher taxes on the people, as it may displease them. — *MS* VII.139

> The rate of the tax should be determined on the basis of the expenditure incurred for buying, selling, transporting and preserving the goods. — *MS* VII.127

The traders must get reward for their hardwork. There should be a margin of profit for the businessmen. They should not be over-burdened with taxes.

> There is no sense of fixing such time and method of payment, which do not suit the taxpayers. The tax should be taken in proportion to the income of the taxpayer. — *MS* VII.139

While imposing tax on the people, a king has to take care of the convenience of the traders and farmers. The tax should not cause unnecessary suffering to anyone. At the same time, the cost of the collection should be as less as possible.

> As the leech, calf and insect eat their food little by little, so yearly taxation is to be taken little by little from the subjects by the king. — *MS* VII.128-29

Manu was against imposing additional taxes.

The amount earned through taxes has to be utilized in a proper manner. A king has no right to forget that the survival of the kingdom depends on the taxes collected from the common people. There should not be any misuse of the taxpayer's money.

> It is the responsibility of the king to give something to the subjects in return of the taxes paid by them.
> — *MS* VIII.307-08

A ruler is the guardian of the people living in that country. He has to protect the life, wealth and even the character of everyone.

> As the king is getting the sixth part of the good deeds done by the people, in the same manner he too has to share the bad actions performed by the people. — *MS* VIII.305

A king, who is getting tax from the people and not fulfilling his duties towards them, will surely go to hell. The tax system has to be fair and free of corruption. It should be governed by the policy of give and take. From the point of view of ensuring economic stability, it is necessary to maintain transparency in the tax system.

> Charging the tax in a deceitful manner or by using force or in an illegal way may bring the downfall of the king then and there. — *MS* VIII.309

The characteristic of the tax system should ensure that when national income is increasing, as during the boom, a moderate part of that may be brought under the tax net. Though the normal rate of tax was the sixth part of the total income, during emergency (e.g. war time) the king may enhance tax as he needs more money for protecting the kingdom. Manu did consider this fact very well:

> The king may take the fourth part of the produce as tax and he will not incur any sin as he is going to use that money for protecting his subjects. — *MS* X.118

The sources of raising emergency revenue were used only under exceptional situations. Under those circumstances, the normal tax rate was enhanced. But after the improvement of the situation there was a provision of lowering the tax rate. The flexibility in tax system may prove to be of great help to taxpayers. The tax system is not merely aimed at raising certain amount of revenue, but to collect the taxes from that section of the people who are earning more and may afford to share a certain amount of their income with the government in the form of tax. The burden of the tax should be according to the paying capacity of taxpayers. One may find the parallel of this concept of tax system in *Manu-Smṛti.*

> A king may charge the eighth part of the grains and the twentieth part of the money from vaiśyas, but nothing should be charged from śūdras or from artisans, instead of that they may be asked to do some work. — *MS* X.120

Businessmen of almost all communities are rich enough to pay more tax in comparison to the people depending on daily wages. The high rate of taxation for traders may encourage them to increase their income to compensate for the tax paid by them. At the same time, it will enable the king for tapping the available resources of traders for rainy days. It was a must for every citizen to pay the tax in time. Strict rules were framed for the payment of the tax and the defaulters were harshly dealt with.

> A man, who avoids the payment of tax and lies in the calculation of the due tax, should be fined eight times more of the cheated amount. — *MS* VIII.400

Conclusion

On a careful examination of the tax system presented in *Manu-Smṛti*, one thing becomes very clear that the determination of the tax amount was based on humanitarian ground. The rules pertaining to the payment were simple and reasonable. The proper care was taken of the people engaged in farming or teaching. The people involved in intellectual work were exempted from paying tax. The helpless people like poor, women and people of low-income group were totally exempted from paying tax. The articles required for sacrifices, flowers and fruits used for worshipping the gods, and earning from the craftsmanship were non-taxable. The *koṣādhyakṣa* and *koṣāgārādhyakṣa* jointly were responsible to look after the whole affairs related to the collection of revenue. From time to time, they were supervised by the king and no one was allowed to break the rules formed for the collection of taxes. Manu emphasized at every point that the money earned through tax collection had to be spent for the developmental activities of the state. The public must get good returns on their money paid as tax. The misuse of the taxpayers' money was considered a sin and the public had the right to question the head of the state for the irregularities taking place in spending the taxpayers' money.

In *Manu-Smṛti* there is no clear reference to the proportion of revenue that can be used as expenditure. Perhaps during that time the systematic economic planning was at its initial stage. There is a vague reference that a king should distribute the money found unclaimed, among the people of all castes, but he should keep nothing for himself. The maximum amount of revenue was spent on the maintenance of the army and armoury. The other items on the expenditure side were for the welfare of the state. Some amount was also spent on widows and orphans. The revenue was also used for the construction of dams, roads, cow infirmaries, bridges and rest houses. Factories, mints, mines, forests, schools and temples were maintained with the money received through the revenue collection process. In conclusion it may be said that *Manu-Smṛti* contains several aspects of economics, which are akin to modern economic concepts. Wealth was never condemned by Manu. In fact, it was regarded as a means to discharge the allotted duties in an ideal manner. The ideal manner involved the concept of righteousness to be followed in every system related to different economic activities. The selfless service of the state got utmost priority. Strict vigilance and harsh punishments were the tools for curbing the malfunctioning of different systems. The economic concepts, as presented by Manu, may not be as refined, systematic or mature as one may find in Kauṭilya's *Arthaśāstra* or in later Smṛtis. But one thing is very clear that in relation to economic theories, *Manu-Smṛti* has provided the principle of idealism, while others have given more importance to the practical aspects. Manu advocates that *dharma* should be followed in its wider sense in each and every sphere of life, and economic activity is no exception. It was a middle path to enjoy the worldly life along with spirituality.

10

Codes for Biodiversity Conservation and Ecosystem Stability

INDIAN tradition holds that the Supreme Self projects the whole universe out of Himself. So every object, gross or fine, is "He" in the garb of a particular name and form. The diversity of the universe was created with some special purpose and none of the objects existing in this universe can be considered useless. The whole empirical world, consisting of man and nature, bears the superconsciousness or the energy of the Supreme Self. Hence, everything in this universe is equally venerable and there is an apparent interdependence between all of them. Each one of them plays a vital role in the stability of the ecosystem.

Man as a Member of Biological Community

Our ecosystem is composed of a biological community and the physical environment. The populations of various kinds of organisms living and interacting in a particular area, make up a biological community. Man is an integral component of this biological community. The physical environment includes climate, water, soil, minerals, air, space and energy.

The physical or non-living components of the environment sustain the biological community by providing energy and matter that are essential for the survival of living organisms. On the other hand, the various components of the biological community of ecosystem also influence and modify the physical environment. The organisms present in an ecosystem, their various activities and products, and varied kinds of effects that they exert on the physical environment, determine the stability of the ecosystem. Man and his activities assume the most crucial role in this context. Man has acquired huge capacity to alter the environment; he can improve the environment, he can deteriorate it, and he can destroy it. If the environment is degraded, the life processes will be adversely affected. Thus the success of life on this planet depends on man and his activities in a large measure. Man has also built his own social and cultural world, and has also framed certain social codes that may regulate his actions. So, any consideration with regard to biodiversity conservation and ecosystem stability has got to be anthropocentric. *Manu-Smṛti* is replete with codes which regulate the conduct of man and his behaviour towards the fellow beings, other creatures and even towards non-living components of the ecosystem, and these codes are very relevant to biodiversity conservation and environmental protection.

Ecosystem Stability

It is a well-established fact that ecosystem stability and ecological balance depend on desirable interaction among organisms, between organisms and physical environment, and among various physical factors of the environment. In other words a proper integration of living organisms with their physical environment is a must for maintaining the ecosystem stability. Our ancestors lived in harmony with nature and had realized that each and every component of the ecosystem is important for its proper structural organization and functioning. On the contrary, the modern man does not have that much respect for nature, and he is overusing or misusing the natural resources. The ever-increasing human population and growing need and greed of humans, and ever-expanding efforts to meet the needs of human necessities and luxuries have strained the environment and disturbed the harmony between man and nature. This has resulted in a severe backlash in the form of soil degradation, global warming, depletion of stratospheric ozone, environmental pollution, loss of biodiversity and economic disparities. The irrational use of natural resources has ruined the fertile soil that was earlier covered with dense forests having a variety of trees, shrubs and herbs. It is amazing that Manu had visualized the environmental problems long time back and has put forward a real holistic approach for protecting nature and environment. *Manu-Smṛti*, a digest of social codes, suggests that the protection of nature and environment needs an active participation of the society. The aesthetic and spiritual values formed the core philosophy of nature protection. This concept has its seed in Vedas. *Manu-Smṛti* expanded a number of social codes related to nature protection mentioned in Vedas. According to *Manu-Smṛti*, at the dawn of the creation, the great Brahmā created everything existing in this universe.

> In this terrible cycle of transmigration of living beings, which moves relentlessly on and on, the levels of existence are said to begin with Brahmā and to end with Him. —*MS* I.50

Thus it is an ethical responsibility of human beings to take care of his fellow beings. Ethical values evaluate the relationship, rules and principles that require or forbid certain conducts. Disturbing the nature or destroying the natural resources is a forbidden act. According to *Manu-Smṛti*, a man must observe the righteousness in his conduct. A righteous conduct encompasses the kind behaviour towards every creation, be it a plant or an animal, and even non-living objects. *Manu-Smṛti* stipulates provisions for the protection of plants, animals, small creatures and physical environment and for the conservation of natural resources.

Codes for the Exploitation and Protection of Plants

Plants are the most important component of an ecosystem, as they trap the solar radiation and convert it into chemical energy, which is passed on to the organisms of the higher trophic levels in the food chain, such as herbivores, carnivores and micro-organisms. Except green plants, no other organisms can manufacture their food. They are all dependent on green plants for the supply of food materials. Therefore, green plants are essential for the survival of human beings and all other creatures on this planet. Plants are intimately linked with our culture, religion and social ethos. *Manu-Smṛti* recognizes that plants have internal consciousness as well.

> Enveloped by darkness, which is the result of their own innate past deeds, they (plants) have an internal consciousness and they experience both pleasure and pain.
> — *MS* I.49

This concept has also found support from the experiments of the great Indian scientist Sir Jagdish Chandra Bose.

Plants germinate, grow, develop, mature, reproduce and die. Every plant is a product of interplay between its genetic set-up and its environment and physiological behaviour. Most plants are fixed in a given place and manufacture their own food within the limits imposed by their immediate environment. They depend on how much raw materials and light energy are available to them in the environment. Unavailability or low availability of these factors may make them unhappy. Their unhappiness may be manifested in their poor growth and reduced yield, on account of which human beings and other animals will be deprived of the food which comes from plants, and may also become unhappy. Plants support the life of all other living organisms, and provide to humans many other products besides food. But it does not mean that human beings should keep on exploiting them beyond limit. We have to treat them as the most precious things. Manu advises the restrained use of plants. Anyone indulging in excessive exploitation of plants is committing a crime, and is liable to be punished. Manu says:

> For injuring plants, a fine must be imposed in proportion to their usefulness; that is the established rule. — *MS* VIII.285

Every plant growing in the nature has got some utility for human beings. Man has to recognize this fact. The punishments are made to remind that plants useful to the human beings are worthy of protection. Manu prohibits causing injury to medicinal plants (see *MS* XI.63) as they are very valuable and rare in occurrence. This is a good strategy to conserve the rare species. He also forbids cutting down the green trees for firewood (see *MS* XI.65). It has great ecological significance. The green trees can flower, bear fruit and produce seeds which are responsible for their regeneration. If the seeds are not produced in sufficient quantity, regeneration of tree species will be hampered which will cause decrease in their population. The green trees are like a young man, full of vigour, and cutting them down is similar to the killing of a young person. The plants also have equal right to grow and to reproduce. No one has the authority to hinder their growth and reproduction.

Manu listed several species of plants in *Manu-Smṛti* and asserted that all of them are needed for the welfare and happiness of human beings. Plants contribute immensely to the harmony and peace and their mere soothing presence transmits peace to human mind. A tiny grass or a green moss, stretched on the ground reflects the quietness of nature. They are harmless, and thus no one has any right to harm them. Manu considered harming plants a serious crime and he prescribed atonement for becoming free of that guilt.

> For cutting fruit trees, shrubs, vines, creepers or flowering plants, 1,000 Vedic verses should be chanted.
>
> — *MS* XI.142

Many medicinal plants grow in the wild. They are natural gifts to human beings as they cure many diseases. A man has to realize their utility and should not misuse or overuse them. The overuse may disturb or even disrupt their regeneration causing reduction in growth of their population. Many useful medicinal plants have already become extinct due to their over-exploitation by human beings. The medicinal plants take care of our health and so, they are very important for us. *Manu-Smṛti* brings out the names of medicinal plants used for different purposes (*MS* XI.147-48). In India growing medicinal plants was widely practised for a long time. These plants were considered very precious and needed more care and protection. *Manu-Smṛti* declares severe atonement for destroying medicinal plants.

> For pulling up, for no purpose, medicinal herbs grown by tillage or that grow wild in the forest, a man should serve a cow for the whole one day, living on nothing but milk.
>
> — *MS* XI.142, 144

Different types of plants have their own role to play in maintaining the ecological balance. Every plant has a definite lifespan during which it passes through different pheno-phases. Flowering stage of a plant is more important as it leads to the process of reproduction, which is a prerequisite for its regeneration. Thus, cutting a plant during its flowering phase may hamper the whole process of regeneration.

Codes for Soil Conservation

Man is a terrestrial animal and, so, his life very much depends on the soil. Soil is an essential component of the biosphere, and is the most important medium for plant growth. It must be nurtured and cultivated in such a manner that its production potential is fully realized, and its capability to give good yield is not lost so that with some additional inputs it may sustain good growth of plants in future too. It is one of the most important life-support systems. We cannot imagine our existence without soil. The soil is the complex mixture of weathered mineral materials derived from rocks, decomposed organic molecules and a host of living organisms. These ingredients impart to the soil certain physical, chemical and biological properties that are needed for the proper growth of all types of plants. Soil has to be protected from rain water, high wind velocity and natural disasters, as they take away most of the soluble minerals and organic matter, leaving behind the gravel and coarse sand. If proper conservation measures are not taken in time the land gets degraded. The soil erosion reduces its fertility, causes siltation of rivers and lakes in which navigation is not possible, increases the destructiveness and frequency of floods and turns good land into useless wasteland. Therefore, soil conservation measures and management of land topography need to be undertaken to protect soil. *Manu-Smṛti* brings forth an effective method of controlling soil erosion. According to *Manu-Smṛti,* planting of such trees on the slopes, that have strong, long and ramified roots, can check the water run-off and protect the soil from erosion. Manu says:

> One should make boundaries by planting *nyagrodha* (*Ficus indica*), *aśvattha* (*Ficus religiosa*), *kiṁśuka* or *palāśa* (*Butea frondosa*), *śālmali* or *semala* (*Bombax malabaricum*), *śāla* (*Shorea robusta*), *tala* (*Palmyra palm*) and milky trees (i.e. trees that produce latex). — *MS* VIII.246

Planting these trees on little elevated boundaries has some special significance. All the above-mentioned tree species are perennial and are having long and strong roots. The roots of these plants penetrate deep in the ground and hold the soil firmly. The elevated boundaries may trap the water and allow it to seep into the soil rather than being lost as run-off water.

The planting of thickets and shrubs having strong stems, creepers and runners may also check soil erosion. *Manu-Smṛti* brings forth a list of such plants as well for soil conservation.

> Thickets of various types of bamboos, *śamī* (*Prosopis spicigera*), runners (plants trailing on the soil surface with roots arising from their nodes (for example, *dūrvā* or *dūba* grass, i.e. *Cynodon dactylon*), mounds of earth covered with vines, reeds, thickets of *śara* (a kind of white reed or grass, most probably, *Saccharam munja*) and humpback plants are also good to keep the soil firm. — *MS* VIII.247

The boundary having these plants will not disappear.

Small shrubs and runners provide protective covering to the soil surface to reduce the erosive effect of wind and water. They also reduce the evaporation and may help in conserving the moisture content of the soil. The plants like bamboo and reeds grow with the help of their rhizomes and tubers that keep the soil intact and control erosion.

Man has now become a dominant species over most of the earth. The destruction of natural habitats of plants and animals, and conversion of forests to grasslands and agro-ecosystems are the major causes of biodiversity loss. The activities of man are now causing destruction as well as degradation of the natural ecosystems. However there should be a limit to the disturbance caused by human beings to natural ecosystems, if these are to be saved from further degradation. The disturbances may hamper the natural course of succession or the development of climax vegetation. In many parts of the world including India, forest is the climax vegetation. The loss of forest cover and green patches may have an adverse impact on other ecosystems and this may result in serious undesirable consequences. Human need, greed and ambition have been increasing leaps and bounds, as a consequence of which, the illegal encroachment of natural habitats has also increased. The ecological restoration is needed to bring back the nature in its pristine condition. We have to stop the deterioration of the green landscape. Protecting the natural habitats is essential for ecosystem stability. There is an urgent need to undertake eco-restoration of severely degraded sites. The water resources have to be protected and pollution of all types has to be controlled. These things are needed for maintaining the health of biological community. *Manu-Smṛti* provides many references related to environmental conservation.

Eco-friendly City Planning

According to Manu, while planning a city, one should consider the inclusion of green patches and open spaces. A town should be developed in an orderly and civilized fashion. A town should be the combination of a village and a modern city. The town must have the green belt of forest and fields. According to *Manu-Smṛti,* it is mandatory for every village and town to maintain green patches. Manu says:

> Round about every village there should be a strip of green patch, measuring 100 bows (the bow is four cubits or *hasta*) or even three casts of a staff in width, but for the city, the area should be three times more than the village.
>
> — *MS* VIII.237

The green patches, apart from their aesthetic beauty, minimize the impact of pollution and provide fresh air. They may also help in preserving the biodiversity. The town, with large gardens and open spaces, will look beautiful and will be a habitable place. Nature has a great regenerating power. The small effort rendered by human beings may change the whole scenario. No effort can fructify without the involvement of the society. *Manu-Smṛti* recommends that the work of land reform should be given to the society. In order to encourage involvement of the people some incentive may be given to them (*MS* IX.44). The socio-economic progress cannot be achieved if the resource base is eroded and the environment is degraded. Keeping in view the human needs, economic activities have to be undertaken but we have to keep in mind the overall health of the environment as well. In other words, our planning process must aim at a balanced and sustainable development. The maintenance of biological diversity and smooth functioning of essential ecosystem processes are necessary for sustainable development. Therefore, strategies must be formulated to conserve biodiversity. The protection of natural habitats, critical watersheds, wetlands, forests and unique and fragile ecosystems will go a long way in conserving the biodiversity. There should be a proper integration of man with nature. Man is also an integral component of ecosystem like any other biological species, and should not consider himself the master of ecosystem and perturb or manipulate it at will and beyond repair. We have to cultivate among ourselves the sense of shared responsibility towards protecting the nature, and then only the ecosystem stability and sustainable development can be achieved, which is so essential for bringing peace, harmony and happiness in the entire world community.

Protection of Water Bodies

It is not very easy to motivate people to protect the environment and natural ecosystems. Many a time, a person, guided by his own selfish attitude, destroys the natural resources. The environmental protection needs support of the government too. The laws related to the protection of environment and conservation of natural resources should be strict and effective. The availability of clean and fresh water, these days, has become one of the biggest problems. Most of the ancient civilizations had developed by the side of river banks or big water bodies due to easy availability of usable water. The availability of water determines the location of settlement and activities of humans on the earth, and therefore, the ponds, lakes, rivers and streams need to be protected. The destruction, degradation and disappearance of water-bodies may have serious implications for the biological diversity, productivity and human health. *Manu-Smṛti* contains many examples of communal effort to manage the water bodies. There are several references in *Manu-Smṛti* to harvest rainwater and store it in reservoirs, so that it may be available during dry months or dry years (*MS* VIII.262). According to *Manu-Smṛti,* it was the responsibility of the king to take care of water resources. The person, destroying the water resources was liable to be punished.

> If a man takes away a house, a pond, a garden or field by threatening, he should be fined 500 *paṇa*s, but if he does it unintentionally, he may be fined only 200 *paṇa*s.
>
> — *MS* VIII.264

Manu-Smṛti considers the destruction of ponds as a major crime and pronounces the highest punishment for this crime.

> If a man destroys a pond he should be physically punished by drowning or by simple killing; but even if the criminal repairs it, he should pay the highest level of fine.
>
> — *MS* IX.279

Stealing of water from a pond that was made in former times or cutting off the supply of water to the pond was also considered a crime and provision was made for imposing fine on the offenders (*MS* IX.281).

The rainfall is never uniform and water shortage may have most severe effect on ecosystems. The ground water is a great source of fresh water and is used for agriculture and domestic purposes. The wells and natural springs are the sources of obtaining ground water. The overuse or misuse of ground water causes several problems, such as lowering of the water table which makes the wells dry (i.e. without water), and bringing undesirable changes in the surface water features. *Manu-Smṛti* prescribes atonement for misusing the wells and springs.

> For misusing the water of the well or long ponds, one has to observe *cāndrāyana vrata*. — *MS* XI.163

It is amply clear that water management is given due importance in *Manu-Smṛti* because of its crucial role in sustaining life.

Throwing any impurity or excreting on the royal highways was forbidden.

> If anyone excretes on the royal highways when he is not in extremity, he should pay a fine of 2 *kārṣā-paṇa*s and immediately get someone to clean up the impure substance. — *MS* IX.282

Protection of Animals

Man is not the only organism living on this planet. Many species existed much before the arrival of man on this planet, many more arrived on the scene later, and many of them disappeared due to their lack of adaptation. Besides natural forces that caused disappearance of the species, man's activities and their impact on environment have also contributed to the extinction of a good number of species. We have no power to recreate them, if they become extinct. Every species of the organism down to the smallest ones is an irreplaceable treasure. They all have an *ipso facto* right to exist. Animals are also the important components of biotic community. Animals are intricately interconnected with other components of the biological communities and perform several important functions. Animals form the most important links in the food chain and food web, maintain the ecological balance and contribute to the stability of ecosystems. They also provide us several valuable commercial products. Many animal species serve as barometer for the health of entire ecosystem and play an important role in bio-monitoring of pollution. We cannot afford to deplete the animal diversity by killing them. The endangered animal species need to be fully protected. Hunting, shooting and capturing of animals are to be prohibited by law. We need to save all animals, regardless of their usefulness to humans. We are yet to discover the ecological role and scientific value of many species. The pace of species extinction is so fast that there is a risk that we would lose some of them before their actual scientific worth is discovered. *Manu-Smṛti* has taken the protection of animals seriously and has prescribed many codes for this purpose. The killing of domestic as well as wild animals is considered a major crime. People have to be kind towards all animals. Even the small creatures like bugs and flies are important for the maintenance of the ecosystem of which they are a part. The destruction of natural habitats of wild animals has already caused serious problems in many parts of the world. In the absence of sufficient food and shelter in their own natural habitats, wild animals have been found to enter into human habitations causing loss to humans, their domesticated animals and property.

The killing of domesticated or wild animals, whether intentionally or unintentionally, was considered a crime or sin, and Manu prescribed punishment or atonement of varying magnitudes for killing different animals.

> If a man kills a cat or a mongoose, a blue jay, a frog, a dog, a lizard, an owl, or a crow, he should carry out the vow for killing a śūdra. — *MS* XI.131

Even the brāhmaṇas were not spared of punishments or

atonements for killing animals. According to *Manu-Smṛti*:

> If a brāhmaṇa kills a snake, he should give a black iron spade to a brāhmaṇa; for killing a boar, he should give a pot of clarified butter; for a partridge, a bucket of sesame seeds; for killing a parrot, a two-year-old calf, for curlew, a three-year-old calf; and for killing a goose, a crane, a heron, a peacock, a monkey, a falcon, or a vulture, he should give a cow. — *MS* XI.133-35

> For killing a horse, he should give a garment; for an elephant, five black bulls; for a goat or sheep, a draught ox; for a donkey, a one-year-old calf. — *MS* XI.136

But the punishment prescribed for killing a carnivorous wild animal like tiger was to give a milch cow.

> For killing carnivorous wild animals (such as tiger, etc.), one should give a milch cow as a punishment or atonement, for killing non-carnivorous animals, one should give a heifer (young cow); and for killing a camel, one should give gold equal to the weight of a berry. — *MS* XI.137

Conclusion

A detailed account of punishments and atonements for injuring and cutting different types of plants, and for destroying water-bodies, and for killing different types of animals has been presented in the chapter on punishment and atonement in *Manu-Smṛti*, and so, to avoid repetition those details are not included in this chapter.

It would be seen from the above that punishments or atonements are prescribed mostly for killing those animals that are either very useful for the household, or they are endangered and threatened, or they are the keystone species performing unique functions in different ecosystems. Most of these animals play a very critical role in maintaining the ecosystem stability, and are protected even under the modern laws, acts and rules governing the conservation of animals.

It is quite clear that *Manu-Smṛti* has covered a variety of ecological aspects that are quite topical. It has presented many eco-friendly methods for landscape planning, outlined conservation measures against soil erosion caused by wind and water, discussed the need for conserving plants, animals and water resources, and has prescribed punishments for those who destroy these life-support systems and cause depletion of biological diversity by killing the valuable plants and animals. Manu also prescribed several codes for conserving plants, animals as well as non-living components of the ecosystem. Those who violated these codes were liable to be punished. The extent of utility of different components of the environment, regardless of whether they were living or non-living, was considered the basis for determining the magnitude or severity of punishment (*MS* VIII.285, 297).

The modern man, of late, has lost the desired connectivity with other creatures and has the least concern even for the life-support systems such as, soil, landscape, water-bodies and vegetation. He has been exploiting the resources in an unsustainable manner to meet his ever-growing needs and greed. This has caused several problems such as water pollution, air pollution, land degradation, depletion of biodiversity and climate change as also the shortage of vital natural resources. This has given rise to a situation of conflict and disharmony in the community of nations. In the present scenario, the unique ideas and codes enshrined in *Manu-Smṛti* may help in charting out a viable roadmap towards achieving the goal of environmental conservation and global harmony.

Conclusion

EACH nation is having its own intellectual bent of mind to comprehend different aspects of human existence. The great ancient Indian thinkers have always strived for the socio-spiritual reformation of human civilization. They had a firm faith in Ultimate Reality and they conceived that a man by performing good *karma*s may visualize that Reality within himself. Leading a righteous life was considered as the first step towards achieving this goal. The real spirit of life lies in the merger of spirituality in day-to-day life. Spirituality does not mean mysticism or practising any mystic power, but just to follow a disciplined life and to realize the energy lying within. The philosophical theories must have a follow-up in practical life. The great sages kept on supplying the fresh visions and thoughts depending on the changing needs of society. The new emerging thoughts enjoyed the liberty of criticizing and questioning the existing concepts and were free to introduce something more useful and practical to the new generation. Different views focused on the same truth form different angles. There was also a tendency of synthesizing the old concepts with the new ones. This tendency is clearly reflected in *Manu-Smṛti*. Manu had faith in Vedic practices, but he also wanted to revive them with certain modifications. He wanted to introduce certain new practices through which a person may enjoy the life gleefully and may achieve closeness to that inexpressible and invisible God. The faith in the Almighty and service to humanity can make a person worthy to live in this world and even in the next world.

Vedic philosophy was very simple. The polytheistic character of *Ṛgveda* could not answer many questions related to human existence. The Vedic seers were fully engrossed in the delightful sight of vast nature and did not think much beyond that. They developed a direct communion with nature and had no interest in penetrating into the mystery behind that. Vedic practices could not satisfy fully the ethical aspirations of human being as the main emphasis in Vedas was on the rituals and sacrifices. In order to make Vedic thoughts more practical, Manu concentrated on the word *ṛta* (*satya* or truth). For Manu this word became the standard of morality and he accepted this word as *dharma*. The word *dharma* with its variegated nature has dominated throughout in *Manu-Smṛti*. Manu also had some leaning towards Brāhmaṇa *grantha*s which did not insist on mechanical performance of rituals and introduced few systems for making the life more fruitful by practising morality (see *SataBrā* XIII.7.1.1 and I.1.1.4). Manu took the support of Upaniṣads for extending the arena of *dharma*. Upaniṣads expounded the true nature of reality and provided freshness to the concept of spirituality. Upaniṣads propounded the theory of Advaita and insisted that the whole creation is the manifestation of same God. The external world is not different than *Brahman*. The empirical is a pathway to the Ultimate. The human love is in no way inferior to divine love. There is an intimate binding between the singularity of pure consciousness and outer plurality or physical world. The worldly life is the expression of Self or *Brahman* and, human deeds are the preparation for gaining the knowledge of Self. So, there is no need of denouncing the life.

> Life is a great festival to which we are invited, and we might show *tapas* (self-renunciation), *dāna* (charity), *ārjavam* (right dealing), *ahiṁsā* (non-violence), *satyavacanam* (truthfulness).
>
> — *ChāUp* III.16, S. Radhakrishnan, Indian Philosophy p. 216

In *Manu-Smṛti* the concept of four *puruṣārthas* (*dharma, artha, karma, mokṣa*) got an important place for enjoying the life on the earth. There is no need of discarding desires totally. The desire has to be accompanied by *jñāna* and good *karma*. The needed combination of *jñāna, icchā* and *karma* generates *ānanda* (Supreme Bliss). Manu asserted that the life should have spirit, truth and *jñāna*. The religion and rituals help a person to realize his own position in this world and make him free of *ahaṁkāra*. A person requires a long course of training in moral and spiritual discipline for reaching the state of perfection.

Based on all these ideologies, Manu chalked out a very systematic programming for leading a fruitful life. The four *āśramas* — *brahmacarya, gṛhastha, vānaprastha* and *saṁnyāsa* — represent the different steps by which a man gradually moves away from mundane world and becomes fit for final emancipation. During the first stage of life, i.e. *brahmacarya āśrama*, a young boy has to study under the supervision of a selfless and learned *guru* and has to undergo an ascetic withdrawal from the world. At this stage the *brahmacārī* has to receive tough training and go through physical preparation for leading the rest of the life in an ideal manner. He has to practise severe *tapas* (austerity) as it will help him in restraining the senses. The temptations culminate into vices causing downfall. *Dharmas* prescribed for *brahmacarya* are designed to lay down a strong foundation for future life. The initial training used to be similar for the three upper classes. They were entitled to enter the *gurukula* only after *upanayana*. Their training used to be quite rigorous as they were supposed to bear enormous responsibilities later in their life.

Getting married and leading a life of a *gṛhastha* is also a divine blessing. It was almost mandatory to enter this *āśrama* and fulfil the assigned duties towards gods and ancestors. The home is as sacred as a temple. The rigorous training obtained during the first stage of life enables a person to consider everything as sacred. The love, warmth and affection received from family members prepare a person to realize his responsibility towards the society. It is the time to perform good deeds for making the human life fruitful and meaningful.

Vānaprastha and *saṁnyāsa* were the stages meant for extending spiritual brotherhood. The *saṁnyāsī* was free of caste and nationality and led a detached life. With the power of holiness, humility and detachment he lives in this world as an ambassador of God. The system of the *āśrama*s was based on the principles of making the life more systematic. It provided a perfect timetable for managing the whole life and for making people aware of their next agenda.

The division of class or caste created by Manu carries its own purpose. It did not carry any tint of looking down upon any section of people or to discriminate among different classes of people. The hierarchical composition of the society becomes a boon if it maintains the value system and everyone gets his due share. It was a perfect division of labour. The duties were allotted to different sections of the society based on their capacity, level of intelligence, qualification, interest, aptitude and psychology. The quality and outcome of a job will surely be better if a person performing that work is worthy enough. The uppermost caste of brāhmaṇa was not just for the name-sake. It was based on the brāhmaṇahood. Likewise, the people those were brave, mighty and good in governance joined the line of rulers. The people possessing the best knowledge of trade, commerce and agriculture were known as vaiśyas. The section of the society with less mental capacity did the job of supporting the other three castes. The training which the individuals received in childhood from their mothers and, later on, from their highly esteemed and learned teachers helped them soften their attitude towards division of society into different castes and helped them to refrain from becoming caste conscious.

Manu took much care while dealing with subjects like governance. He was in favour of spiritual governance that comprised faithfulness, truth, justice and adherence to allotted duties. There was no difference between a *ṛṣi* and *rājarṣi*. Governance was treated parallel to penance. Kings were also supposed to be the master of higher philosophy. Kings like Janaka and Ajātaśatru are known for holding religious congresses to discuss complex philosophical topics (*BṛUp* III.7). Kings not behaving in desired manner were always reminded of going to hell. Manu has presented a very compact and advanced process of judiciary, which is close to modern judiciary. Judiciary was kept away from the interference of kings. King used to be the member of *sabhā* and was responsible to deliver justice based on the decision taken by the members of *sabhā*. Priesthood and power were never contradictory to each other; they were complimentary. Priests helped the king by giving him guidelines of *dharma*. Violation of human rights was taken due care. Manu wanted to maintain a balance between the powerful and the powerless. This concept is an example of how all members of the society may walk together without showing their supremacy in any manner.

The biggest problem that we are facing today is the increasing rate of crimes in modern society, and tardy process of awarding exemplary punishment to criminals. Different agencies involved in controlling the crime are only partially successful. Ordinary people are frustrated and feed helpless. The system of punishment as presented in *Manu-Smṛti* is quite capable of checking the growing crime. Manu has often been criticized for his harsh codes of punishment. But many a time it becomes necessary to form strict codes of punishment. The lack of suitable and deserving punishment is the main reason for the growth of crime. Manu advised to punish criminals based on the prima facie evidence in serious cases like violence and murder. There is no need of keeping the terrorists unpunished for a long period just for the reason that a proper judicial procedure has to be followed.

Manu-Smṛti is a social code covering all aspects related to human life. Manu has supported the idea of earning money and leading a comfortable life. His main concern was that a person should not forget the value system and ethics while getting engaged in any work. The money should not be earned by vice means. Manu had a strong faith in the philosophy of *karma* and rebirth. One may collect *puṇya* by doing good deeds for securing his next birth. Any work done by a person has an impact on the society. Therefore, one must consider what impact his actions would have on others.

Manu was aware that in a society every person would not be equally pure and free of vices. That is why he has given guidelines for each and every endeavour to be carried out by a person. Indian philosophy is optimistic in true sense. Once a person realizes his mistakes he becomes free of guilt. The concept of *prāyaścitta* is a unique method of bringing a change in the person who has not followed the prescribed *dharma*. Apart from this relaxation, Manu has also made a special provision of *āpad-dharma*. This provision has often been wrongly interpreted. *Āpad dharma*s were not meant for normal situations. They were to be used only in emergencies and that also in a controlled manner. Many a time *āpad-dharma* was used to save one's own life or save the life of others.

Manu-Smṛti is regarded by many critics as a work full of contradictions. But they forget that *Manu-Smṛti* is based on the practices that were prevalent in society during a particular period. Indian tradition had the liberty of introducing changes in consonance with the needs and convenience of the society. Though Manu introduced his own codes, at the same time he also included the practices that already existed in the society that could not be ignored. The context sensitivity is needed for understanding the real gist of the notion presented by Manu. It will not be fair to pick up one statement at random from somewhere and come to the conclusion just based on that. It becomes necessary to give some relaxation. It depends on a person to choose the relaxation depending on his wisdom. With regard to flesh eating, for example, Manu did not deny animal sacrifice and offering flesh to ancestors (*MS* III.123, IV.28). But at the same time, he asserts that guests should be offered food and water without troubling any other creature. During later Vedic period there was a tradition of offering to guests the flesh of animals used for sacrifice (*ŚataBrā* II.7.1-3; *MS* V.39-44). Manu was not totally in favour of Vedic practices and he gave the option of welcoming guests with just food and water.

Many scholars have criticized *Manu-Smṛti* for its lack of coherence. Making this type of comment is not fair. An author uses his own vision and style while producing his work which should not be challenged. A reader must give some allowance for judging an ancient text like *Manu-Smṛti*. Quite often a reader fixes himself on one part of the text and draws his partial conclusion. All topics dealt by Manu are interwoven with a single thread of *dharma*. The text needs to be comprehended in totality. Bringing in a paradox, reaching to negativity and then coming to a positive conclusion, is a typical Indian style of writing classical texts.

It is unfortunate that very often, Manu and *Manu-Smṛti* have been caught under severe criticism. It has happened because of the critics' ignorance of Indian culture, inadequacy in existing translations, dominance of irrational political agendas, and desire or craze to bring out something entirely different from the well-known thoughts. Many translations have been done by well-known Western scholars. They are not much aware of complex Indian culture which is entirely different from the rest of the world. The facts of Indian life become fantasy for Westerners and they consider those as fairy tales or primitive or barbaric concepts. They try to put their logics and fallacious arguments (Vitaṇḍāvāda) which do not merit any serious discussion. It is their ignorance. Indian culture is dominated by deep-rooted philosophy. In India philosophy was never a dogma but was a part of day-to-day life. Indian thinkers have always fought for the truth and were against falsehood. The philosophers were mostly social reformers and they kept on guiding the common people through their own conduct. It will surely be a futile effort to compare the Western modern life with ancient Indian lifestyle. It is also not fair to criticize a particular custom prevailing in any society without having a sound knowledge of cultural and religious ethos of that period. Manu belongs to a remote past. The social codes presented by him were meant to cater to the requirements of the contemporary Indian society of his time. An author always sets his/her aim before starting any monumental work. Manu might be having some thoughts in his mind to attain the objectives set forth by him. He had before him the great Vedic tradition with enormous following. It was not possible for him to change the whole system abruptly. He supports Vedic thoughts, but apart from that, the text also contains many other useful concepts. Many critics are the victims of false notions and they do not want to deviate from their pre-conceived ideas. Thus arguing with them on the subjects like priestly rituals, metaphors used for depicting certain ideologies, vegetarianism and non-violence, rebirth and theory of *karma*, or what Manu said about women is meaningless.

Indian commentators of *Manu-Smṛti* have followed a *paramparā* (tradition). There is not much difference in content and elaborations between the commentaries of Medhātithi (ninth century CE) and Kūlluka (fifteenth century CE). It happened so because of their cultural affinity, personal involvement and command on the source language. It is a must to follow authentic commentaries. Many a time, the authors do not explain the words in detail and that creates difficulty for the translator to explain the meaning. In such cases at least two commentaries may be compared. Reaching closer to or assuming author's intention or his philosophy for giving any statement is not an easy task. That is the reason for disagreement between any two commentaries. At this point, a translator has to be very careful. He needs to follow the context and provide his own interpretation. The translator should retain the original spirit of the text. It is not very easy to translate Sanskrit text to any foreign language. Semantic proliferations are very common in Sanskrit and the vocabulary is also very rich. Single verbal root may have several meanings. The problems occur when the translator does not get the exact meaning befitting to the context. Many translators exploit this situation and try to impose their personal interpretation and thus change the whole flavour of the original text. It has happened many times with *Manu-Smṛti*. The translator must avoid dishonesty.

Getting exact rendering of many Sanskrit words is also a difficult task. In *Manu-Smṛti* the words like brāhmaṇa, *dvija* and *purohita* contain different meanings. But while translating, the word "priest" has been used for denoting all these words. Similarly, rendering the word *dvija* as "twice born" changes the whole philosophy lying behind the word. Bringing out literal translation also creates problems for a reader. For example, the word *phala* translated as "fruit" falls short in conveying the meaning. The rendering of the word *śuci* as "unpolluted" spoils the purity of the word. The words like *Brahman, dharma, karma, manas, tapas* and *saṁskāra* cannot be rendered. Manu has used many technical words in different contexts. They should not be translated literally to English or any other foreign language as it creates confusion (e.g.

cakravṛddhi vyāja translated as "wheel or compound interest"). In these cases the translator must use the original Sanskrit word and English rendering of that word can be put in brackets. The translator should not hinder the original sense of the word. He is free to ponder over different meanings of a given word, but should select and re-enforce the correct meaning of the word by applying his own wisdom.

While interpreting a text like *Manu-Smṛti*, one needs to be free from all types of personal, social, religious and political prejudices. Even one has to keep himself away from the narrow dogmas propounded by different cults. Interpreting or translating *Manu-Smṛti* has to be done with a fresh mind. The interpreter has to be honest while giving his opinion. He should not depend on the borrowed ideas and should not be guided by any personal gain or loss. Many a time people depend on baseless pre-conceived notions without going through the text themselves. Borrowed philosophies are always deceptive and harmful. They cripple the normal function of the brain and put a person in the state of acute obsession. Obsession is not a normal function of the brain and the judgement given under this state may be incorrect. There is also a good number of crazy people who, just for gaining popularity, try to produce something unconventional or very new. These people usually create a riot of new ideas and produce senseless piece of work. These works create a turmoil in the society by initiating political conflicts. It is a real misuse of creativity and one should remain away from such practices. *Manu-Smṛti* is precisely a social code covering ideologies of social evolution of different periods. It did not intend to generate a line of followers.

Manu-Smṛti is an attempt to deal with perennial problems taking place in the social, political and religious spheres of human endeavour. It will be wrong to say that modern society is free from those problems. Human psychology has not changed much and the conflict between vices and virtues is still going on. The graph of the problems is moving upward making the life more and more difficult. Most of the people are aware of the reasons behind these problems and are coming closer to Manu's ideologies. People have begun to acknowledge the relevance of different ideologies propounded by Manu related to value system and harsh punishment for serious crimes. For Indian tradition, *dharma* is not just a concept, but a way of life. People of all sections of the society, in general, have accepted it. Considering this tradition as Brāhmanism or orientalism will be narrowing its scope. The *dharma* propounded by Manu is *sanātana* signifying its adaptability. The relaxations and choices given by Manu provide an opportunity to the people to use them at different periods and in different situations. Manu's codes are the balanced combination of *pravṛtti* and *nivṛtti* as well as *śreya* and *preya*. They are not idealistic and dreamy vision. His synthetic outlook has brought together all components from different ancient texts for improving and smoothening human life.

Manu understood human psychology and had studied human impulses, emotions and actions minutely. Division of four *āśrama*s is the finest example of his keen observations with regard to changing psychology of human beings at different phases of their life. His speculative and analytical mind was capable of understanding the things, both good as well as bad. He wanted to train human minds so that they can improve their life on their own. He laid more emphasis on spiritual discipline and self-examination to enable a person to judge himself. India always practised reverence for the past and, Manu too had inclination towards the past tradition and he had maintained the traditional faith and trust throughout his work. Few of his theories may be stale or unacceptable to the present generation, but there are so many pertinent and joyous theories which may add value to the quality to present-day life. While going through an ancient text like *Manu-Smṛti*, the reader has to be open-minded and has to give some allowance to the statements related to Vedic sacrifices and untouchability, which are not befitting to the present-day life. As for the Vedic sacrifices, unfortunately, they are still in practice in some places. But even in Vedic age *śraddhā* (faith) in all ceremonies was necessary (*ṚV* VI.55.5). It becomes very difficult to challenge the religious practices as they are based on faith. In Vedic age people considered gods just like human beings and wanted to offer them every type of food, but offering flesh to gods was not a very common practice. Even for Aśvamedha *yajña* no animal was sacrificed and the ceremony was performed with the repetition of several *mantras* (*Sāmaveda* I.ii.9.2). Animal sacrifices became a part of rituals only during the later Vedic period. At present, people in India are not in favour of animal sacrifice and this practice may come to an end gradually. The practice of untouchability becomes untenable once we realize that the same *Brahman* is pulsating in the body of everyone. So, there is no sense of discriminating a person on the basis of caste. At present, the people of lower caste in India are availing all types of facilities and are enjoying equal status in the society.

Manu always supported the philosophy of submission and tolerance. He prohibited all kinds of violence, be it mental or physical, against not only human beings but all other creatures. Manu had a firm conviction in the continuity of life and has emphasized that immoral actions would have bad consequences. In order to re-enforce this concept he linked it with *karma-phala* and *punarjanma* (rebirth). The nature of the next birth is determined by the deeds performed in the present life. By indulging in unwanted actions, a person would ruin his next birth and may suffer a great deal. The material forces of the world cannot subdue the spiritual strength developed through morality. Self-discipline strengthens the good impulses and weakens the bad ones. It is the most valuable and everlasting doctrine suggested by Manu. The fear of God keeps a person abstain from vice deeds and motivates him to move on the path of righteousness. *Jñāna,* which provides energy, is not different from righteousness (*dharma*). The actions performed in the spirit of *dharma* will always be beneficial to everyone. The ideologies presented in *Manu-Smṛti* are based on the zenith of Indian philosophical thoughts and will never lose their charm and utility. It becomes our duty to bring them closer to us for a better understanding. In order to extract the essence of Manu's thoughts one has to educate his mind in a proper manner by broadening the vision.

Bibliography

Primary Sources

Please see Introduction.

Secondary Sources

Acharya, R.K., 1976, "The Theory of Punishment in the Dharmasutras", *Journal of G.N. Jha Research Institute*, pp. 1-8.

Agarwala, V.S., 1970, *India as Described by Manu*, Varanasi: Prithvi Prakashan.

Altekar, A.S., 1952, *Sources of Hindu Dharma in Its Socio-Religious Aspects*, Solapur.

———, 1958, *State and Government in Ancient India*, Delhi: Motilal Banarsidass.

Bagchi, S.C., 1933, *Juristic Personalities of Hindu Deities*, Calcutta.

Banerji, N.V., 1980, *Studies in the Dharmaśāstra of Manu*, New Delhi.

Betai, R.S., 1976, Evolution of Criminal Law-Transition from Manu to Yājñavalkya", *Journal of G.N. Jha Research Institute*, pp. 34-49.

Colebrook, H.T., 1810, *The Law of Inheritance According to Mitāksharā*, Calcutta: Hindustana Press.

Das, R.M., 1957, *Woman in Manu and His Seven Commentators*, Varanasi.

Dhar, Somnath, 1957, *Cāṇakya and Arthaāstra*, Bangalore.

Dutta, M.N., 1908-62, *The Dharmaśāstra or the Hindu Law Codes*, Calcutta.

Ghose, J.C., 1919, *Principles of Hindu Law*, Calcutta.

Ghoshal, U.N., 1947, "The Status of Shudras in Dharmasatras", *Indian Culture*, 14(1): 21-7.

———, 1947, "The Status of Brāhmaṇas in Dharmaśāstras", *Indian Historical Quarterly*, 23(2): 83-92.

Gupta , A.S., 1970, "Manu on the Duties of Kings", *Journal of Indian History*, 48(2): 399-404.

Hazara, R.C., 1959, "Dharma: Its Early Meaning and Scope", *Our Heritage*, 7(1): 5-35.

Hopkins, E.W., 1969, *The Great Epic of India*, Calcutta, repr.

———, 1887, "The Position of the Ruling Caste", *JAOS*, XIII: 10-11.

Jayaswal, K.P., 1930, *Manu and Yajnavalkya: A Comparison and Contrast*, Calcutta.

Jha, G.N., 1931, *Hindu Law in Its Sources*, Allahabad.

Kane, P.V., 1930-62, *History of Dharmaśāstra*, 5 vols., Poona: Bhandarkar Oriental Research Institute.

Kangle, R.P., 1964, "Manu and Kautilya", *Indian Antiquary* (n.s.) 1(1).

Ketkar, S.V., 1909-11, *History of Caste in India.*

Law, N.N., 1914, *Studies in Ancient Indian Polity*, London.

Moghe, S.G., 1991, *Studies in Dharmaśāstra*, Delhi: Ajanta Publication.

Mukherji, P., 1961, "Property Right of Woman as Recorded in Kauṭilya's Arthaśāstra and Manusmṛti", *Our Heritage*, 9(1): 49-60.

Patavardhana, M.V., 1968, *Manusmṛti: The Ideal Democratic Republic of Manu*, Delhi.

Radhakrishnan, S., 1922, *Indian Philosophy*, 2 vols., London: Oxford University Press.

———, 1968, *The Principal Upanisads*, London: George Allen and Unwin.

Raghavan, V., 1859, "The Manusmṛti", *The Cultural Heritage of India*, I: 335-63, Ramakrisna Mission, Calcutta.

Ramamurthy, R., 1974, "Concept of Punishment Under Manusmṛti", *Indian Philosophical Quarterly*, pp. 51-64.

Rangaswami Aiyangar, K.V., 1949, *Some Aspects of Social and Political System of Manu*, Lucknow.

Sen, P.N., 1918, *General Principles of Hindu Jurisprudence*, Calcutta.

Sen Gupta, N.C., 1914, *Sources of Law and Society in Ancient India*, Calcutta.

Sharma, S.D., 1976, "The Concept of Justice in Manu", *Indian Sociological Journal*, pp. 47-68.

Sreedhara, B.H., 1971, "Manu's Theory of Kingship", *The Journal of Karnataka University*, pp. 43-53.

Srivastava, V.C., 1976, "Socio-Juristic Position of Atatayi Brāhmana", *Journal of G.N. Jha Research Institute*, pp. 69-91.

Tiwari, C., 1963, *Sudras in Manusmṛti*, Delhi.

Tiwary, U.K., 1990, "A Note on R.C. Hazra's Article 'The Sources of Dharma'", *Journal of the G.N. Jha Kendriya Sanskrit Vidyapeetha*, XLVI: 216-28.

Visvanathan, S.V., 1925, *International Law in Ancient India*, London.

Vedic Texts cited in the Book

Aitareya Brāhmaṇa, Ānandāśrama Sanskrit Series, 32, Poona, 1931.

Aitareya Āraṇyaka, Ānandāśrama, Poona.

Āpastamba Dharma-Sūtra, ed. U.C. Pandeya, Chowkhamba Sanskrit Series, Varanasi, 1969.

Bṛhadāraṇyaka Upaniṣad, Swami Ranganathananda Advaita Ashrama, Calcutta, 2005.

Kauṣītaki Upaniṣad, S. Radhakrisnan, *Principal Upaniṣad*.

Mahābhārata, Bhandarkar Oriental Research Institute, Poona, 1933-60.

Vālmīki Rāmāyaṇa, Baroda, 1960-75.

Ṛgveda Saṁhitā, Chowkhamba Sanskrit Series, Varanasi, 2002.

Sāmaveda Saṁhitā, Chowkhamba Sanskrit Series, Varanasi, 2002.

Śatapatha Brāhmaṇa, 5 vols., Bombay, 1940.

Śvetāśvatara Upaniṣad, S. Radhakrishnan, *Principal Upaniṣads*.

Taittrīya Ārarṇyaka, 2 vols., Ānandāsrama, Poona, 1981.

Taittrīya Upaniṣad, S. Radhakrishnan, *Principal Upaniṣads*.

Index